JUNE - '1

To CHERYLE —
THANK YOU!

(BARRY ZeVAN)

THANK YOU, JERRY STILLER...
for urging me to write this book

THANK YOU, JERRY STILLER . . .
for urging me to write this book

Barry ZeVan
My Life Among
The Giants,
A Memoir

The really overwhelming life and lives of
Barry ZeVan (the Weatherman) **by Barry ZeVan**

**Entertaining, enlightening,
educational, insightful,
powerful, quality stories and
significant vignettes you've
probably never known.**

4 square
books

First published in 2016 by 4 Square Books, an imprint of Ebooks LLC.

Copyright © Barry ZeVan, 2016

The moral right of the author has been asserted

ISBN 978-1-61766-265-2

Copies of this book are available through Amazon sites and through the trade.

Please address orders for bulk copies or any enquiries to 4SquareBooks@gmail.com

Contents

This book is dedicated with love and gratitude to:

My late dear mother, Selma, for everything, who instilled
The Golden Rule's admonition in me from the time I could
understand its meaning.

Jerry Stiller and Anne Meara, for the honor and privilege of
Jerry's genuine friendship, encouragement and caring,
with Anne always warmly and kindly echoing his feelings.

Carol Lawrence and Bob Newhart, who launched my career's
most significant "parades".

Ed Ames, Tino Barzie, Suzy Chaffee, Joe Delaney, Sam Donaldson,
Verne Gagne, Robert Goulet, Vera Goulet, Peter Jennings,
Quincy Jones, Howard Keel, Ted Koppel, Billy Kidd, Jerry Lewis,
Peter Nero, Wayne Newton, Louis Nye, Louis Prima, Tony Randall,
Don Rickles, Joan Rivers, Willard Scott,
Frank Sinatra, Jr. and Ambassador Ardeshir Zahedi, who
were always welcoming and available.

Others who believed (and still believe) in me, keeping me
glued together in almost perpetually tough times.
They know who they were, and are.

Daughters Shaunda and Lisa, grandchildren Ryan, Maritsa,
Chelsea and Brady, great-grandchildren Wesley, Reagan, Emma,
Hunter, Shelbea, Abby, Chevy and Presley.

Ellen, my wife and champion, listed last, but definitely not least.

Acknowledgments

The following people, all with whom I've had personal times
. . . some fleeting but most *not*, most famous and *some* not,
most still alive and many not . . . are appreciated for their
having taken the time to bless me with their kindnesses to
like me enough to include me in their "real people" lives and
moments, *most* of which have been shared with you herein,
and listed here in alphabetical order:

John and Shane Adams, Marlene Adler, Jim Agostino, Chadi Aladi,
Eddie Albert, Marty Allen, Woody Allen, Stephanie Allensworth,
Steve Allen, Ojibwe Chief Marge Anderson, Marc Angell,
Kofi Annan, Loni Anderson, Louie Anderson, Ivan Annenberg,
Ted Anthony, Mike Appollon, Robert Armao, Louis Armstrong,
Ina Balin, Pete Barbutti, Barbara Barrie, Julie Bartkey,
Dennis Belafonte, Harry Belafonte, Steve and Joyce Bell,
Warren Berlinger, Lyle Berman, Andre Bernier,
Victoria James Bivens, Rudy Boschwitz, Tim Braun,
Charlie Brill, David Brinkley, Madeline Broderick, Mel Brooks,
Cecil Brown, Peter Buffett, Kathy Bushkin Calvin, Steve Cannon,
Eric Canton, Eddie Cantor, Marilyn Cantor, Kitty Carlisle,
Gretchen Carlson, Bob Carroll. Jr., Leslie Caron,
Raul and Chuy Carrera, Jack Carson, Suzy Chaffee, Charo,
Eugene Chase, Patricia Chase, Spencer Christian, Dick Clark,
Gage Clark, Nic Clarke, Rac Clark, Nick Clooney, Rosemary Clooney,
Chuck Connors, Perry Como, Tim Corder, Chuck Costa, Gina Costa,
Gail Cottman, Wally Cox, Joseph and Lorie Croft, Pamela Curlee,
Jamie Lee Curtis, Keith Dare, Delmer Daves, Madelyn Pugh Davis,
James Dean, Gloria DeHaven, Joe Delaney, Marjel DeLauer,
Dom and Carol DeLuise, Catherine Deneuve, Sam Donaldson,
Serge Dubois, Jimmy Durante, Steve and Melanie Edwards,
Chris Egert, John Ehrlichman, Queen Mother Elizabeth, Linda Ellerbee,
Duke Ellington, Jim English, Heinz Eppensteiner,
Stein Eriksen, Arturo and Debi Ruiz-Esparza, Timmy Everett,

Frank Fahrenkopf, Frank Faylen, Adam Fell, Bob Finkel,
Eddie Fisher, Henry Fonda, Gerald Fors, Bob Fosse, Pete Fountain,
Redd Foxx, Bill Fyffe, Francesca Gabor, Zsa Zsa Gabor, Frank Gallup,
Kathy Garver, "Rusty" Gatenby, Karl Gensheimer, Frances Gershwin,
Steven Geray, Raphael Ghermezian, Don and Nancy Giacchetti,
Bob and Elmer Gill, Elliott Gould, Robert Goulet, Cary Grant,
Kathryn Grayson, Abner "Abby" Greshler, Merv Griffin,
Buddy Hackett, Ed Hall, Patrick Hammer, Scott Hansen, Phil Harris,
Major General John Hawley, Vinton Hayworth, Jr., Tippi Hedren,
Les Heen, Jane Helmke, Dwayne Hickman, Arthur Hiller,
Donnette Hilton, Doug Hofman, Joan Holman, Dan Holter,
Kirby Grant Hoon, Bob and Carol House,
Genevieve Hovde-Rugo, The Stanley Hubbard Family,
Howard Hughes, Buck Humphrey, Hubert H. Humphrey,
Skip Humphrey, Chet Huntley, Tippi Huntley, Gunilla Hutton,
Shirley Hutton, Marty Ingels, General "Chappy" James,
Harry James, Hal Janney, Peter Jennings, J. Allen Jensen, Jim Jensen,
Brad Johnson, Jan Jones, Quincy Jones, Shirley Jones, Phyllis Kahn,
Herb Kaplow, Don Kaulia, Danny Kaye, Howard Keel,
Betty Lou Keim, Gene Kelly, John Kerry, Billy Kidd,
Dorothy Kilgallen, Henry Kissinger, Eartha Kitt,
Senator Amy Klobuchar, Jim Klobuchar,
Marguerite and Al Knickerbocker, Jill Konrath, Ted Koppel,
Gregory Lafayette, Jim Lange, Michael Laughlin, Manny Laureano,
Carol Lawrence, Paul Laxalt, Norman Lear, David Letterman,
Carol Lynley, June Levant, Daryl Lewis, Jerry Lewis,
Art Linkletter and family, Denny Long, Jeff Lonto, Sophia Loren,
Marion Lorne, Carl Low, James MacArthur,
Frank and Brent Magid, George Maharis, Gia Maione, Jack Malisow,
Henry Mancini, Iris Mann, Tom Marsland, Svetlana Masgutova,
Rudy Maxa, Liza Minnelli, Mitzi (Steiner) McCall, J. Elroy,
Marion and Craig McCaw, J.B. "Buck" Macdonald,
Frank and Josh Mankiewicz, Bill Maus, Sr., Art and Kerry McGinn,
Phyllis McGuire, Anne Meara, William "Fishbait' Miller,
Susan Miller, Sal Mineo, R. Garrett Mitchell, Peter Molson,
Vice President Walter F. Mondale, Marilyn Monroe, Jack Morgan,

Russ Morgan, Art Mosby, Charlie Moss, Senator Edmund Muskie,
The Ted and Betty Nathan Family, Peter Nero,
Eric and Barbara Neville, Bob Newhart, Megan Newquist,
Bob North, Deborah Norville, Louis and Anita Nye, Ted O'Brien,
Peggy O'Connell, Donald O'Connor, Maureen O'Hara,
Edward James Olmos, Rosemary O'Reilly, Tom Oszman, Betty Otto,
Empress Farah Diba Pahlavi and children, Gregory Peck,
Governor and Mrs. Rudy Perpich, Michelle Phillips,
Tom and Kay Poston, General Colin Powell, Leonard Prescott,
Louis Prima, Al Primo, Juliet Prowse, Bill Putch and Jean Stapleton,
John Putch, Heather Randall, Tony Randall, Josh Raphaelson,
Dan Rather, Maureen Reagan, Sumner Redstone, Sandy Reedy,
Reginald Reeves, Carl Reiner, George Richey, Chris Riddle,
Thelma Ritter, Joan Rivers, Jerome Robbins, Al Roker,
Mickey Rooney, Dr. Judith-Rae Ross, Steve Rossi, Bob Ryan,
Tom Ryther, Eva Marie Saint, Heidi Sanders, Vineeta Sawkar,
Bob Schieffer, George Schlatter, Lada Shabunina, Eunice Shriver,
Maria Shriver, Charlie Sheen, Jean Shepherd,
Dave Wayne and Pat Siebenmark, Dewain Silvester,
Senator Paul Simon, Judge John Sirica, Jack Slattery, Jean Smart,
Marvin D. "Mark" Smith, Jimmy "The Greek" Snyder, Roy Southwick,
Karl Spring, Cris Stainbrook, Rod Steiger, Carl and Joy Stern,
James Stewart, Pepi Stiegler, Jerry Stiller, Susan Strasberg,
Bob Stupak, Patrick and Penny Sweeney, Mark Sweet, Bob,
Dee and Kelly Syers, Senator Herman Talmadge, Nya Terry,
Phil Tonken, Lou and Priscilla Torok, Van Tran, Arthur Treacher,
President Harry Truman, Linda Twiss, Jim Tyne, Leslie Uggams,
Lucretia Whelan, Joe Valandra, Dick Van Patten, Jimmy Van Patten,
Jo Van Patten, Pat Van Patten, Sarah Vaughan, General John Vessey,
Edward Villella, Christopher Walken, Kenny Walken, Harvey Weinstein,
Tuesday Weld, Lawrence Welk stars, Denis and Jean Wiesenburg,
Randy Wile, Andy Williams, Joe Williams, John Williams,
Mary Alice Williams, Alice Wlliamson, Lizz Winstead,
David Winters, Bobby Wooten, Rudi Wyrsch, Henny Youngman,
Ambassador Ardeshir Zahedi, Tawnja Zahradka and Si Zentner.

Author's Personal Notes

1. I'm in the midst of writing this after just learning Anne Meara, Jerry Stiller's cherished wife and life-partner for 61 years, passed away yesterday, May 23, 2015, making these memories all the more profound and this book more difficult to write without considerable sadness. Her passing has numbed me and so many, of course, incredulously trying to accept the fact she's not here anymore.

2. The reason for this book's above-title (so above-titled with Jerry's kind printed permission) is to not only thank Jerry for urging me to write my story, but also to emphasize he kindly cared enough about *me* to acknowledge me as one of his friends in *his* autobiography, *Married to Laughter*, published in late 2000. He, God bless him, circled my name in red pen on the acknowledgments page. I had no idea Jerry was writing a book, but it arrived here in the mail from him in early January, 2001, inscribed, *"To Barry ZeVan, To Ellen ZeVan: You are very much part of my life. Love, Jerry Stiller, 1/2/2001"*. (Please see photos section) What an unexpected honor, to say the least, for which I've been, and am, more than humbly grateful. Jerry is one of the few "real" human beings in a business fraught with "fakers". In Jerry's book, he stated his father didn't like "fakers". Obviously, that thought attached itself to Jerry, as he's as far from being a "faker" as anyone could ever be. To have the privilege of his caring and friendship is one of the major blessings of my life and I can't think what the other blessings would be.

3. I've just successfully completed chemotherapy treatments for chronic lymphocytic leukemia and am in remission in perpetuity, according to the VA Oncologist.

"You're an express train that hasn't reached its destination." and *"You remind me of 'June Is Bustin' Out All Over'."* I still have Jerry Stiller's

letter from 2010 that contains those heartwarming statements he kindly expressed about me, shown later in these pages. Two *additional* unsolicited statements Jerry made to me during one of our phone conversations in February, 2015, prior to my beginning to write this memoir, were, *"You're a self-made man"* and *"You should be more recognized"*. His comments, based on years of *his* profound successful career and life experiences, were, to me, a signal this writing *should* be accomplished, perhaps the sooner the better, since I'm aged 78!

Jerry has been a true friend, for which I'm more than blessed. I've had the honor, privilege and joy of his friendship since the early 1980s, but our *professional* history had its genesis during our "making the rounds" acting days beginning in the early 1950s when he and the now late Anne Meara, his brilliantly talented and wonderful wife, were beginning to deservedly become national treasures via television.

As to which previously alluded, had it not been for Jerry's many urgings, I would never have begun nor completed writing this chronicle about my very unusual life, continually and simultaneously blessed and cursed, maximally, at both ends of the spectrum, personally involving more world-renowned icons than imaginable, but all true. Thank goodness there are many still alive who know all I've written is fact, not fiction, not embellishment nor delusion. It's simply insight as to "how they were, *when*", either before or after they became icons, the previously unknown *non-embarrassing* stories they shared with me, as well as how I came to be part of their lives and vice-versa.

This book also pays homage to many *not*-famous people who cared enough to keep me glued together when times were tough and were great teachers who had no idea they were teaching me. They, too, were (and those alive still are) iconic people to me. The many places I "pitched my tent" (as my friend Peter Jennings once publicly referred to my ubiquitous lives) are also filled with unordinary memories I hope you may consider interesting.

As previously stated, with his kind printed permission, conveyed to me in a February, 2015, email via his assistants, Jody and Dawn, Jerry allowed me to above-title this book. The *"thank* you" to him in the above-title is genuine and stated with *eternal* gratitude for his urging me to write my story. Hopefully, if you choose to read this memoir to its conclusion, you'll, as previously stated, understand why he admonished me to write it and I finally decided it was time to do so. I thank him, again and always.

Aside from unique personal stories about the iconic people of whose lives I was a part, and vice versa, many of them long before they became famous and afterward, and the stories they told me, as well as the places I've worked and lived, this book will also possibly help people who suffer from timidity, self-doubt, depression, pervasive fear of rejection and uncertainty, overcome and defeat those demons. I also hope it will illustrate and echo what actress Maureen O'Hara admonished to me during a special week together in Jackson Hole, Wyoming, in 1963, i.e., "to never ever give up". Memories of that time are also among the stories I relate in these reflections, as well as why and how those times "happened".

Ironically, there have been others who have echoed Jerry's admonitions I should write this book, but never sinking-in as profoundly as Jerry's. One came from former co-worker and longtime national overnight radio personality, George Noory, host of the nation's most popular program about the paranormal. George told me years ago, "I want you to be more noticed". I still have that email.

Longtime friend, the late actor Tom Poston, to me in front of others at his then temporary residence in Stratford, Connecticut: "You should be President of a network."

Another insightful comment about what I consider my possibly *too*-extraordinary life, and an additional "seed planter" to write this book, was stated by Kim Thomas, now of London, England. Kim was one of my directors at WJLA-TV during my on-air Washington, D.C., television years (1974 to 1977) and has been, I'm happy to state, a dear friend since. Kim was also my mother's next-door neighbor during those D.C. years. During dinner one night in the 1990s at an outdoor restaurant on The Croissette in Cannes, France, I began recalling many disparate things about my eclectic life, after which Kim asked something that has resonated deeply to this day, i.e., "How many people *live* in that body, Barry?" She then smiled, as did I, but I also realized it was a valid question, the answer to which you'll hopefully care to learn her insightful reason for asking.

What I've written involves a lifetime of being welcomed into literally dozens of circles of the world's most powerful individuals, globally, with vivid (and provable) memories of how they were as "people". Rather than "name-dropping", the memories I'm sharing are related *in awe and gratitude* of my privilege to have had (and still have, with those still alive) their private selves be shared with mine, and vice-versa, personally and professionally.

My memories will also attest many people who had endured anything resembling my perpetual roller-coaster ride would have jumped off at the highest point and enjoyed their demise. Again, when and if you continue reading, hopefully you'll know and understand why Jerry and some others felt my story should be told. I'm grateful to *them* and for *your* kindness to continue reading.

Reiterating what Jerry kindly stated to me in the afore-mentioned letter, "You're an express train that hasn't reached its destination". Well, dear friend Jerry, here we go. That train is almost ready to leave the station, so, dear *reader*, please come aboard for one very unordinary, unexpected, unpredictable, hopefully educational, thought-provoking and possibly inspiring ride.

Barry ZeVan
Minneapolis, Minnesota
December, 2015

Stories Preview

As is the case with so many people these days, and perhaps throughout history, it might be interesting for those who know or *don't* know me, I have many personal demons I battle and have battled daily, especially depression, sadness, more hand-to-mouth living than not, handling rejection and other extreme thoughts. Those sorts of thoughts have been often present and perhaps, after reading this book, you'll understand why. Hopefully, this book may also serve as a guide to why some of us never give up.

In 2002, a Phoenix, Arizona, palm reader, whom I visited on a whim during a national play tour stop there, stated one very true observation: She told me many people have been, and are, very jealous of me, and have almost begrudged me any successes. She quickly followed with the added observation, "It's not they don't *like* you, but it's definite they, for some strange reason, either don't *want* you to be successful, or are jealous of any of your many successes". She made these statements without knowing what my profession or history was. Interesting, because, without paranoia, and for the most part, it's true. Discern if *you* might feel the same way after reading what I have to tell, including many private stories about private moments with some of the most celebrated figures contemporary history ever produced, from entertainers to world leaders. They were friends (some of them from their youngest years), acquaintances, colleagues and, sometimes, temporary enemies. One of the amusing elements is most people who *think* they know or knew me, or what I've been through, or accomplished, don't have a *clue*, but they *will*, now, again thanks to Jerry strongly encouraging me to write about it.

In addition, when a television anchor friend named Mike Binkley once asked me how I'd like to be remembered, I had never thought of it to that minute, but responded spontaneously and truthfully, as follows: "*I* only ever wanted to become successful enough to have enough clout and influence to help *other* people become successful."

It's still true and I hope can someday be achieved to the fullest. I strongly agree with the credo that giving is far more rewarding than receiving, and have "lived it" as much as possible.

Some of the stories I'll share in this book, include:

—*I Love Lucy*'s writers, Madelyn Pugh Davis and Bob Carroll, Jr., telling me how they arrived at the idea to create the candy factory scene for Lucy and Ethel and also how Madelyn was responsible for Steve Allen's big break, getting him from Phoenix to L.A.

—Art Linkletter telling me the story of how Art became even more of a multi-millionaire because Walt Disney was too broke to pay Art to emcee the opening of Disneyland.

—Having President Truman tell me, and others, why he was furious with President Roosevelt the day after Roosevelt died.

—Having Catherine Deneuve and Jacques Cousteau as seat partners during a flight from Paris to New York, including a smile-evoking anecdote regarding Ms. Deneuve and yours truly. Same for my high school contemporary and seat partner, Susan Strasberg, on a flight from New York to Paris.

—Having Stefan Lorant, one of the six original members of the Nazi Party, tell me how he convinced Hitler to not have Lorant as a member, but rather becoming Hitler's personal photojournalist to the end of Hitler's life, even though he personally hated Hitler and what Hitler was doing.

—Having Frances Gershwin, George, Ira's and Arthur's sister, tell me about life in the Gershwin homes and how she became George's "tooter" for *An American in Paris.*

—Having coffee with James Dean and George Maharis the day before James left for Hollywood to make his first film, *East of Eden* and what George had to say about show business before our social coffee meeting ended.

—Having Duke Ellington kiss me on the lips, with witnesses still alive.

—Being on New York television as a performer with Bill Cullen and John Reed King in 1946, two years before the entire U.S. got television in 1948.

—Producing a ski tourism film in 1977 for The Shah of Iran in Iran's Elburz Mountains, seen on HBO for a year, until the Khomeini revolution began and maintaining a cordial relationship with the Shah's wife (now widow), Empress Farah Diba Pahlavi. Also having President Nixon be my "delivery boy" to get the film to the Shah in Mexico after The Shah's exile, and my friendship with John Ehrlichman, including a story that will shock Nixon-lovers.

—What it was like to work for Howard Hughes and learn he was a "fan" of my work.

—What it was like to have MGM Grand owner Kirk Kerkorian as a one-time tennis partner in Las Vegas as well as hitting golf balls more than one time with Pearl Bailey at The Dunes driving range.

—How Howard Keel, Robert Goulet, Louis Nye, Tony Randall and I became lifelong friends and the stories they shared with me for decades. (I acted with Tony as one of the students on *Mister Peepers* for two years. He took me under his wing for 50-plus years.)

—Sharing great years with my second cousin, Cecil Brown, who was one of Edward R. Murrow's "boys" in London during WWII. He has a star on the Hollywood Walk of Fame and was ABC-TV's first anchorman in 1953. Peter Jennings and I were like brothers, with Chet Huntley, Ted Koppel, Steve Bell and Frank Reynolds honoring me with *very* close personal friendships and significant social times together. Lots of great stories there, too. Same for SFO's KGO-TV weatherman, Spencer Christian (my *best* friend) and Willard Scott. Great story about Willard riding in my Rolls Royce during very halcyon days in D.C. when we were locally opposite each other on television there. Illinois Senator Paul Simon was a passenger of mine in the Rolls, too, which is *another* story that will be told.

—Calming Woody Allen's fears and driving him safely through a flood in Las Vegas after directing him in a television show there.

—Pierce Brosnan's kindness and astute observation before we even first said "Hello".

—Being written about in two books, regarding how I was responsible for actor Sal Mineo's break into feature films. Sal was among my high school classmates at a New York school for children who were professionally acting and couldn't attend regular classes. Our other school friends included Leslie Uggams, Tuesday Weld, Charlie Moss (he in later life created the I♥NY ad campaign), Charlie Brill, Carol Lynley, Sandra Dee, Patty Duke, Kenny Walken (Christopher's brother) and Chris Walken (when Chris was age 6 and I was age 17), among others.

—Privately advising Peter Molson in his Quebec home, at his request.

CHAPTER ONE

"Who *am* I, anyway?"

Partial lyrics from the song of the same name in A Chorus Line

"*I*never got a good job I didn't create for myself."—Actress Ruth Gordon (stated to me at New York's Russian Tea Room in Jerry Stiller's presence after Jerry treated me to lunch there in the 1990s and introduced me to Ms. Gordon and her husband, playwright Garson Kanin.)

Reiterating, *on purpose*, my author's note, numbered 2 in this book's Prologue, the reason for this book's above-title (so above-titled with Jerry's kind printed permission) is to not only thank Jerry for urging me to write my story, but also to emphasize he kindly cared enough about me to acknowledge me as one of his friends in *his* autobiography, *Married to Laughter*, published in late 2000. He, God bless him, circled my name in red pen on the acknowledgments page. I had no idea Jerry was writing a book, but it arrived here in the mail from him in early January, 2001, inscribed, *"To Barry ZeVan, To Ellen ZeVan: You are very much part of my life. Love, Jerry Stiller. 1/2/2001"*. (Please see photos section) What an unexpected honor, to say the least, for which I've been, and am, more than humbly grateful. Jerry is one of the few "real" human beings in a business fraught with "fakers". In Jerry's book, he stated his father didn't like "fakers". Obviously, that rubbed off on Jerry, too, as he's as far from "faker" as one could ever get. To have the privilege of his caring and friendship is one of the major blessings of my life and I can't think what the other blessings would be.

There are about ten-million people in this country (especially in Minneapolis-Saint Paul, Washington, D.C., Detroit, Las Vegas, Seattle-Tacoma and Idaho Falls) and parts of the *world* who have known me from being on television, radio and/or in print as either "Barry ZeVan, the Weatherman", a talk show or music show host, actor or singer on major television series and in films (or on stage), multimedia film critic/reviewer and/or columnist, blogger and/or opinion commentator. For the other almost six-*billion* who have no idea who I am or why reading this book should matter, I think it best at least a small fraction of those billions who might be reading this know from where I'm coming and what has made and makes me "tick". It may help them, and you, understand and possibly validate why Jerry kindly encouraged me to write these memories in book form.

Some favorite sayings and admonitions which have helped guide my life:
> *When does God laugh the loudest? When He hears our plans.* (A friend)
> *It's never too late to be who you might have been.* (George Eliot)
> *Great spirits have always encountered violent opposition from mediocre minds.* (Albert Einstein)
> *I've never been poor, only broke. Being poor is a frame of mind. Being broke is only a temporary situation.* (Mike Todd)
> *The truth is incontrovertible. Malice may attack it and ignorance may deride it, but in the end, there it is.* (Sir Winston Churchill)
> *Do unto others as you would have them do unto you.* (The Golden Rule, most important, in my opinion)
> *We never stop learning.* (Me)
> (More life-shaping sayings or witticisms are stated atop the beginning of each chapter, hopefully helpful as gently thought-provoking.)

Some favorite movies which have constantly inspired me, starring many of whom I got to know, warmly and personally, in later life:
> *The Red Shoes*
> *An American in Paris*
> *The Search*
> *Picnic*
> *The Life and Death of Colonel Blimp*
> *Carousel*
> *Lawrence of Arabia*
> *Rhapsody in Blue*

Limelight

Inglorious Basterds (For those unaware, "Basterds" is the way writer-director Quentin Tarantino chose to spell it for the film's title.)

It's A Wonderful Life

Music that has constantly inspired me and with which I've been blessed to have strong personal relationships with their vocal artists, composers, musicians and/or families (also chronicled in this book):

Anything "Gershwin", but especially *Concerto in 'F' for Piano and Orchestra, Rhapsody in Blue* and *An American In Paris*

Richard Wagner's *Prelude to Act Three of Lohengrin* and *March of The Meistersingers* from *Die Meistersinger*

Anything Peter Nero

Anything Leroy Anderson

Anything Frank Sinatra

Anything Robert Goulet

Anything Nikki Yanofsky

Anything Quincy Jones

Any great symphony orchestra's performances

Anything Tchaikowsky

Any Sousa march

Favorite places in North America:

Monument Valley, Arizona-Utah

Death Valley, California

The Grand Canyon, Arizona

Anywhere in Nevada

New York City

Boston

Glacier National Park, Montana

Anywhere in Quebec or Alberta, Canada

Favorite places outside North America:

Monte Carlo, Monaco

Cape Town, South Africa

Singapore, Singapore
Anywhere in England
Chile's Andes Mountains
Mount Dizin, Iran
The Royal Albert Hall, London, England
The village of Luss, Scotland
The village of Eze, France
The villages of Mayrhofen and Lilienfeld, Austria

From *very* humble beginnings, I'm in *awe* of having had the privilege
to be more than a passing part of the lives of the most powerful icons
in the entertainment, broadcasting, journalism and political arenas
and to have been to all the "favorite places" named, and then some,
very often when poor as a church mouse, which few ever knew.
I'll share how the icons were thinking as "people" when I was with
them in social private times, sometimes in their homes as an invitee,
mostly *not* as an interviewer, as well as the stories and thoughts
they were kind enough to share with me. None of what I've written
is embarrassing, tawdry or "tell all", but rather bemusing and very
introspective. I spent much of my childhood and adolescence with
many of them before and after they became world famous. The stories
I'll share, and about whom I'll share, will be, I promise, unpredictable
and the people named a major surprise in many instances.

There's rarely a movie, movie on television, television show,
special television feature, major newscast or anything in media
or "live" on stage with which I haven't had, or still have, a strong
personal connection, with either the stars, the featured players,
subjects of the stories, the writers, producers, anchors, reporters and/
or directors. Frankly, it sometimes drives me crazy, in a melancholy
way, seeing all those icons and remembering my personal times
with them, most of them chronicled herein and listed in the Stories
Preview preceding this first chapter and Acknowledgments at the
beginning of the book. I never asked any of them for help when so
many times in my life were very lean financially. Two of them came
through, though, voluntarily, as gifts, without my asking. Another

made me a "loan", for which I *did* ask, to help me maintain some self-esteem and whatever dignity existed at that time.

It might also be good to know my many "down times" were *very* down, almost to the point of ending it all, as previously stated, but, in my opinion, can't be too often emphasized. More will be related about *those* days, too.

CHAPTER TWO

Pittsburgh, via Ukraine and France

Some people were born with a golden spoon in their mouth. I was born with a plastic fork in my mouth.—Me

As part of the lyrics to *The Sound of Music*'s song, *Do-Re-Mi*, state, "Let's start at the very beginning, a very good place to start". In that context, Barry Noel ZeVan is my real name. It's on both my birth certificate and the State of Pennsylvania Notification of Birth Registration document. I always hated my name. I thought it sounded too "affected", but, indeed, to *add* to the affectation I've identified, my dear mother felt it necessary to make my *middle* name what it was, but pronounced as the French word for Christmas, i.e., "no-ell". It makes sense (not), since I was born August 5th, 1937, at 6:06 a.m. at Western Pennsylvania Hospital (known as West Penn, colloquially) in the Pittsburgh enclave of Bloomfield.

My father, nee William ZeVan, was born in Marseilles, France, arriving in this country in 1890 when he was six months old. He was a theater architect and my mother, at the time I was born, a housewife, but a graduate of the University of Michigan who studied languages to teach. Sadly, she never achieved her goal to teach *professionally*, but certainly taught *me* throughout my life, including French becoming my "second language". When I was sixteen months old, my father left the apartment one Sunday morning to get a newspaper and never returned. We later learned he was simultaneously married to at least three women other than my mother. What we subsequently learned of *his* history would make a book. We learned he died somewhere in Kansas in 1950.

Regardless, my grandfather, John Nossokoff, who had opposed my Mom's marriage to William ZeVan, also had a history, and a colorful one, in only the most positive sense. He was born in Kiev, Russia (now identified solely as Ukraine). When his family arrived at Ellis Island in 1890, my grandfather was *also* only six months old, the same age as my father when he and *his* family arrived at that fabled gateway to begin trying to live the American dream. For whatever reason, my great-grandfather decided Pittsburgh was the place to begin and flourish in the family's new American life. There they settled.

In downtown Pittsburgh, my great-grandfather, Morris Nossokoff, created the first barber college in the United States, with 12 chairs. My grandfather, on the other hand, was more into music than sartorial thinking, from the time he could lift a violin, although still very dashing, sartorially. He became a child prodigy on the violin and later had his own orchestras performing throughout western Pennsylvania, all in his late teens. He also became an agent for another violin prodigy named Dave Rubinoff, who became nationally famous. Others my grandfather "booked" in his post-teen years were Milton Berle, George Burns and Gracie Allen and a songwriter and his nightclub-act wife. Their names were Lou Handman and Florence (Florrie) Lavere. *In my pre-teen years, and for years afterward, Lou and Florrie became "Uncle" Lou and "Aunt" Florrie. Lou had been a song-plugger for Irving Berlin . . . directly working with Mr. Berlin . . . and the most famous song for which "Uncle" Lou wrote the lyrics was,* Are You Lonesome Tonight? *When Elvis Presley recorded that song, a few years after "Uncle" Lou passed away, "Aunt" Florrie lived a very good life and didn't pass away destitute, thank goodness, and thank Elvis. I met Elvis later in my life, but that story comes later!*

My grandfather wasn't the only music prodigy in the family. Two others were my grandfather's brothers, Irwin ("Toots", as they called him) and Harry. Toots eventually had a big band of his own, but simultaneously, with Harry, took piano lessons with Oscar Levant, another Pittsburgh native. Toots told me Oscar was so short they had to place a phone book on the piano bench that allowed him to reach the keys. *In later life, I had dealings that involved Levant, his wife, June, and Frances "Frankie" Gershwin, but* those *stories you'll* also *see later in this compendium of memories.*

(Also in later life, I learned from singer Ed Ames, who became a longtime friend to me, my great-grandfather, Morris Nossokoff, afore-mentioned and Ed Ames's grandfather co-owned a Kiev brewery named Nossokoff and Yurikoff, until the pogroms chased them out of Russia in 1890. Yurikoff was the Ames family's original last name. I'll relate how The Ames Brothers chose their Americanized last name later in this book, told to me by Ed during dinner one night in Las Vegas, circa 1968.)

When I appeared on the scene in 1937, all was going swimmingly with the family, and remained so until World War Two commenced in earnest for the U.S., beginning December 7th, 1941. The announcement Pearl Harbor had been bombed is my first memory, hearing it on Pittsburgh's KDKA radio that fateful Sunday afternoon, about four, Pittsburgh time. I remember the sun streaming at a slanted angle through the south window of our third-floor small apartment in a private home. When she (and I) heard the radio bulletin, my mother jumped up from her single bed, crying and running across the small room to my bed. She hugged me and said, "Oh, my baby. I hope you'll never have to go to war!" At age four, I didn't think that possibility was imminent, but I was all my mother had and her melodramatic heart was certainly in the right place. Although she's been gone since 1987, I still love, miss and cherish her every day.

Ironically, when listening to the KDKA Pearl Harbor news bulletin that Sunday afternoon, I never knew I'd be a boy singer on that station, less than two years hence. Two years earlier, in 1939, when Hitler was threatening to bomb Great Britain, there was a U.S. National War Bond Drive and tour to try to help the Brits deter Germany from bringing the war to their shores. One of the cities on the tour was our beloved Pittsburgh. Among the celebrities who were beating the drum to help Great Britain's anti-war effort was a very notable Brit himself. His name was Arthur Treacher, a revered motion picture character actor who later became known as Merv Griffin's sidekick on television's *The Merv Griffin Show*. Because my grandfather, as previously noted, was deeply immersed in the entertainment industry, my mother and I were invited to be both on stage and backstage during the tour's performance at Pittsburgh's Stanley Theater, now known as Heinz Hall. My mother and grandfather told me Arthur Treacher lifted me up over his head,

mother immediately got a job as a secretary in Allegheny County's Recorder of Deeds office and was, again, the "star" typist and linguist. Her boss, John J. Exler, had been a recent World War Two veteran who had been disabled during his service. My grandfather had, by the early 1940s, morphed from entertainment into politics and worked for The City of Pittsburgh as a health inspector focusing on restaurant cleanliness. His influence with then Mayor David E. Lawrence helped my mother get her position with the city. Mayor Lawrence, a mega-Democrat, later became Governor of Pennsylvania and was truly right out of "central casting". He was a true powerhouse in every sense and justifiably revered by almost everyone in the political arena, be they Republican or Democrat. With my grandfather present, I met him once or twice in my pre-teens and knew he was "power personified". (At age eight, I had no idea President Truman would tell me about the atomic bomb drops, in person, as well as other pertinent events during his presidency, just 18 years later, in October, 1963. The story of that time with Mr. Truman is related later in this book, including a very special picture taken after the interview which he graciously signed with a kind message to me, and seen on the second page of this book.

Two weeks after V-J Day (victory over Japan ending World War Two) my mom took me on vacation to New York City for my first visit there. It was a month after a plane had crashed into the Empire State Building's 79th floor, July 28th, 1945. I remember being in awe to see in person, from 34th Street ground level, the gaping hole about which I'd heard on Pittsburgh radio, being repaired right before my eyes. Hey, at eight years of age, everything (in those days, at least) made one awestruck. Regardless, my mom and I stayed the first night at a cockroach-infested hotel, The Somerset, on 46th Street between 7th and 6th Avenues, but for only one night before she wisely decided to move us to a better hotel a couple blocks away. She had remembered The Somerset to be a better hotel from her youthful visits to New York in the 1920s with my grandfather. Ironically, in better days, it was the hotel in which actress/comedienne Rose Marie had lived. My mom moved us to The Edison Hotel, a half-block west of Broadway, on 47th Street, a stone's throw from Duffy Square (the North end of Times

Square) that was, in later life, soon to mean even more to me than being the second place I'd ever stayed in New York, to be explained later. (The Edison Hotel was also where a then-unknown clarinet and saxophone player named Alan Greenspan was a member of Henry Jerome's Edison Hotel "house band", which my mom and I watched play for a while one evening during our first stay at The Edison. Greenspan would later become the well-known Federal Reserve Chairman from 1987 to 2006 under several U.S. Presidents and marry NBC News correspondent Andrea Mitchell. I occasionally dated one of Greenspan's nieces, Judy, who was a nearby neighbor of ours on the Upper West Side, during my teenage acting years in the 1950s in New York. I met Ms. Mitchell only once in later years.)

We stayed in New York for a week that year and returned to Pittsburgh to continue life post-war. The following summer, timed to make their vacations coincide with Labor Day (to get an extra vacation day, with pay), my mom took me to New York again, but this time my grandfather was with us. We stayed at The Edison. During that stay, the film, "Rhapsody In Blue", the romanticized story of George Gershwin's life, starring Robert Alda (Alan Alda's father) was playing, along with a stage show starring Mr. Alda, at The Strand Theater, the stage door for which was right across the street from The Edison. Our room was on the eighth floor. One late afternoon, I looked out our window and saw Mr. Alda below, standing outside the stage door. Not being bashful, and encouraged by my mother to do so, I shouted, "Hi, Bob!" To my surprise, he looked up, saw me and shouted, "Hi! What's your name?" I shouted back, "Barry!" He shouted back, "Hi, Barry!" with a big smile on his face and in his voice. We did that for the next five days at just about the same time each day. I later told this anecdote to his son, Alan, during an interview I did with him for one of his feature films and Alan seemed to enjoy hearing it. Alan was also one of the speakers at my later-in-life friend, Peter Jennings's memorial service at Carnegie Hall. During Alan's eulogy that day, he referenced how down-to-Earth Peter really was, with Peter once insisting on washing the dishes by hand after a large party at Alan's home on Long Island. There's much more about Peter's and my friendship, later.

During that 1945 trip, my mom took me to a live broadcast of
a popular CBS radio show called Give and Take. *It starred a radio*
"giant", in those days, named John Reed King. The announcer was
another Pittsburgh native, Bill Cullen, who later went on to legendary
fame as a television game show host and panelist. My mom and I had
listened to it every Saturday at home in Pittsburgh, now here we were at
the show itself! It was broadcast from a very classy radio broadcasting
theater located in New York's Barbizon-Plaza Hotel. When we got into
the theater, someone from the show asked my mother if she'd approve
of my being a contestant on the show. She said, "Yes". That was an hour
before the live show was broadcast, thus we had time for a snack in the
hotel coffee shop. Sitting next to me at the counter, on my right, was
Bill Cullen. I knew Give and Take *was sponsored by Chef Boyardee*
Spaghetti Dinner, so I precociously asked Bill, "What are you having
for lunch, Bill?" Bill replied, as though he was reading my mind, which
he was, "It sure as Hell isn't Chef Boyardee Spaghetti Dinner!" He then
gave me a warm smile, and that was that. In later years, I was blessed
to be with Bill during several occasions, both professional and social.
I then was coached about how to behave on Give and Take, *a quiz*
show. Coast-to-coast, CBS radio listeners heard me answer questions
correctly and win prizes of my first bicycle, a classic Schwinn, and a
set of luggage, which I gave to my mother. Those quality suitcases are
still in my garage. The "punch line": Just after the Give and Take *show*
was over, the producer asked my mother if she would allow me to be
on television that night. It was August, 1946, two years before the
entire U.S. would get television. We didn't even know what television
was, but my mom said, "Okay". We were given directions to the studio,
scheduled to be there at 6:30 that evening. It was a show named King's
Party Line, *again hosted by John Reed King and announced by Bill*
Cullen. The studio was on the second floor of The New York General
Building, the tall building at the south end of Park Avenue and attached
to the north side of Grand Central Station. I was told before the show
that a viewer was going to try to guess my hat size, which was 6⅞. If
the viewer guessed correctly, all I was coached to say, was, "That's right,
Mr. King." If the viewer guessed the wrong size, I'd reply in the negative.
Also appearing on the show was a female zither player. The lights in the

studio were gigantic and hot scoop-style, thus we got paid in as much Coca Cola we could drink, even while the live show was being aired. It started at 7 p.m., ended at 7:30 and a man from The Bronx, the first caller to be asked about my hat size, guessed correctly and I said my line. That was my television debut, two years before the rest of the nation got television. I was later told New York City had 600 television sets in existence that hot August night. I never thought, at the time, that show and that appearance would be considered part of television history, but indeed that was the case. Anne Cullen, Bill's widow, is still alive at this writing, to corroborate what I've just related. Two other incidents that would become serendipitous during a subsequent New York trip in August, 1949: My mom took me to the then famous Dinty Moore's Restaurant for lunch. She whispered, "Frank Faylen is sitting at the next table." I recognized him from movies in which he'd acted, but of course never expected in later years he'd portray Dobie Gillis's character's father in The Many Loves of Dobie Gillis *which would star a person with whom I'd have a very close and warm friendship in later years, i.e., Dwayne Hickman, more about which later. Also on that show was Tuesday Weld, with whom I'd share her pre-high school days, and almost a date, in New York in the mid-1950s, about which I'll also relate more, later. The second "incident": My mom also recognized Mickey Rooney's father, Joe Yule, sitting in the lobby of The Edison Hotel, where we were staying, as previously mentioned. She struck up a conversation with him and he said he'd be playing the title role in a national tour of* Finian's Rainbow *in October that year (1949). He said Pittsburgh's Nixon Theater would be one of the tour's performance venues, thus if she brought me to the theater when the tour arrived, he'd make sure I could perform as one of the children dancing around the wishing well for all seven days of performances there. It happened, and the wonderful photo he signed to me after the play had concluded is seen later in this book. In later years, I worked with Mickey several times throughout my crazy career, most notably when I was one of The Ray Charles Singers on* The Perry Como Show *in 1955-56-57, about which much more about those times will also be related later.*

I attended and graduated a straight-A student from H.C. Frick grade school in the Pittsburgh suburb of Oakland, having been presented, upon graduation, the American Legion's Scholastic Award, that body's highest educational honor. Frick was a teachers training school, less than a half-mile east of Forbes Field, then home to the Pittsburgh Pirates baseball team (still my favorites at age 78, but with some fondness and allegiance now to the Minnesota Twins) and a half-mile or so west of The Pittsburgh Playhouse. In those days, The Pittsburgh Playhouse was one of the two most admired semi-professional theaters in the country, the other being California's Pasadena Playhouse. Both theaters are still held in high regard and were the launching pads for the careers of some very accomplished and world-renowned stars.

One Friday night in late August, 1948, my mother told me she'd read an ad that day in the Pittsburgh Sun-Telegraph The Playhouse was accepting walk-in sign ups for children to attend acting classes there. The classes would be held every Saturday morning, with chances for the young students to be cast in plays there. She told me we'd go to The Playhouse the next morning and enroll me in the acting class. My mother made spontaneous decisions, although based on laser-beamlike intuition and life experiences. She could look at a person for ten seconds and know if they were "real" or trustworthy. It's another trait I eventually inherited from her, although more gullible and trusting for more of my life than I'd like to admit.

Regardless, she took me to sign up that Saturday morning for my first class. There were three instructors for different facets of acting. Their names were William (Bill) Leach, Joseph (Joe) Ruskin and Bill Putch. The latter, with whom I would eventually act in several plays at The Playhouse, later became the lifelong husband of noted actress Jean Stapleton, whose most memorable role was that of Edith Bunker on CBS Television's *All In The Family*. (The late Joe Ruskin's daughter, Alicia, is now a well-established agent in Hollywood. Joe eventually went on to be a featured actor on *The Untouchables* and other iconic television series.)

At the conclusion of my very first class, Bill Leach told me they wanted me to have a part in the next Playhouse production, entitled *Strange Bedfellows*, circa autumn, 1948. I acted in three additional plays at The Playhouse from 1948 through 1951.

One of the then not nationally known but now justifiably revered world-beloved stars I knew "when" was Shirley Jones. Shirley took her first acting lessons at The Pittsburgh Playhouse during the same years I studied and acted there, 1948-1951. We shared instructors and classes. Shirley became Miss Pittsburgh in 1952. The preceding year I acted in her first play entitled Wonderful Good. The play's musical composers and pianist accompanists were named Ken and Mitzie Welch. They later became Carol Burnett's musical directors on CBS Television's The Carol Burnett Show. The Playhouse's scene designer and silk-screen sign maker, Gino Conte, with whom I kept in touch for life, eventually became NBC-TV's head of production services in Burbank. In 1948, I used to stand beside Gino when he was in a dark attic section of The Playhouse, fascinated with his silk-screen sign making. Who knew he'd become one of NBC-TV's biggest "wheels". In later years, Gino told me he gave Lorne Michaels the final green light to start SNL. Gino's son, Courtney, with whom I also had some fun times in later years, thanks to Laugh-In creator and producer, George Schlatter, who also became a longtime friend (still is, as of this writing), became an executive with Carsey-Werner Productions in Hollywood during the 1980s heyday of TV sitcoms. The Playhouse's Director, one Frederick Burleigh, was the best Director ever. I'm happy to say Shirley and I have kept in touch and seen each other sporadically since then. Two wonderful photos she signed for me, with delightful inscriptions, are included in the photos section of this book and the locale and story behind them described. When those photos were taken, in 2013, in Omaha, Shirley and I reminisced about the Playhouse days and she concurred with my assessment about Fred Burleigh being the best Director ever, with a resounding, "Yes, he was". In later years, Shirley would also share the silver screen with my best high school-years friend, Timmy Everett, when he portrayed the young boy befriended by Robert Preston's character in The Music Man, more about which will be told later. Ironically, when my mom and I moved to New York in 1951, after Wonderful Good, I started part of one year at Forest Hills High School. Long before Shirley met or knew him, one classmate of mine who protected me in lunch line, for whatever sweet reason, was a kid named Marty Ingels. Marty, as most people are aware, became

Shirley's husband (twice), but sadly Marty passed away in October 2015. Shirley and I keep in touch, sporadically but warmly, to this day. The aforementioned Bill Putch, a drama teacher for Shirley and me, as well as a fellow actor, several years later married actress Jean Stapleton, aforementioned. One of my daughters had one "date" with Bill and Jean's son, John Putch, when we visited them in 1976 at Bill's and Jean's Jennerstown (PA) Totem Pole Playhouse, during my Washington, D.C., television days. John Putch now directs the television show, Cougar Town. *Bill Putch and I also acted together in summer stock during those years in a couple plays at The White Barn Theater, near Irwin, Pennsylvania, about an hour's drive east of Pittsburgh. The White Barn Theater was owned by two actor/producers named Clay Flagg and Carl Low. The latter became a giant presence for 15 years as the character, Dr. Bob Rogers, on the television soap opera,* Search for Tomorrow. *(Ironically, in the early 1980's , I also had a one-time part on that show, and which can be seen on one of Minneapolis-based Tom Oszman's TCMedia web-site clips. I played a policeman whose wife had just given birth and I was looking for the delivery room. At our first rehearsal, actress Marie Cheatham, a longtime regular on the series, almost fell on the floor laughing at my opening line, which was, "Where do they keep the babies?" I was very appreciative for her reaction, to say the least. The Pittsburgh Playhouse restaurant was also the site of my first meeting with a major-league baseball player. His name was Ralph Kiner, a Pittsburgh Pirate, who, with 54 home runs, was the runner-up to reaching Babe Ruth's home run record at that time. Ralph's hand was bigger than half my arm when we shook hands that evening in 1948. It was a thrill for this fledgling 11-year-old actor. Ralph, as most sports fans know, died the year I'm writing this book, and was one of the New York Mets's most revered play-by-play announcers.)*

My mom and I moved to New York in the summer of 1951, after concluding my first year of high school at Peabody High School in the Pittsburgh enclave of East Liberty. My art teacher at Peabody was a first-class, very elderly lady named Jean Thoburn, who knew I had been acting at The Pittsburgh Playhouse. Because of that, she said she felt compelled to tell me she had been Gene Kelly's art teacher at Peabody, too. *Ironically, my grandfather knew the Kelly family very well, from the time Gene left for Hollywood in the 1930s. I met Gene just one time (an honor for even one time with him) when I was on television and radio in Las Vegas from 1967 through 1970. I interviewed him for KLAV radio in his dressing room at the relatively new Las Vegas Hilton in 1970. He was in a white plush bathrobe and we sat down for the one-on-one interview. The calves on his legs were like the pistons on a steam engine: strong, muscular and solid from all those years of dancing, as well as, in his early career, boxing. Gene told me he considered himself as much an athlete as a dancer. He also remembered our mutual art teacher, Ms. Thoburn, fondly. We also discussed Gene's use of our fellow Pittsburgher and family friend, Oscar Levant, in An American In Paris. He jokingly said, "Well, we sometimes have to keep it as much in the Pittsburgh family as possible." Followed by that infectious smile he had. When I had just completed the interview, Dick Martin, of* Rowan and Martin's Laugh-In, *came into the room. Obviously, he and Gene were longtime friends as they began jovially conversing in both French and English when I was packing up my interview microphone. French is my second language (thanks to mom) thus I understood every word, none of them derogatory. It was fun banter within a private time for the three of us there. Ironically, I would also, in later years, have the honor to have a longtime friendship with* Laugh In's *creator and producer, George Schlatter, previously referenced and more about which I'll happily relate later in this memoir.)*

Memories that make me smile about those innocent days at Peabody: Our high school song, the lyrics to which were, *Our alma mater, Peabody High. Our thoughts are with you, they will never die. We'll stand beside you, we will never stray, from our alma mater, maroon and gray*; Peabody's rousing football fight song's lyrics were, *Run the team across the field and show that Peabody's here. Come on and set the Earth reverberating with a mighty cheer –rah, rah, rah. Hit them hard and see how they fall, never let their team get the ball, Hail, hail the gang's all here, so hurrah for Peabody High*. Being a novice to football and to kids with "normal" lives who attended the games, I attended only two. The next football game I attended was in 1976. It was the Army-Navy game in Philadelphia, with his personal tickets given to me by soon-to-be-elected Vice President Walter Mondale.

I emceed his pre-inaugural banquet in January the following year,
1977. More about that honor later, too. I'm proud to state he and I still
maintain a warm friendship. (Please see photos section.)

I also remember the lyrics to the Pennsylvania state song.
In my opinion, and in my heart, truer lyrics were never written:
Pennsylvania, my native state, to you we pledge our devotion.
Pennsylvania, my loyalty is boundless as the ocean. Pennsylvania,
Pennsylvania, strong and true. Pennsylvania, Pennsylvania, hear our
song to you: There is beauty in your mountains, there is peace upon
your hills, and where e'r I roam, my only home is Pennsylvania.

My grandfather had contacted "Uncle" Lou and "Aunt" Florrie
(Handman, as referenced in Chapter One) asking if they could help
my mom and me find a place to live in New York as I was about to
continue my acting career there. They introduced my mom and me to
a lady named Lorraine Stanley, who had the upstairs of her attached
house available for rent. Lorraine was a "bachelorette" and one-half
of a statuesque redheaded dancing duo named The Stanley Twins.
The other half, her twin sister, was named Loretta. They entertained
the troops during World War Two and were also popular on the
vaudeville circuit. The latter is where "Uncle" Lou and "Aunt" Florrie
had met and worked with them. Ironically, Lorraine and Loretta were
born in St. Cloud, Minnesota, 70 miles from where I would live most
of the last half of my life, i.e., the Twin Cities of Minneapolis and
Saint Paul. Lorraine's and our address was 88-30 62nd Drive in Rego
Park, Queens. *Many years later, during one of numerous television*
interview junket trips to New York, I decided to take a subway ride to
visit "the old neighborhood". When I got there, I was aghast at how it
had changed. When we lived there, Queens Boulevard, not far away,
still had farms lining part of its length. I wish it were the early 1950s
again . . . always.

Prior to moving into Manhattan in 1953, my mom enrolled me
into Forest Hills High School for my sophomore year. There was
more than one fellow student there who would go on to national
and international fame, and were in my classes. One was named
Ina Rosenberg, the daughter of a surgeon. She would later become
known as Ina Balin. The other was named Marty Ingels, about whom I

referenced in Chapter Four. *Ina was very sweet to me in school. After I moved into Manhattan with my mom in 1952, I still maintained contact with Ina, frequently, especially during my* Mister Peepers *days in 1952, 1953 and 1954. In 1956, Ina told me she was going to give up trying to get acting parts. I told her she'd be a star and to not give up. I also told her I'd introduce her to a wonderful agent I knew, named Tom Ward. Tom became responsible for landing Ina her big break in a 1957 Broadway play entitled,* Compulsion. *Just after* Compulsion *opened in October, 1957, I had just landed my first local radio broadcasting job in Helena, Montana, and was excited to tell Ina about it over lunch or dinner before I left for the "Wild West". She very coldly told me she had no interest in having lunch or dinner with me. It hurt, to say the least, since I was glad my recommendation to Tom Ward had helped her get to her first big rung on the show business ladder. It was the second time I encountered that sort of ego directed at me. I never tried to reach Ina again. She died at age 52 in 1990. The only other time I encountered that hurtful sort of ego will be described later, during my high school days in New York.*

During the early summer of 1952, I was cast to play the role for which my mother and I had originally moved to New York to understudy, i.e., Bibi in *The Happy Time*. The one-week production was at The Corning Summer Playhouse in Corning, New York, adjacent to the world-famous Corning Glass Works, makers of world-class Steuben Glass items. The Corning Summer Playhouse was operated (and I think owned) by a Rochester, New York duo named Dorothy Chernuk and Omar K. Lerman. They were first-class, as was the theater. In order to pay for my train ticket to and from Corning, I washed dishes for two weeks at a diner on Woodhaven Boulevard, two blocks from Lorraine's house. One of the actors in the play was one of my former Pittsburgh Playhouse drama teachers and fellow actors, Joe Ruskin, previously referenced (please see photos section). The lead actress was a lady named Barbara Barrie, who later went on to portray Hal Linden's character's wife on the successful television series, *Barney Miller*.

During a lull in rehearsals one afternoon, I wandered into a spacious sitting area in the adjacent Corning Glass Works building where one of the stagehands was seated, listening to a vinyl recording (the only kind we had in those days) of George Gershwin's *Concerto in 'F' for Piano and Orchestra.* It was the Andre Kostelanetz-conducted version with the New York Philharmonic and our fellow Pittsburgher and, previously referenced, my great-uncles Harry and Irwin's piano-lessons pal, Oscar Levant, at the piano. I had never heard it, but it changed part of my life significantly in the 1970s, about which I'll relate later, including my significant time with Frances Gershwin, also previously referenced. I wish I could remember the name of that young stagehand, and how his appreciation of that great piece was a partial "life changer" for me. Thank you to him, sadly anonymously. (In my opinion, *Concerto in 'F' for Piano and Orchestra* was the best and most powerful piece George Gershwin ever composed. Oscar Levant is seen and heard playing the most powerful part of that piece in MGM's *An American In Paris.* Oscar, with the great sense of sarcastic humor he perpetually displayed, parodied and satirized himself . . . or his character in the film . . . by conducting himself and that filmed orchestra for the Concerto.)

My mom had known about New York's Professional Children's School (PCS) for many years. She wanted to enroll me there after we moved into Manhattan in late 1952, but the tuition was too expensive for her pocketbook, thus, God bless her, she found another school similar to PCS, named Lodge Professional Children's School. Lodge was located only a couple blocks north of PCS, at Broadway and 63rd Street, with classes held in a very spacious room (a former ballroom) on the mezzanine floor of The Empire Hotel. Both New York State-accredited schools were founded to allow kids who were acting to get accredited educations with schedules that could accommodate their rehearsal and performance schedules doing live stage, television and radio acting. My attendance there, along with my other classmates, allowed me to make the rounds visiting agents and casting directors, as well as rehearsals for television shows as a regular cast member and even one or two films in which I acted or appeared, including the first Cinerama film, *This Is Cinerama*, backed by Lowell Thomas, with whom I'd have a pleasant professional and personal relationship later in life during my radio year in Wenatchee, Washington and afterward. Mr. Thomas's letters to me from his home, Hammersley Hill in Pawling, New York, adjacent to the Rockefeller estate in

Pocantico Hills, are very treasured mementoes as was one great conversation with him in Las Vegas, which was not an interview, but personal. Among my classmates were Sal Mineo, Carol Lynley, David Winters, Judson Rees, Betty Lou Keim, Charlie Brill, Charlie Moss (nee Moskowitz, who in later life created the iconic *I [heart] New York* ad campaign. Charlie is still alive as I write this book, and to whom I spoke on the phone only three weeks ago.) There's much more to relate later about Sal, below. He's actually the reason I'm where I am now and why he's sadly no longer with us, having been murdered in 1976.

What I remember most about the Lodge classmates and PCS days is more easily recounted by personality as follows. First, Lodge:

Sal Mineo—*This memory was also almost correctly written about in two books, to be acknowledged later in this book. The biographers even spelled my name correctly, thanks to Sal graciously telling them what happened . . . and how to spell my name.* Sal was one of my best friends at Lodge. His father owned The Universal Casket Company in The Bronx. His mother, Josephine, was a very sweet lady, but whom I met only once. Sal's brother, Mike, also went to Lodge. Why, I don't know, because I never heard Mike had acted in any play or television show, but was a nice person and classmate, regardless. Sal had played Prince Chulalongkorn in *The King And I* on Broadway, replacing a PCS actor named Ronnie Lee (nee Leff), who I also got to know during our collective high school years.

In the late summer of 1954, I got a call from an agent named Frances Robinson, telling me I was chosen to play Tony Curtis's character as a young boy in a new Universal Pictures film entitled *Six Bridges To Cross*. It was the story of the infamous Brinks truck robbery in Boston, which had taken place in real life a few years earlier. Ms. Robinson told me to come to her office on 42nd Street to just visit briefly in person. When I got to her office, she asked me to look at a "head shot" book showing professional head shots (pictures) of actors and actresses. She then asked me to suggest two actors who I might know who would be good to play "extras" in the movie, and who, like me, looked like juvenile delinquents. We all had "D.A." hairstyles in those days (D.A. was short for Duck's Ass), with enough grease on our slicked-back heads to complete a lube job on any car. I pointed to my school pals, Sal and Mike Mineo. She said they'd be perfect for the extra parts and that was that. Ms. Robinson then told me I'd have a "cursory" reading for the film's Director, named Joe Pevney, at the (then) Universal Building on Park Avenue at 56th Street the following week. She gave me the script, told me to study my few lines and said the reading was "cursory" because I'd already had a lock on the part.

The following week, I went to Universal to do my "cursory" reading. When I got off the elevator at the designated floor, I saw Sal sitting on a bench outside the main doors into the Universal offices. I got a sinking feeling that his presence wasn't "good". I let the receptionist know I was there, exchanged a couple pleasantries with Sal and then was rapidly ushered in to where Mr. Pevney was waiting to hear me do my "cursory" reading. Mr. Pevney greeted me warmly and had me read the few lines of the part. One line I remember well was, "Nothin' for nothin' with me." (I wish I'd remembered that line the remainder of my real life throughout later years.) When I concluded the reading, Mr. Pevney said, verbatim and smiling, "Excellente!" with a proper Hispanic pronunciation. He then said the studio would be in touch with me in a few days and that was that.

I left the room and walked out into the waiting area near the elevators. Sal was still sitting on the bench. We said some pleasant goodbyes and that also was that. Four days later, I received a call from Frances Robinson telling me my kindness to recommend Sal and Mike for extra parts didn't pay off. She told me Pevney chose Sal to play the young Tony Curtis part and because Sal and I looked so much alike at that time, I wasn't chosen to play even an extra role. As the saying goes, "No good deed goes unpunished." I didn't begrudge Sal's selection but always wondered if I hadn't suggested him and Mike (the latter who wasn't cast) if indeed it would have been the beginning of a strong motion picture acting career for me. Instead, it motivated me to join the U.S. Air Force a couple weeks later, more about which I'll relate later and which also was a life-changing event.

Also cast, as an extra, in *Six Bridges To Cross*, was another of my Lodge classmates named Charlie Moss, previously referenced. (Joe

Pevney, in later years, directed almost all of *Star Trek*'s episodes. I wish I'd kept in touch with him!)

Carol Lynley—Carol, for all her eventual fame, was a very quiet girl at Lodge, and almost shy. I remember her to be very studious, too. We didn't have much interaction, but meeting her many years later at a function in North Hollywood, I reminded her of our Lodge days. She smiled and asked, "You survived Lodge?" Carol was (and is) a very nice person for whose successes I've always been happy.

David Winters—David took me under his wing. David was on the first (and all subsequent) *Mister Peepers* episodes and responsible for introducing me to his agent, a wild but successful man named Archer King, who had landed David his part as "Walter Murdoch" on *Peepers*. Archer called NBC-TV and told them I should be cast as one of the students. Archer's pronouncement was immediately green-lighted, and my national television acting career commenced, thanks to David's kindness. Between late summer, 1952 through spring, 1954, I was on 14 episodes of *Peepers*, portraying one of Wally Cox's character's students. My favorite episode was one featuring Wally's character describing the spider crab on a blackboard. We "students" began to giggle silently and almost broke Wally up, which would have been horrible on live television. No retakes on live television and Wally wasn't giggling after that show. We all deserved to be chewed out and never got out of our characters again.

Mister Peepers *had significance for me for much of the rest of my life, especially because the show was responsible for my having the blessing of a lifelong friendship with actor Tony Randall. Peepers was "live", and telecast from The RKO Center Theater (now converted into offices), part of Rockefeller Center, but facing Sixth Avenue (then The Avenue of the Americas) one of the best television theaters, ever. That theater was where* Your Show Of Shows, *starring Sid Caesar, Imogene Coca, Carl Reiner and Howie Morris was performed, with later to be giants, Mel Brooks and a teenager named Woody Allen as two of the writers. It blows my mind in later years I got to know all those people named, except for Howie Morris.*

We actors had to be there at seven a.m. to begin rehearsals each Sunday for that evening's show, which was telecast at seven p.m. I had to pick up my scripts every Thursday on the third floor of the then RCA Building. The Peepers *offices were only a few doors past the* Howdy Doody *studio. One of the joys was to, like clockwork, walk by George "Gabby" Hayes sitting outside that studio on my way to pick up the script. He was always sitting with his knees up and every time I walked by, he'd always say in that inimitable "Gabby" voice, "Hello, sonny!" I'd of course respond with a friendly "Hello, Gabby", and that was that. The door to the* Howdy Doody *studio was always ajar enough to see some live action going on with the characters Buffalo Bob and Clarabelle, the Clown. Clarabelle, of course, was actor Bob Keeshan, who later created and starred in CBS-TV's iconic morning children's show,* Captain Kangaroo. *In 1998, I interviewed Mr. Keeshan for a documentary I was producing about television's first fifty years. I reminded him of the joy of seeing Gabby so often. He affably smiled, then told me some of* his *history in the business, starting as a page at NBC just after World War Two. He told me his Marine Corps buddy and best friend during their combat days in World War Two was actor Lee Marvin. Perhaps war and politics make strange bedfellows. I thought it was fascinating, though, and hope you found it so, as well.*

Regarding Tony Randall, from the very first time we met on set, during breaks in Mister Peepers *rehearsals, he would invite me to sit next to him in the empty semi-dark theater and just totally open up to me about world events, acting, the important parts of life and humanity in general. In sum, he took me under his wing as somewhat a mentor and I was very honored, to say the least. We were together socially and professionally many times in later years, almost to the time when he became mortally ill, passing away in 2004. Some of the fascinating and revelatory stories Tony shared with me will be related later in this book (please see photos section).*

It might also be interesting to know our Peepers *writers, Jim Fritzell and Everett Greenbaum, in future years wrote many episodes of* The Andy Griffith Show, *and Mr. Greenbaum was also one of the frequent writers of* M.A.S.H. *episodes. Whenever I see their names on MeTV or Antenna TV re-runs these days, the memories back to the* Peepers *days immediately emerge. For one of the documentaries I wrote and produced in 1998, i.e.,* Television: The First 50 Years, *I interviewed Everett in Art's Delicatessen on Ventura Boulevard in Studio City, CA, over corned beef sandwiches and matzo ball soup. We reminisced for an hour about those wonderful* Peepers *days. Not too much later, when I'd heard Everett was dying, I called Tony to let him know. Tony was as devastated on the phone as I'd ever heard anyone be. I'm certain part of that reasoning was because Everett's* Peepers *words catapulted Tony into riches he never imagined.*

David, his mother Sadie and I had Chinese food every Friday evening at a restaurant on the second floor of a building on the west corner of Broadway at 42nd Street. David was born in England. His mother, Sadie, still had a strong British accent, and David's was a combination of Brit and Brooklyn. He was a phenomenal actor and dancer, energy personified. He later went on to portray Baby John in the original Broadway production of *West Side Story* and A-Rab in the movie version of the play. Little did I know in those days that Carol Lawrence, who portrayed the original Maria in the stage-play version of *West Side Story* would later become the personal catalyst (and a friend) for my immersion into the lives of mega-stars during my on-air Las Vegas television days and all subsequent years of my life. (More details about those events later.)

The last time I conversed with David in person was in November, 1957, on the west side of Sixth Avenue near Rockefeller Center. He saw me walking on the sidewalk and pulled over to greet me in his new silver Corvette convertible to say hello. *West Side Story* had just opened and everyone was "flying high" with its success. David asked what I was doing then. I told him I was about to leave for Helena, Montana, to start my local professional broadcasting career as a disc jockey and news director for $55 a week. The next time we spoke was on the phone during my Las Vegas television days (1967 through 1970). At that time, he was Ann-Margret's choreographer and was staying at The Riviera Hotel, where she was performing. I called his room, he answered and I announced my name. He very politely said he did not remember me. I unfurled all we'd been through together, but he still said he didn't remember me. I couldn't believe it, and was saddened about it, but that was that. David's had a continued very successful career the reminder of his life and I will always be grateful to him for my break on *Peepers*, but very saddened he didn't remember those 1950s years together, very memorable to yours truly, especially because of his kindnesses to me.

Archer then became one of my agents. He was one of the premier agents in the business, under the wing of the agency for which he worked. It was The Louis Shurr Agency, located on one of the upper floors of The Paramount Building on Broadway in Times Square, just across the street from where ABC-TV's Good Morning America is telecast. Every time I watch GMA, I'm flooded with memories of my times in the building I see every morning in the GMA background shots. Louis and his brother Lester's clients were Bob Hope, Bert Lahr, Jack Warden, Gina Lollobrigida and so many other "giants". I literally hung around with all of them many times, for over two years, in that office. They were all very nice to me, and supportive with encouragement I'd get big breaks soon. The really big breaks never happened, but I was happy they were "in my corner", rather genuinely or solicitously. Some of the shows in which I acted, thanks to Archer, were live television dramas such as Playhouse 90, Studio One *and* The Big Story. *In 1971, I asked Bob Hope do a promo for me . . . free . . . during my Minnesota television days. He did it. I was known, as stated in the preface, as Barry ZeVan, The Weatherman, and thus wrote the following for Bob to deliver on camera: "I know what Barry ZeVan's forecast is going to be: Blinding sunshine, or maybe that's just the glare from the top of his head!" One can still view that bit on the Internet. He did it in a remote spot on the Minnesota State Fairgrounds with the not-so-happy broadcasting mogul (and my boss at the time) Stanley E. Hubbard, Sr., looking on. He and Hope had struck a performance deal several years earlier and Hope never showed up, but he kept the $50,000 advance money Mr. Hubbard had paid him. Both before and after Hope did the promo, each of them looked daggers at one another. I thought a shoot-out reminiscent of* High Noon *would occur any second. It didn't, but it was a lesson in watching giants staring each other down. Mr. Hubbard had driven me to the site for the filming (no tape in those days). On the way back to KSTP-TV, he told me the "no-show" story about Hope.*

Regarding West Side Story, *one of my other agents was Dick Van Patten's mother, Jo Van Patten. I got a rushed call from her at The Hayes Registry one late afternoon in the summer of 1957. The Hayes Registry was an office where many actors waited to get their agent's calls to audition for parts. No cell phones then, of course. Jo told me to get to an address just a couple blocks away and meet Jerome Robbins, the famous director/choreographer, to let him see me for a part in a new play called* West Side Story. *I had not heard of the play and didn't know what types they were seeking. When I walked into the room, Mr. Robbins was sitting behind a table, with some of his assistants on either side. He asked me to tell him something about myself. A few sentences in, he stopped me and said, "Kid, you're perfect for any of the parts, but you sound just like Jimmy Stewart. Very sorry." I was devastated, because had Jo told me the types for whom they were looking were tough New York street kids, I could have easily sustained a tough New York accent and would have been in the show. I was furious with her for not letting me know, because in addition to David Winters, I would have been acting with Carol Lawrence, as well as one other person I would get to know in later years, dancer/actor/director Tony Mordente. More about that, later, too!)*

In addition, even though I had met Dick Van Patten once or twice during his I Remember Mama *television show days, I had no idea I'd be double-understudying Dick and fellow Pittsburgher . . . and grade school pal . . . Frank Gorshin, in a national tour of* The Sunshine Boys *in 2001 and 2002, while also playing a small part in the play. Dick and I moaned and groaned about his mother not telling me how to speak when I met with Jerome Robbins that fateful day in 1957. More about* The Sunshine Boys *national play tour later. Sadly, while writing this book, I just learned Dick had passed away today, June 23rd, 2015. He, his wife Pat and his youngest son, Jimmy . . . a truly great actor . . . were all wonderful to me throughout many years. It was a joy to have Dick and Jimmy have dinner at our Minneapolis dining room table during a play tour break. Dick was a delightful man, filled with energy and humor, with not a phony bone in his body. His wife, Pat, had been one of The June Taylor Dancers on the iconic* Jackie Gleason Show *during 1950s television.)*

Judson Rees—Jud was one of the kids on *I Remember Mama*. He and his divorced mother were both very nice to me. We were nearby neighbors in Queens. Jud's mother always wanted to lobby for me to get more parts, for which I was very grateful. I'm not certain Jud was happy about that, but, nonetheless was cordial and introduced me to some relatives of his who were high up the Washington, D.C. social ladder in those days and very warm to me for many years thereafter. Jud had no reason to have any trepidation about my getting any parts for which he might be considered. He had thick, wavy blonde hair. My hair was black and my complexion darker skinned. I looked Jud up in the 1980s during a trip to New York. It was the last time we saw each other in person. We had lunch at The Four Seasons on Park Avenue. Jud had become an executive with a major cosmetics company and living the good life, but was no longer swashbuckling in appearance. Age had taken its toll and it was truly surprising to me how much his appearance had changed. Regardless, he looked nothing like Quasimodo and the visit was pleasant. We later connected by phone, in the 1990s, when he'd moved to Florida and was heading a Mystery Shopper company.

Betty Lou Keim—This is tough to recount. Betty Lou was the epitome of class without having her nose in the air. She was intuitive, very intelligent and always had or made enough time to talk and make a person feel as though they were worth the time it took to listen. She married one of the PCS kids, named Warren Berlinger. Warren was Milton Berle's nephew and a truly brilliantly talented actor, who, in my opinion, should have become a major star. He and I still keep in touch. I'm 20 days older than Warren, thus he always listens to me implicitly. In all seriousness, I actually had a crush on Betty Lou, about which Warren knew nothing until I confessed to same last year. Sadly, Betty Lou died in 2010 from lung cancer, thanks to much-too-much smoking. During frequent trips to L.A. in subsequent years, Betty Lou, Warren and I would have dinners, and when not supping together, I'd have long phone conversations with her about how we both felt about certain movies. It wasn't until after Betty Lou passed away I learned she played Frank Sinatra's character's niece in *Some Came Running*. When I've since watched it on TCM, seeing her brings back very special memories of her friendship and our classes together at Lodge. It's also very difficult to watch, knowing she's gone. I could never sufficiently extol her genuine excellence as a human being and was honored for her kind and true friendship.

Charlie Brill—As was true with my friends Shirley Jones (see photos sction) and Marty Ingels, both of whom I'd known at different times in their lives before they ever met one another (previously referenced) Charlie, from Brooklyn, married a girl with whom I acted in 1948 in my first play at The Pittsburgh Playhouse, *Strange Bedfellows* (also previously referenced). Her name was Mitzi Steiner (then) but became Mitzi McCall when she became nationally known as Charlie's comedy partner and wife, appearing on *The Ed Sullivan Show* and other national shows of that era, as well as at least one feature film starring Jerry Lewis, for Mitzi. Before Charlie ever knew Mitzi existed, he and I were great pals in school and afterward, to this day, and the same for Mitzi and me. The only times I was ever in Brooklyn was when Charlie would have me accompany him to the St. George Hotel's super-Olympic size swimming pool to swim in the early evenings after school.

The most memorable times with Charlie were when we decided to go into Times Square on two consecutive New Year's Eves, circa 1953-54 and 1954 transitioning into 1955. In those days, there were no barricades set up for crowd control, thus we squeezed our bodies into the Square at about 11:45 each of those years. The crush of people against us was almost life threatening. One could never have fallen down with the push of the crowd so intense. One of the funniest things I ever heard anyone say was when Charlie, at the top of his lungs, shouted, "Everybody stop havin' fun!" It was a classic and a few people around us laughed or smiled at his "admonition". He, Mitzi and I reunited in the late 1960s when they were featured in their nightclub act at The Tropicana Hotel in Las Vegas. I called the room and Charlie answered. I asked if he, Mitzi and I could get together for a snack after their show that particular night. He said "Yes" and we got together, but when we did, they both told me they had a fun discussion asking when each had first met me. "I knew him first", "No, I knew him first", was what they told me they exchanged after my phone call. He and I and Mitzi still speak on the phone occasionally. They're still as delightful as ever. (Much more about my wonderful and blessed friendship with Jerry Lewis later.)

Charlie Moss—Charlie was fun and easy going. He was also one of those kids you knew would become successful. He, as I previously referenced, got a part as an extra in *Six Bridges To Cross*. He was tall, lanky and had a huge mop of thick black hair. School days were the last I saw Charlie in person until he acknowledged me at a Detroit Advertising Club luncheon I attended in the early 1980s. He was the guest of honor because he had several years earlier created the I (heart) NY campaign (previously referenced) while Vice President of the Wells, Rich and Greene ad agency in New York and had become an advertising "game" icon, justifiably so. He told the audience it was true he and I were high school mates and friends. I remarked he still had his hair and everyone gasped. They had no idea Charlie and I were close enough to allow that fun remark to be uttered. He also took it good-naturedly and we conversed a bit afterward. Every time I see an I (heart) NY or anywhere slogan or T-shirt, I think of my pal Charlie.

For the PCS kids and us Lodge kids, it was almost as though we were all going to the same school regarding times before and after school. Being almost directly across the street from each other's schools and being in the same business of attending special schools to accommodate our rehearsal and acting schedules, we not only all socialized but also performed charity events together. Several of those times were on Riker's Island, entertaining the prisoners with a couple song and dance numbers. "Another Opening, Another Show", was one of the numbers. My singing partner (and still friend) was Leslie Uggams (then known to us privately as Leslie "Uggams" Crane, Crane being her real last name). Others included a PCS kid named Kenny Walken (Christopher Walken's older brother. Chris was also in school at PCS, but in first grade when we were all sophomores and juniors). Kenny was a great guy and occasionally brought us kids some baked goods from his family's business, Walken's Bakery in Queens. Kenny and I acted on one NBC-TV episode of a live drama entitled *The Big Story*. Wesley Addy, who would later become a television drama star, was the featured player on that Christmas Day, 1953, episode. We performed in one of the studios of the then RCA Building, next to Studio 8H, where, in later years, SNL would be housed.

Among PCS's other kids with whom we all socialized and sometimes acted were Patty Duke (at a time we never knew she was under the Machiavellian spell of her agents, Mr. and Mrs. John Ross, and about whom she wrote in her autobiography, *Call Me Anna*), Elliott Gould, Sandra Dee, Timmy Everett, Natalie (Campana) Trundy, Iris Mann, Warren Berlinger (previously referenced) Tuesday Weld (also previously referenced), Joey Walsh, Josh White, Jr., Beverly White, Vinton Hayworth, Jr., Alan Tobias, Bobby Gusikoff, Ivan Cury and MGM studio President Dore Schary's niece, Patty Baumholz, who taught me how to lindy/jitterbug. That jitterbug lesson was given to me in the apartment living room of a wonderful husband and wife named Theodore (Ted) Reade Nathan and his wife, Betty, as well as their daughters who attended and graduated from PCS, Joy and Gay. Every time I see a movie on TCM that was produced, directed or written by Dore Schary, my mind always warmly takes me back to those days in the Nathan's apartment at The Parc Vendome on West 57th Street, dancing with his niece.

As was the case remembering most about the Lodge classmates, recalling the PCS pals is more easily by personality. Here we go again, with almost *no* degrees of separation:

Theodore (Ted) Reade, Betty, Joy and **Gay Nathan**—Mr. Nathan was a PR man extraordinaire, with clients ranging from Nelson Rockefeller to the aforementioned Edison Hotel. He was also very connected to PCS as a trustee and was Billy Rose's Executive Assistant during some of the years when Mr. Rose owned his famous Diamond Horseshoe nightclub in New York and was married to Fanny Brice (later to be known on Broadway and on film as *Funny Girl*). During the years I was one of the Ray Charles Singers on *The Perry Como Show* (previously referenced with more to be described later) Mr. Rose had an apartment on the top floor of the original Ziegfeld

Theater on Seventh Avenue in the upper 50s, where we did *The Perry Como Show* live every Saturday night at 7. During those years (1955-56-57), I never met him, but all knew the legendary Mr. Rose housed himself there, primarily. Betty Nathan was the personification of class and dignity combined with sweetness and warmth. Daughters Gay and Joy inherited both their parents' traits. Gay in later years moved to New Mexico and taught American Indian children in Pecos, just east of Santa Fe. Joy married NBC-TV Law Correspondent, Carl Stern, and we're still close friends, having re-connected when I began my D.C. television weathercasting days in 1974. Joy and Carl still live in D.C. Both Ted and Betty Nathan have passed away, but Heaven must surely be more joyful because of their presence.

The Nathans hosted PCS and Lodge after school parties at their apartment almost every Friday evening. The parties mostly consisted of hosting us kids above-mentioned, more detailed memories about whom follow and not previously chronicled:

Leslie "Uggams" Crane—Leslie was one of the sweetest, outgoing, energetic and talented among all the PCS kids. She's still wonderful. I was one of her singing partners, along with other PCS kids, when we'd occasionally entertain prisoners on Riker's Island. The song that commenced the performances was *Another Opening, Another Show*, an uplifting and lively number I still sometimes sing around the house or in the shower. (I know, way too much information.) Leslie's mother chose me to take her home from the parties at the Nathans because she said I was the only one she trusted. Her thinking was flattering and valid. Those Friday night parties usually ended around 11 o'clock. Leslie lived on the Upper East Side around Lexington Avenue above 125th Street. I had to get her and me to that side of town via a 57th Street bus, then take the (then) IRT train from 57th and "Lex" to her stop, then walk a couple blocks East to her brownstone, bid her goodnight making certain she was safely inside the brownstone door, then head back to the West Side where we lived, on 100th Street between Broadway and West End Avenue, getting me back to my Mom's and my one-room apartment about 12:30 each Saturday morning. That routine was repeated at least ten times throughout a two-year period. Let's just say I was naively "brave" during those sojourns.

Every three or four weeks during the 1954 school year, Leslie was also one of my dance partners on *Paul Whiteman's TV Teen Club*, telecast from WFIL-TV in Philadelphia on the then fledgling ABC-TV network. It was the precursor to Dick Clark's *American Bandstand*. Dick Clark was our announcer! The PCS kids and some of us Lodge kids were bused to Philadelphia on those Saturday afternoons when we could all make it as invitees to dance on that show. I never told Mr. Whiteman he had been one of my pre-teen heroes when listening to his orchestra on Pittsburgh radio at night during the early 1940s when my mom was working for The War Department (previously referenced). I wish I had, because he was such a close friend to George Gershwin, my all time music "hero" and whose sister, Frankie (Frances) I would get to know later in life (story be related later). Mr. Whiteman's orchestra had performed the world premiere of *Rhapsody In Blue* at New York's Aeolian Hall, with George at the piano and at George's request.

In later years, Leslie and I coincidentally wound up in the same places when she was touring, from Las Vegas to Pittsburgh to, of course, New York. One of my favorite memories about Leslie and her mother is Leslie's Pittsburgh "gig" was at a nightclub in Monroeville, PA, a Pittsburgh suburb. I happened to be in Pittsburgh, truly coincidentally, when I saw her name on a television promo announcing where she'd be performing. I called the venue (a Monroeville hotel) and asked for Leslie's room. Her mother answered. I asked, "Mrs. Crane?". She said, "Yeah, this is Mrs. Uggams." I didn't say anything about her response except who I was and we had a nice reminiscent conversation.

In 1999, Dick called me at our Minneapolis house to respond to a thought I'd had for New Year's Eve special to air December 31st, 2000, to "officially" welcome the 21st century, which really began January 1, 2001. There was never a year "zero". My wife, Ellen, took the call and said "Dick Clark's calling you!" Calls from Dick didn't happen often to many "little people" like me, thus we were both happy he'd taken the time to discuss my thought, which I'd originally broached to him

*in person at a broadcasting conclave in New Orleans a few months
earlier, where we also reminisced about our mutual 1954 days with
Paul Whiteman. Dick liked my idea . . . said it was "beautiful" . . . but
also said there was no sufficient budget available via his production
company to execute it properly. My later-in-life friend, Peter Jennings,
would have hosted it. It could still be done and would be produced with
Leroy Anderson's* Belle Of The Ball *composition as the platform for
the unique 24-time zone piece, still totally storyboarded and in my file
drawers. Another addition to the bucket list!*

Elliott Gould—Even though we reunited years later at a film event
honoring Elliott in Minneapolis, what I remember most about Elliott
was how genuinely "sweet", quiet and almost bashful he was when
I knew him in those teenage years. Almost every day after both our
schools ended their respective school days, we gathered for sodas
(literally!) at a teenage-type malt shop on 57th Street, as memory
serves. Maybe it was 58th Street. Oh, some "Senior Moments" do
occasionally prevail. And oh, so what? Regardless, I was unaware
Elliott was a chorus boy in one of the Broadway plays because he
never called attention to himself or what he was doing. He was just,
and still is, "flat out", very likeable (please see photos section).

Obviously, when Elliott married Barbra Streisand, it was a big
"Wow" for some of us. I've been told, even though long-divorced,
Elliott and Barbra continue to maintain cordial connections because
of their son Jason and the health issues he's endured. Elliott kindly
recorded a congratulatory message to me, which was played on
a Twin Cities radio station in February, 2003, acknowledging my
then 60th anniversary in broadcasting. His message included the
word "endured" referencing the number of years I'd "endured" as a
broadcaster. His willingness to ad lib that message was, and is, deeply
appreciated. *"Aunt" Florrie and "Uncle" Lou's niece, Allison Caine,
in later years married a man named Carl Gottlieb, who co-wrote the
screenplay for* Jaws. *Allison and I got together for dinner a couple times
when I was on visits to L.A. in the 1990s, and she told me she was a
"looper" (creates background audio) for Barbra and her films. The
connections never end.*

Sandra Dee—I only met Sandra in passing during our impromptu double-school social times, but remember she was truly a sweet girl and very loved by her PCS classmates. Ironically, her future husband, Bobby Darin, had a very personal interaction with me in Las Vegas in 1970.

Bobby was appearing at The Desert Inn that summer. He was a magnificent talent, but also had a "wandering eye", as the saying goes. Bobby was scheduled to appear on my morning talk show and weathercast one day and evening. When I told my then significant other at the time, an "information" telephone operator for Central Telephone Company, she said, "Well, you'll be interested to know Bobby just called asking for a number, then made a pass at me on the phone, asking for my number. I told him I wasn't interested." I thanked her for the information, which came very close to the time I was to call Bobby to confirm his appearance on my shows. I reached him in his Desert Inn suite and confirmed the appearance, then told him what my s.o. had told me. He said, "Oh, I was just kidding, but sorry about that". I didn't say anything else about it and we then confirmed the appearance for a couple days hence. The next day, Bobby because seriously ill and actually had to cancel performances at the D.I., as it was lovingly known in those days. He died very soon thereafter. In my opinion, Kevin Spacey's phenomenal characterization of Bobby in Kevin's film about Bobby and Sandra, Beyond The Sea, *was superb and should have been much more well-received at the box office. Apparently, quality of that caliber is definitely not recognized nor appreciated. Seeing that film, in my opinion, should be on everyone's "bucket list".*

Timmy Everett—Timmy was my very best friend from the PCS group of kids. He was an actor/dancer who spent many weekends at my mother's and my small apartment on the Upper West Side until he teased my mother talking softly on the phone to her boyfriend one Saturday morning. It was the last time Timmy stayed, but it didn't wreck his and my friendship. As earlier referenced, Timmy went on to portray the young boy Robert Preston's character, Professor Harold Hill, befriended in *The Music Man*. Shirley (Jones) and I talked about Timmy reverently during our time in Omaha in 2013 because, at age 39, Timmy committed suicide.

I also learned in later years, Timmy was Jane Fonda's boyfriend (for five years) just after high school years had ended. I wish I had known that when I spent some very pleasant private time with Jane and her then husband, Ted Turner, at a special party in New York in the mid-1990s. Of course, with both of us aware Timmy had taken his own life, it would have hardly made for pleasant conversation. I was shocked when I heard Timmy had taken his own life, not only because of the deed itself, but also because, as anyone can still see in *The Music Man*, he was a brilliant talent who could have given the world so much more joy. Timmy's sister, Tanya, was a dancer, too, in *Fiddler On The Roof*, but I never met her. Another irony, Timmy was born in Helena, Montana, where I began my local broadcasting career in 1957.

Natalie Trundy (Campana)—Natalie was a truly beautiful girl. I was only at parties with Natalie and just once years later outside a talent agency office in L.A. In later years, I learned she and I share/shared the same birthday, August 5th. Natalie, three years my junior, carried herself with an almost aristocratic air and during after school parties often dated a PCS classmate of hers, and friend of mine, named Alan Tobias. (Alan's father was Wally Cox's accountant, more to be described about that later.) Natalie appeared in numerous Broadway productions, commercials and feature films. She married major film agent/studio executive, Arthur Jacobs, providing a very comfortable life, but also had her share of tragedy and physical problems. Glad to state she's still alive as I write this.

Joey Walsh—Joey's father sold tour bus maps in Times Square and was justifiably very proud of his son. I visited with Mr. Walsh on that street corner often, and basked in his pride for Joey. Joey had a presence about him that was truly compelling. His most famous role was in *Hans Christian Andersen*, which starred Danny Kaye, portraying a young boy Hans befriended. Joey also performed in several of the live television dramas of the day and was liked by all of us, again with good reason. (More about my own special time with Danny Kaye later.)

Vinton Hayworth, Jr.—Vinnie (he was often nicknamed "Dink") was a nearby neighbor to us when we still lived in Rego Park, Queens, which, in later years, I learned was television mogul Fred Silverman's home "town". Vinnie lived with his parents in Forest Hills, but attended PCS. His father, Vinton Hayworth, Sr., was a handsome, debonair major television actor and brother (yes, it's true) of Rita Hayworth, although all the biographers list her last name as Cansini. Look it all up, on Google! Young Vinnie's love for quality mood music was shared with me often in the Hayworth house. One of the instrumentals to which he introduced me became one of my favorite radio theme songs during my DJ days in later years, entitled *Beyond The Next Hill*, with Tito Acquaviva's orchestra providing that great music. I still have that "78rpm" vinyl record. It's one of those many memories that instantly activates very vividly to me. Indeed, a blessing and a curse, the latter because I know those quality days are unlikely to ever return.

Josh (Donny) White, Jr. and **Beverly White**—Josh/Donny and Beverly were the children of legendary guitarist, singer, jazz performer, actor and civil rights activist, Josh White. I recently learned Mr. White also became the closest African-American friend and confidant to President Franklin D. Roosevelt. He was wonderful to all us kids, but little did we know how much "power" he had, viewing the humility and playfulness with which he always adorned us. Josh/Donny and Beverly were two of the most delightful people I ever knew, and in later years, during my Detroit on-air television days (1978-1983) Josh/Donny and I reunited frequently for coffee or just a visit, since he had settled in Detroit later in life. Sadly, I didn't socialize with Beverly very much, but what occasional times I had with her during the New York school years, were pleasant.

One of the fondest memories was when one late spring evening Mr. White piled four or five of us kids (including Josh/Donny and Beverly) into the rear seat of Mr. White's white Cadillac convertible on 125th Street in Harlem, then driving us down that street with the radio blaring jazz music full blast and at proper beats. Mr. White made the car "dance" by pumping the brakes at the synchronous beats of the music playing. It was a blast and a smile-maker to remember.

Iris Mann—Iris and I still maintain our communication and friendship. I was with her just two months ago, prior to beginning to write this book. She was on the cover of *Life* magazine when she was only nine years old. She was, and is, an extraordinarily gifted actress and has deeper interests in subjects far distant from show business. She's also a gifted writer and has been a longtime commentator for National Public Radio. Iris and the aforementioned Betty Lou Keim were best friends during our mutual school days. Sadly, Iris told me she was supposed to have been picked up to attend Betty Lou's funeral by another former PCS schoolmate and that individual, who shall be nameless here, didn't do so. It made Betty Lou's passing even more heart wrenching for Iris. Iris is also a cousin of actress Scarlett Johansson.

Warren Berlinger (previously referenced)—One of Warren's uncles was Milton Berle, although Warren never mentioned it during our high school years. I also never mentioned to Warren my grandfather had been one of Berle's agents in his early performing days (previously referenced). I was with Milton several times during my New York acting days, and even a few times afterward, many years later, the last time in D.C. in the mid-1970s. He was very funny, as everyone knows, as "Mr. Television" and in films, but not well liked by a lot of people in that very jealousy-ridden and ego-filled business. Regardless, Warren, in my opinion, and the opinion of many, truly surpassed Milton's comedic and acting abilities by light years. He acted in major Broadway plays, with major parts and with all the "giants", not only on Broadway, but also in major television productions and in films.

During one of the six years I was on television in Detroit, Warren called me to let me know he'd be co-starring in a national tour of the great Neil Simon play, *Plaza Suite* and had a free ticket waiting for me at will-call to see the performance at Detroit's then newly-revamped Fisher Theatre. I can honestly say there has never been a more memorable performance of *any* part than that which Warren gave that night. He's a brilliant talent who should have been a major film star. I'm 20 days older than Warren, so when we speak occasionally on the phone, we joke that he still always pays attention to me as one of his "elders". Right.

Tuesday Weld (previously referenced)—Tuesday once asked me for a date when she was 11 and I was 17. The setting was another "malt shop". She was seated at a table and I had just arisen to leave when she told me there was an event that night that required dates and she didn't have one. "How about you?" she asked me. Knowing that age 11 was definitely considered "jail bait" as it used to be known when one dated a girl younger than age 16, I fairly rapidly declined the invitation. Ironically, and as many people will remember, Tuesday later portrayed a character named Thalia on the hit television series, *The Many Loves Of Dobie Gillis*, which starred Dwayne Hickman, as previously noted. Sometimes I wish I'd kept in touch with Tuesday, who now lives near Aspen, Colorado, since Dwayne and I became friends when we were both working for Howard Hughes in Las Vegas in the late 1960s. More about Dwayne's and my friendship later, but for now, suffice it to say there has never been anyone more genuinely real and nicer than that man, in or not in, show business. *I guess I could have kept in touch with Tuesday in later years, but just didn't. I don't know why. It would have been relatively easy to re-connect because Tuesday married conductor/violist Pinchus (Pinky) Zuckerman whose baton guided the St. Paul Chamber Orchestra during some of the years I was on television in the Twin Cities.*

Alan Tobias (previously referenced)—Alan was a genuinely unaffected kid from a very "well-to-do" family, whose father was the accountant for Wally Cox, as previously noted. I don't recall Alan ever doing any acting, but he was definitely enrolled at PCS, possibly because of his father's stature with some of the more popular television stars of that era. Regardless, because he knew I was portraying one of the students on *Mister Peepers*, he told me Wally always allowed him to visit Wally's apartment (Alan had a key) and it might be fun for me to visit Wally's apartment with Alan some evening, too. The one visit I had there with Alan was a good one, kept in my memory bank and now related here.

The year was 1953. Wally's roommate at the time was Wally's longtime friend, Marlon Brando, who took Wally under his wing years earlier and helped Wally be at the right place at the right time when Wally got his big break to star on *Mister Peepers*. Wally's and

Marlon's second-floor walk-up apartment was on 58th Street, just west of Fifth Avenue, across from the south side of The Plaza Hotel. The apartment was almost "hospital clean-room" clean, with all white walls and cabinets. Alan and I only stayed in the living room adjacent to the open kitchen space. Boyhood curiosity had me opening one of the kitchen cabinets. On one of the shelves was one can of unopened tuna fish. That was all the food there was in the entire apartment!

Wally had just become engaged to Marilyn Gennaro, choreographer Peter Gennaro's sister. There were at least four note pads (predecessors to Post-It notes) scattered around the living room on end tables with the name Marilyn (in Wally's handwriting) written at least ten times on each pad. I thought it was wonderful to get a glimpse of Wally's humanity and romantic feelings toward his wife-to-be. Alan and I just sat around talking as there was no television set in the apartment. We were there for about an hour and at about 10 that very rainy evening, Wally entered the apartment and asked, "What are you children still doing here? It's time to go." He wasn't irritated, but he was correct: It was time to leave and I knew it was a privilege to know we had spent that time there.

When Alan and I were leaving, halfway down the long flight of stairs leading to the apartment's street exit, Marlon was coming up the stairs with a racing bike on his right shoulder and dripping wet from the heavy rains that were falling. He was wearing a white T-shirt and jeans, a la On The Waterfront. *He said, "What are you kids doing here?" Alan immediately reminded him of Alan's association with Wally via Alan's father and I just nodded my head. Marlon said , "Oh. Yeah," and that was that. The next and last time I was with Marlon was in front of Saint Paul, Minnesota's Ramsey County Courthouse in the 1970s during my first Twin Cities television days. He was in St. Paul defending the American Indian Movement's Russell Means (the latter with whom I spent significant time in the 1990s, to be later described). Marlon had written a book, so I asked him to sign it and reminded him of the night at his and Wally's apartment. He just grunted, signed the cover of the book in ballpoint pen and that concluded the encounter. Every time I see him on screen, large or small, the memories just described evoke a smile of how privileged I was to know him in "real life" situations.*

Once again, the connections never stop with apparently no degrees of separation for yours truly: I learned recently Marilyn Gennaro also danced in The King And I, *the original Broadway version, in which my friend Sal Mineo had advanced to the role of Prince Chulalongkorn (previously referenced). She was also part of the original Broadway cast of* The Pajama Game, *starring John Raitt, with whom I would later have a great and very long friendship beginning in the 1970s.*

Bobby Gusikoff—Bobby died of a stroke, October 20, 2006, in Los Angeles. The final years of his life he was bound to a wheelchair. In my opinion, it was an ignominious and cruel end for one of the most fascinating and first-class people I ever had the privilege to know. He was the ultimate world's champion table-tennis (ping-pong) player and to watch him demolish others at a major table-tennis parlor on Broadway was watching greatness in action. We Lodge kids were often invited by Bobby's PCS classmates to watch Bobby in action after school. His prowess was truly mesmerizing. One could watch for hours. Though he chose and excelled at ping-pong, Bobby had a huge show business pedigree: Brought up in a very musical family, his mother's father had played the cornet for John Philip Sousa; his mother was an accomplished pianist and his father was a noted violinist and symphony orchestra conductor. Despite an almost fatal aneurysm and subsequent paralysis committing Bobby to life in that wheelchair two years earlier, he proved able to courageously receive in person the first Mark Matthews Lifetime Achievement Award for more than 50 years of contributions to the sport of table tennis. He was presented the award in 1999 at the Stratosphere Hotel in Las Vegas. Again, with *no* degrees of separation for yours truly, the Stratosphere's construction was begun by Bob Stupak, the son of one of my grandfather's friends in Pittsburgh and completed by one who was my boss at that time, named Lyle Berman. Berman also created the popular World Poker Tour television series.

Ivan Cury—Ivan was (and still is) a brilliantly talented actor, later turned director and professor. In 1953, Ivan and I acted together in a Boy Scout training film called *The Time Of Their Lives*, which starred

Alan Hale and was shot at the International Scoutmasters Training Headquarters in Mendham, New Jersey. In later life, Ivan directed Jerry Stiller and Anne Meara in a series of commercials, as well as, for many years, George Zimmer's Men's Wearhouse commercials. Ivan will be happily surprised (I hope) to see his name in this book and know we had a strong connection to Jerry and Anne at different times of their and our lives. Because Ivan and his mother knew we were poor, even during my New York acting days on national television, Ivan's mother hired me to earn extra money as a Saturday stock boy in her Madison Avenue dress shop, for which my mother and I were very grateful.

Patty Baumholz (MGM studio President Dore Schary's niece)—Patty had a delightful personality, was very attractive and never gave the impression she "knew who was her Uncle". One evening at a Nathans party, the very first of the rock 'n' roll hits was playing on the Nathans record player. It was on a 45rpm record and the song was *Sh-Boom*, recorded by Canada's great rock 'n' roll foursome, The Crew Cuts, who really started rock 'n' roll. Patty saw me sitting on a chair and said "C'mon, I'll teach you how to Lindy!" Lindy, of course, for those who remember, was another name for jitterbug, or in today's jargon, swing dancing. It was a door opener for me, as even with a hip replacement I can still do most of the moves. Thank you, dear Patty. (I hope she's still alive. What she taught me brought a lot of joy into the remainder of my life.)

During those Lodge and PCS kids years, there was a six months interruption, but extremely significant in regard to much of the remainder of my professional life. Here's what happened:

High school days concluded for me when I lost the *Six Bridges To Cross* part to Sal, but that loss became an eventual win, as losses often do, thanks to Uncle Sam and The Korean War.

After losing the part, I became very despondent. It was the beginning of my senior year at Lodge, in 1954, when my mother said she was certain Sal would now get all the parts for which I would audition, thus she thought I should try to study a trade on which I could fall back if acting ever "dried up" as a choice to make a living.

I had just turned 17 and had already been working professionally for almost 12 years! My mother suggested joining the service to learn my "backup" trade. Her suggestion came a day before I decided to not attend school the following day.

While loafing in the apartment that day, I heard an Air Force recruiting announcement stating anyone at least age 17 could now join, get all the G.I. Bill benefits from the just concluded Korean War, learn a trade and be on active duty for just six months, followed by seven-and-a-half years in the Air Force reserves. Without telling my mother, since it was early in the day, October 17, 1954, I took the subway to The Battery station stop which was only a block from my mother's place of employment, the Lower Manhattan office of the IRS, in the U.S. Custom House, where she was an auditor. (One of my mother's clients was CBS News icon Eric Sevareid, with whom my cousin Cecil Brown, as I earlier noted, had been a colleague during World War Two in London as one of Edward R. Murrow's "boys". I interviewed Sevareid for a documentary in later years and he said he fondly remembered my mother, regardless of her status as an IRS auditor!)

Exiting the subway train, I rushed upstairs to walk to the Air Force recruiting office, which was directly across the street from my mother's workplace. I passed all the tests and joined. I called my mother to let her know. She asked, "You did *what*?" Even though she'd suggested two days earlier that I join, she obviously never thought I'd do it. In retrospect, I should have granted her the common courtesy to tell her my plan prior to simply forging ahead, but I didn't. If there's anything in the world I never wanted to do, it was to have caused my mother any hurtfulness, thus have regretted that bad decision ever since.

I left for basic training two days later. The training base was Sampson AFB in upstate New York, near Geneva, on Lake Seneca, and had been abandoned by the Navy in 1948. To fully describe my basic training experience would fill another book, so suffice it to say my initial service days were more like a Francis, The Talking Mule, army comedy film than not.

One memory of "basic" that's always remained with me was the impeccable class of our squadron T.I. (Tactical Instructor). His name was Robert O. Fryer, A1C. He was the epitome of spit-and-polish, taught us discipline in every element of our 11 weeks there, probably starched his underwear (he *did* starch his fatigues and fatigue caps) and no one could count marching cadence better. I still count cadence as he did when just taking exercise walks. Airman Fryer whipped us into shape with dignity and even had me entertain one night at an Officers Club dinner. When I returned to the barracks that night, I found my bed short-sheeted, but I expected it. Airman Fryer is one of my life's "heroes". I'm certain he never knew it. Thank you, Bob. You were a great role model.

At the conclusion of "basic", everyone is "alerted" to what his or her service job will be. A barracks buddy of mine and I had not been alerted on the scheduled day, thus I asked a new friend I'd made, named Worley, who was in the "alerting office", what our jobs would be. He told me there had been a delay because so many of the jobs were filled rapidly at that time. He then told me the only two jobs that were open were Motor Pool and Meteorology. In my childhood, I had always thought it would be great to be a Greyhound bus driver, thus the Motor Pool thought intrigued me briefly. Then I remembered my lifelong fascination with Astronomy. Astronomy's scientific cousin being Meteorology, I chose that subject to be my Air Force "job", never thinking it would mean anything to me after I was discharged. That's what some of us get for 'thinking", since becoming a television weatherman was my primary "meal ticket" from 1958 through 1988.

My very first airplane rides involved coming home from basic on a DC3 (Elmira, NY to Newark, NJ) in a snowstorm (Wow, did we bounce) and preparing for the flight to Chicago a few days later, also in a snowstorm, but on a much bigger plane. I took my Meteorology course to become a Met Tech (Meteorological Technician) at Chanute AFB near Rantoul, Illinois. One of those in my classes would become Good Morning America's first weatherman, John Coleman. John and I became close acquaintances in later years after he had departed GMA. In the 1980s, John even visited me in my Minneapolis house, contemplating a business venture together, which never materialized. Other places I was stationed on TDY (temporary duty) were Cheyenne, Wyoming; Anchorage, Alaska and Denver, Colorado, where I was discharged, April 18, 1955, six months and one day of the required six months active duty for my enlistment, with seven-and-a-half years in the Air Force reserves to follow. I also got my high school GED diploma there. (During my D.C. television days in the mid-1970s, close friend Peter Jennings and I discussed the fact Peter never graduated from high school, not even with a GED, which, of course, wasn't available in his native Canada. More about our truly great friendship later.)

CHAPTER FIVE

The First Survival Adventure

If you want to understand today, you have to search yesterday.
—Authoress Pearl S. Buck

When I was discharged from the active Air Force, I decided to visit friends in D.C. (not knowing I'd be enjoying a blessed and successful run there as a television weatherman fewer than 20 years later). I liked D.C., so got my first post-service job as an Elliott Fisher operator at the Mayflower Hotel. My job was to log in guests on a special typewriter called an Elliott Fisher machine. That job in late April, 1955, lasted a month. It was boring (almost as boring as this book!). My one-room studio living quarters at 1919 G Street NW were depressing. That building has now been torn down and the address part of George Washington University's campus. It was time to get back into show business as fast as possible.

One of the Universal executives involved with *Six Bridges To Cross* told me he felt I should have been cast in even a "small" part in that film, and told me if he could help me in later years I should call him and get out to Hollywood. His name was Phil Benjamin. I called Phil from D.C., told him I was going to buy a used car and come to see him at Universal as soon as I could buy the car and get my driver's license. He said he'd be looking forward to it.

To make a much longer story as short as possible, for 90 dollars I bought a used 1946 Ford from a girl named Winifred (Winnie) Farrar. Her father was a naval officer stationed at The Pentagon. The car had a stick shift. Winnie taught me to drive around and around The Lincoln Memorial. In those days, one could do that. Not being used to driving, or using a clutch to shift gears, it took a while before I mastered it. Every time I'd shift gears without the clutch pressed all the way to the floor, she'd say, "Grind me a pound." Just something else I'll always remember from so many who helped me grow.

When I went to take my D.C. driver's license test, I flunked it. Because I wanted to get to Hollywood as fast as possible, I drove there without a driver's license. There were no freeways, thus my primary routes were U.S. 40, 54 and the fabled 66. In those days, what have now become retro icons were very real, from "teepee" motels to Minneapolis-created Burma Shave signs. I had almost no money, impulsively and impetuously driving to Hollywood without that driver's license. Luckily, I had a shirttail "Aunt" who owned a boarding house in Las Vegas, primarily housing people who would soon become divorcees. "Aunt" Ora (Prichard), took me in for two nights (free, thank goodness) and fed me. Her boarding house was located on the patch of land where the Clark County Courthouse now stands. Ora eventually did very well, thanks to that choice of construction site. Regardless, as I was about to continue the final leg of my "illegal" drive to Hollywood, she asked, "You need money, don't ya kid?". I embarrassedly said, "Yes", and she gave me twenty dollars. In the spring of 1955, that was a lot.

I forgot to mention the 1946 Ford I bought from "Winnie" boiled over every half hour or so until I got it fixed in Tucumcari, New Mexico, on my way to Hollywood via Las Vegas. Regardless, after leaving Las Vegas at four o'clock that twenty-dollar morning, I ran out of gas on L.A.'s Arroyo Seco Freeway at rush hour. Fate provided me with the blessing of a priest driving the car behind me, who literally pushed me off the nearest exit and into a gas station in the heart of downtown L.A. That was one of many times in my life I survived, thanks to what I'm certain has been Divine Intervention.

Excited to finally arrive in L.A., regardless of how, I immediately went to a pay phone and called Phil Benjamin at Universal. I told him I had no money and no place to stay but was appreciative for his suggesting I come to Hollywood to begin the resumption of my acting career. He said, verbatim, "Get a job as a bag boy at one of the supermarkets and keep in touch with me from time to time." It was the first of a few times in my life when the words "hurt" and "insensitive" weren't strong enough. I think I even asked, "Bag boy?" then hung up. Sometimes having immediate intuition regarding resilience, that was one of those times. I asked the gas station attendant if he knew about any places that housed young people who needed temporary shelter and food. Again, Divine Intervention, in my opinion, surfaced and he guided me to the Junipero Serra Boys Mission in downtown L.A. When I got there, I told them my only "mission" was to get back home to Pittsburgh where I'd then sort out the rest of that part of my life. They allowed me to stay for two nights while I waited for my grandfather to wire me what I thought would be enough money for gas and food to get me back to Pittsburgh. The wire arrived and I started my trip back to Pittsburgh, via Las Vegas again, still without a driver's license.

In a nutshell, what my grandfather wired wasn't enough, thus I needed to ask him for more help when I got to Columbus, Ohio. A lot more happened between Las Vegas and Columbus, including being offered a gas station manager's job in Nara Visa, New Mexico, by a young man whose name I never forgot and with whom I actually spoke on the phone this past year (thanks to looking him up and finding his contact information on the Internet's white pages), but I'll spare you the remainder of other details, except to say I had two candy bars and three bottles of Dr. Pepper for sustenance for almost two days between the afore-mentioned Nara Visa, New Mexico and Terre Haute, Indiana. Keeps making a person tougher, sometimes.

CHAPTER SIX

At The Top, Then . . .

Life's a banquet and most poor SOBs are starving to death (I cleaned that up! BZ)
—A line from the play, *Mame*

When I got back to Pittsburgh, I immediately took my Pennsylvania driver's license test and passed it. Having just driven back and forth across the continent without a license, or an accident, I guess I knew what to do! I told my grandfather the story about Phil Benjamin. He told me he had some friends in the L.A. area who were "connected" and felt I could probably stay with them for a while if I got a job and began to pursue acting again. They also had a friend who was a highly respected talent agent in Hollywood. He called them and they said they'd do everything they could to help me. I packed up the car and headed toward Hollywood again, but this time a bit better "armed" with sufficient cash (again borrowed from my grandfather, which makes me ill about which to think).

I got to L.A. again and my grandfather's friends were wonderful to me. I found a night job as a gas station attendant (Al Rogers Chevron) at the corner of La Cienega and Pico Boulevards. One of the weekly gas station customers was a heavy-set lady with a German accent. When she presented her Chevron credit card, it was labeled Mr. and Mrs. Randolph Scott. She told me she was their housekeeper. Whenever I see Randolph Scott in a movie re-run on television these days, it makes me smile, remembering his housekeeper and the weekly fill-ups and windshield cleanings I provided her.

Thanks to a connection of my grandfather's friends, I rented a studio apartment on Crenshaw Boulevard from a man named Packrose, who was an M.D. My grandfather's friends also set up a meeting with that talent agent and his wife. The agent's name was Al Ochs, with offices on Hollywood Boulevard near Vine Street. In later years, I would be around that neighborhood a lot, but at that time, late spring, 1955, the surroundings were all new to me. Ochs and his wife immediately signed me to an exclusive representation contract.

They genuinely liked me, which blew my mind, and accompanied me to several meetings within a few days of signing. The meetings were with some very big decision-makers at the major film studios and most important, the most prolific and respected casting agent of all time, a man named Lynn Stalmaster.

Lynn Stalmaster was diminutive in physical stature but the giant of all casting directors. His name appears on the credits of almost all iconic movies and television series. Mr. Ochs took me to meet Mr. Stalmaster in his very long, spacious office trailer, on the Columbia lot. Al and I were with him only two or three minutes at the most, but Stalmaster's final comment to Al was, "You keep a short leash on this one. He will definitely work in this town." We all smiled, shook hands and that was that. Stalmaster came through for Mr. Ochs and me, but my lack of enough money to stay in L.A. stuck another life-changing knife into my acting life. Here's what happened: I'd heard nothing from Mr. Ochs for a couple weeks following the Stalmaster meeting, was making only enough at the nighttime gas station job to survive and decided I had to leave "Hollywood" to get back to Pittsburgh or New York, near enough to family to have possibly better chances to get back into the business. Thus, one fine morning, I loaded the car and headed back east again. My rent was paid up and my landlord told me he'd take any calls or messages that might come in after I'd left. The next morning, I had already reached the New Mexico border, found a pay phone at a gas station and called my landlord to learn if there were any messages. He said Mr. Ochs called and told him I'd been cast (by Stalmaster) in an episode of *The Loretta Young Show*, which would star Rod Cameron. The landlord told me he told Mr. Ochs I'd left and Mr. Ochs was saddened to learn the news. I never had the courtesy nor guts to call Mr. Ochs and apologize. That was more than wrong and it's been in my memory ever since. Had I stayed, it would have (not woulda, coulda, shoulda) been the beginning of a long and successful career under Messrs. Ochs and Stalmaster's "wings". Leaving was the first of two of the worst career decisions I ever made. The other, which occurred 19 years into the future, will be addressed later.

I did have family in L.A. They were my Mom's half-sister, my Aunt Arlene and her husband, Phil Seegall. Uncle Phil was an animator for Disney and the nicest person on the planet. Unfortunately, he was married to the opposite, who had been very nasty to my mother her entire life. I chose to not even get in touch with them all the subsequent years I was back and forth to L.A., except for one brief visit . . . ten minutes . . . in 1963.

When I arrived back in Pittsburgh, I knew it would be for only a short time, aiming to get back to performing in New York. Most of the Lodge and PCS kids were becoming more established on television and Broadway. My grandfather then had a brainstorm: He contacted his friend and former business partner named Bill Finkel, asking Bill if he'd contact his son, Bob Finkel, to see if Bob would help me get a break back into television acting (or singing) in New York. Bob said, "Yes", and I was off to New York again.

Bob was a giant in the industry and producing *The Perry Como Show* when he said "Yes". He had directed Dean Martin and Jerry Lewis in the iconic *Colgate Comedy Hour* and directed and produced other major television dramas and series in later years, including *The Andy Williams Show* and *Andy Williams Christmas Specials.* Bob gave The Osmond Family their first break on national television, via *The Andy Williams Show.* (I got to know Olive Osmond, the mother, during my Las Vegas years, to be referenced later, but not any of the other family members.) Bob told me the first time he met Dean and Jerry, they walked him to the corner of Sunset and Vine, lifted him in a prone position over their heads, and twirled him around two or three times. Bob said it scared him half to death, but also let him know "anything would go" with Dean and Jerry. Bob, since he was producing *The Perry Como* show at that time (late 1955), had me meet him in his NBC office at a building in Rockefeller Center . . . not 30 Rock . . . and asked me if I could sing. I told him I could (can't remember what song I sang for him in his office) and he told me I could be one of The Ray Charles Singers, Perry's backup group on the show (and on Perry's recordings, none in which I ever participated, but only on the television show) beginning the following Saturday night. That lasted for me for over two years, until mid-November, 1957. On Google, I'm even listed as a soloist, which I was, briefly, on Perry's 1956 Christmas show. Some of those on that show included

Bishop Fulton J. Sheen and the aforementioned Ina Balin, but we didn't have a chance to exchange any dialogue.

Talk about halcyon days doing the *Como* show! We did it "live" every Saturday night at 7, Eastern Time, at the Ziegfeld Theater, home of the original Ziegfeld Follies. It was a truly magnificent theater on Seventh Avenue in the upper 50s, revamped for television with three camera runways, similar to the afore-described RKO Center Theater where we did *Peepers*. Billy Rose, Ted Nathan's former boss (mentioned earlier) still had an apartment on the top floor of the theater, but we never saw him.

My fondest memories include working with Perry, of course, another fellow Pennsylvanian, born not far from our previously mentioned mutual friend, Shirley Jones. Perry was born and raised in Canonsburg, Shirley born in Charleroi. And, of course, Bob Finkel was a Carnegie Tech (now Carnegie Mellon) graduate, thus we native Pittsburghers and other Pennsylvanians certainly had a somewhat familial relationship throughout. Perry was as laid back off camera as he was on. I heard him "swear" only once. It was during a break in rehearsals one Saturday afternoon. I told him my mother, grandfather and I were on a brief driving trip earlier in the week and had to stop in Montebello, Quebec, to ask some driving directions from a priest who befriended our lost plight. The priest asked me what I did for a living and I told him about being a singer on *The Perry Como Show*. He told us Perry had dedicated the church in that small town a few years earlier. When I told Perry about where we were, he asked, "How in Hell did you find that place?" As I said, that's the only time I ever heard him swear. Perry, Mitch Ayres (our orchestra leader who was struck years later by a car that killed him and his female companion in Las Vegas) and Greg Garrison, our Director, always broke from rehearsals at 4:30, went to a nice watering hole next to the theater and returned very mellow at 6 to prepare for the live show that would air at 7.

Other fond memories include working often on *Como* with Rosemary Clooney, George's aunt and Nick's sister. I remember sitting behind her, her sister Gail and singer Brenda Lee during a break in rehearsals, listening to her give gentle advice to them about stage presence and calming their fears, since it was the first "big" telecast appearance for both of them. In later years, Rosemary had me emcee a special event in Edmonton, Alberta, at which she was the focus. She was one of the most wonderful people one could ever hope to know and left us much too soon. In my opinion, the death of any we love is never the "right time" for those of us left behind.

I'd worked with the aforementioned Mickey Rooney several times, but most often on *Como*. One of the fun moments was after one of the shows when my mother happened to be watching from the sidelines on stage. Mickey had just done his part, saw my mother and kissed her (a big one) right on the lips. My mother was visually less than gracious regarding his action, but, thank goodness, didn't yell at him or punch him, the latter of which she would be capable.

Those were truly fantastic career days for me, working with every star who *was* a star every Saturday night, and also able to do a bit part here and there, once again, on some of the dramatic television shows of the day. By 1957, Sal, however, had become a major star following *Six Bridges To Cross*, starring in *The Private War Of Major Benson* alongside Charlton Heston and Julie Adams (the latter with whom he had also acted in *Six Bridges*), the iconic *Rebel Without A Cause* starring the equally iconic James Dean, Natalie Wood, Dennis Hopper and Jim Backus and *Giant*, again co-starring James Dean, along with Elizabeth Taylor and Rock Hudson.

Sal's successes again lead to, perhaps, the most profound turning point in my career, thanks to advice from Perry's announcer, Frank Gallup, WOR and Mutual network announcer/personality Phil Tonken and my mother.

Jerry Lewis—*The memories are legion, from our first brief meeting in Denver at the Brown Palace Hotel in 1963 (not then knowing about our mutual friendship with Bob Finkel) to television interview time backstage at a nightclub where Jerry was performing in a Twin Cities suburb in the early 1980s to a memorable 1990s wrestling interview in Las Vegas for air on international television (please see photos section). The "punch line" regarding the nightclub interview is coming, to wit: After Jerry and I recalled days of yore, I wrote him a note telling him how much he had truly inspired me with some of the things he said* *about life in general. A couple weeks later, I called Jerry's then manager, Joe Stabile (bandleader Dick Stabile's brother) to ask if Jerry had received my note. Joe said, "Yes", and that was that, but not really. A year later, I got a call from the station for which I'd done the interview and they said "Jerry Lewis wants you to call him at home. Here's his number". I thought it might be about my letter, but didn't know for certain. I called (I still have his number but won't print it) and he said, "Hi, ya, Barry" in his inimitable style. I said "Hi, Jerry. To what do I owe the honor of you wanting me to call you?" He said, "We were just going through the tapes of last year's tour and your letter to me fell out of the box. I swear to you I have never seen that letter until just now and didn't want you to think I would ever ignore such a beautiful letter." I was floored and grateful that he would take that time to make certain I knew what he'd just told me. I thanked him, after which he asked how I was feeling. I told him there were lots of ups and downs. He then said, verbatim, "Well, I'll tell you what. You now have my home phone number, so whenever you're feeling down, call me and we'll pump each other up." How beautiful and a demonstration he had the true heart he displayed so often, especially during the MDA telethons he created so many years before. I thanked him and told him I'd do that, and that was that. We spoke occasionally through the years thereafter.*

James Dean—*One late summer afternoon in 1954, I was invited by my friend George Maharis to have coffee with him at a small coffee shop named Al-Jo's, just a few doors east of where he and I hung out with other actors waiting for agents messages and calls for acting jobs. The place we "hung out" was called The Hayes Registry. George told me the reason for the coffee was to say so long to another actor who was leaving for Hollywood and his big break the next day. When we entered the coffee shop, facing us and sitting in the first booth on the right was a good looking young man who definitely had an "actor's face". George led me straight to that booth and introduced me to the young man, who was James Dean. None of us, except Dean's friends, a la George, had ever heard of him, let alone surmise he'd become a well-deserved Hollywood icon. Regardless, Jimmy (as he said I should call him) told us about the film in which he would be co-starring and introduced to* *international film audiences, i.e., East Of Eden, to be directed by Elia Kazan. Jimmy was very soft-spoken and played with his coffee cup a lot, twirling it full in the saucer. I congratulated him on his big break and also told him about my big break not happening a few weeks earlier in regard to Sal and Six Bridges To Cross, neither of us knowing, of course, Sal and Jimmy would eventually act together the following year in Rebel Without A Cause. Jimmy said he felt badly about my losing that part but told me he was sure I'd get a good break someday. That kind comment from Jimmy sparked George to state what a rotten business show business was, that he was fed up with all the big shots and the phonies and was going to get out of it. He really vented, using four-letter words that haven't yet been heard since, nor invented, but he stormed out of the coffee shop after we said our goodbyes to Jimmy. Fewer than ten years later, George was co-starring with Martin Milner on the hit CBS-TV series, Route 66, which premiered while I was doing television talent and directing work in Idaho Falls, Idaho, much more about which later. I was happy George decided to not quit the business. After the Al-Jo "coffee" I never saw either of them again, in person, and was devastated, along with everyone else who loved his work, to hear about Jimmy's premature death just a bit over a year from when we had that coffee.*

I had met Kazan briefly during a brief alley-way stage door-area chat with a friend who was acting in Tea And Sympathy on Broadway, which Kazan, directed. I nodded a brief "Hello" to Kazan, as well as to actress Deborah Kerr with whom Kazan was chatting at the time. It was the only time I was with either of those two, but fun to remember. In that memory, I also remember both Kazan and Kerr were very "short" in height, but obviously very tall in the show business firmament.

As I mentioned previously, Sal Mineo's film successes again lead to, perhaps, the most profound turning point in my career, and life, thanks to advice from Perry's announcer, Frank Gallup, WOR and Mutual network announcer/personality Phil Tonken and my mother.

It all commenced during a break in *Como* rehearsals when Frank Gallup and I were sitting alone together on one of the stairways at

The Ziegfeld, just "chewing the fat". Frank told me I looked unhappy. I told him I was and mentioned the reason, i.e., Sal. He said, "You have an excellent voice. Why not forget acting for a while and get into the announcing business at a small station somewhere, and in two or three years you'll be back here in New York announcing on one of the big stations." I thanked him for his confidence in me but told him I wouldn't know how to find all the stations in the U.S. Frank said, "I'll get you a book that lists all those stations and you'll have it next week." True to his word, the following Saturday Frank presented me with a thick, beautifully bound gold-colored book that listed every station in the U.S. and all contact information for each. He told me my mother should write letters to stations in places I might like, get audition tapes made and send them to the station managers. *Addenda regarding Frank Gallup: He had one of the most magnificent broadcasting voices ever, but was not a broadcast announcer until much later in his life. Frank told me he had been a full time stockbroker in Boston when someone approached him in one of the brokerage offices after hearing Frank speak. That someone was an NBC vice president offering Frank a full time job as an announcer on the NBC network in New York. Frank said he was flattered and accepted the offer almost immediately. Frank was tall, thin and lanky, had a great sense of humor and was affable to everyone. I was very blessed for his concern about my future, to say the least.*

Needing to make an audition tape (reel-to-reel in those days), my mother contacted one of the WOR and Mutual Network radio personality/announcers who had known us since we arrived in New York in 1952 and whom I was blessed to visit often at WOR. His name was Phil Tonken and was one of the nation's busiest and most recognizable commercial voices, too. Two days later, Phil arranged the audition taping, selected the commercial and news copy and I taped with a WOR engineer doing all the work. I still have the tape, and if I'd been any station manager listening, I wouldn't have hired me. Of course I was very grateful to Phil (am to this day), the engineer made 20 dubs (free, as a favor to Phil) and my mother was now ready to type those "pitch" letters. *Addenda about WOR: WOR is where I also got to know radio genius Jean Shepherd, who wrote the film,* A Christmas Story. *During a 1980s AFTRA union national broadcasting convention at The Bond Court Hotel in Cleveland, Jean invited me to have breakfast with him and catch up on old memories. He then told me he was in the midst of writing a screenplay about his childhood in that part of the country, and focused on Christmastime and a "Red Ryder single-shot bolt- action BB gun", surely the remedy for putting one's eye out, as that delightful movie preached. The film was the aforementioned* A Christmas Story *and the rest is history. Every time I watch that classic, I smile, as I am now, remembering he allowed me to be in on the genesis of its creation. Other great memories of WOR were a couple times meeting and speaking with Dorothy Kilgallen, the "Grande Dame" of all syndicated society and entertainment journalists/ gossip columnists, as well as regular panelist on CBS-TV's* What's My Line? *She also co-hosted a weekday mornings radio show on WOR, entitled* Breakfast With Dorothy And Dick. *Dick was Broadway actor and producer Richard Kollmar. I met him, too, but he wasn't quite as "open" as Ms. Kilgallen, who, several years later, died a very mysterious death, about which not many know or about which talk, but related to President John F. Kennedy's assassination. The news of her passing in any mysterious way was very disturbing to learn, because she was a sweetheart in person. One of the strongest other WOR memories involves probably the only time I ever saw Phil Tonken rattled. It was when Phil was hosting an afternoon talk show using the pseudonym, Alan Grainger. Phil invited the incomparable Danny Kaye to be a guest on Phil's ("Alan's") talk show and kindly invited me to be in the control room to watch the "interview". That "interview" was two solid hours of Danny Kaye "owning" the station. His antics were too hilarious to describe with his sandaled feet atop the broadcast studio table most of the time. Forget any "schedules": Danny* was *the schedule. The final "big" memory was when Phil ("Alan") had actress Thelma Ritter as his talk show guest. Ms. Ritter had been featured in numerous major feature films as a character actress. One of them was one of Alfred Hitchcock's classics,* Rear Window, *which starred James Stewart and Grace Kelly. (I had very personal times and connections with each of the latter, too, later described. Sorry, it never ends.) While doing her interview with Phil ("Alan"), Ms. Ritter frequently looked at me while I was sitting next to Phil ("Alan"). For whatever reason, afterward she warmly asked if I was an actor. I replied in the affirmative and she told me to call her husband, "Tony"Moran, then a giant executive with one of the major ad agencies that not only represented client sponsors for television shows but also did the casting. She wrote his name and number for me on a piece of paper and told me to call him, referencing her and my conversation. I thanked her, profusely. I called and left several messages for him during the next two weeks, but never got a return call. Apparently, it was not meant to be.* What *was* meant to be, and then some, is described in the next chapter, with my express train moving onto a different track. That new track opened more aspects of life and new relationships than I could have ever predicted or conceived, all adding to the building blocks of what were to be some very blessed and somewhat challenging years.

CHAPTER SEVEN

Weather!

No one can make you feel inferior without your consent.—Eleanor Roosevelt

After hearing what I considered my amateurish reel-to-reel audition tape and having had multiple copies made, thanks to Phil Tonken at WOR, my mother, God bless her, typed 75 individual letters to radio station managers asking if they'd consider hiring me, and if so, if they'd wish to receive my audition tape. I had selected 75 stations from the book Frank Gallup had given me, all in the Midwest or Intermountain West. Eight station managers responded, from Wichita, Kansas, to Fort Collins, Colorado, Idaho Falls, Idaho, to Helena, Montana and others. (The broadcasting business is so small the person to whom we had sent a pitch letter in Idaho Falls eventually became one of my bosses in that town three years later at a station competitive to the one at which he worked when he received my pitch letter. His name was Dewain Silvester, another truly class act in the broadcasting business, but, sadly, now long-deceased.)

In early November, 1957, Helena's KCAP radio station was the first to offer me a job. The job was offered via telegram, stating, "If you're still interested in Helena, Helena is interested in you". The telegram was signed by Lou Torok, the station's General Manager, with the starting salary to be fifty-five dollars a week. I was ecstatic. Somebody actually wanted me, even after listening to that awful audition tape. *I learned in later years, after having had the honor to be inducted into The Society of Montana Broadcast Legends in 2011, two of the other "legends" had also started their broadcast careers on that station. They were Donna Kelley, former CNN anchor and Jack Womack who became Vice President of CNN's News Division. I've been in touch with both of them frequently since then, collegially and pleasantly. Donna kindly sent me an email in 2014 stating I was "a real talent." I was honored to have her write that.*

In late November, a week prior to Thanksgiving, I bade farewell to my mother in New York and drove to Pittsburgh to bid farewell to my grandfather, too, on the way west to "seek my fortune". I drove him to work on Pittsburgh's north side, he got out of the car and the last time I ever saw him was in my rear view mirror, waving goodbye. It was the last time I ever saw him and as I write and think about this, tears are welling up in my eyes.

My drive to Helena, because it was now just three days prior to Thanksgiving, was mostly snow filled, stopping overnight in motels in Crystal Lake, Illinois; Anoka, Minnesota and concluding in Mandan, North Dakota. *In the 1970s I would be Anoka's Halloween Parade Grand Marshal because of my blessed success as a weatherman and ski show host in the nearby Twin Cities. Anoka is known as The Halloween Capital of the World, and is also the birthplace of NPR's Garrison Keillor, Fox News anchor, Gretchen Carlson and former Congresswoman, Michelle Bachmann. I met Keillor only once, but have had good interaction through the years with Gretchen Carlson. I never met Congresswoman Bachmann. While in the Anoka motel, I watched the 10 p.m. news on KSTP-TV, not knowing I'd be succeeding the weatherman who I watched that night, named Johnny Morris, in July, 1971, more details about which later, except to say when I watched that news team that night I thought to myself, "I'll never make it to a market this big." I'm glad the fates proved me wrong.*

My last "overnight" on my way to Helena was in Mandan, North Dakota, having just entered the Mountain Time Zone. I'd driven through a fierce ground blizzard early that morning west of Fargo, but also pulled into a small café for breakfast. It was one of my most memorable breakfasts and the all-time least expensive: Two large pancakes, orange juice and coffee, all for the cost of 19 cents. Those are the sorts of times I remember most vividly, with smiles.

It was a below-zero cold morning when I left Mandan, the day before Thanksgiving. One of my other memorable stops was at Badlands National Park. At about 8 in the morning, with absolutely no one else around, I got out of my car to see what there was to see from a tiny viewpoint stand wrapped with chicken wire nailed to that creaky wooden framed structure. I felt like I was the only person left on Earth that bleak morning standing in front of that Badlands scenery. I got back in the car after about only a couple minutes and continued westward.

I'd forgotten from my Meteorology days that Chinook winds warm the prairies east of the Rockies. They're "down-slope" winds, as they're named, that come howling down the eastern slopes of the Rockies bringing warmer air from aloft, thus the farther I got into Montana, the warmer it got. By the time I reached Helena at 11 that night, the temperature there was 70 degrees. I was dressed like the Michelin Man in a thermal red snowsuit because I thought it would be proper attire for what could have been Arctic-like temperatures I'd typically encounter upon arrival there. When my new temporary roommate, who was a KCAP announcer named Wayne Schultz, exited the movie theater where I was supposed to meet him, he burst out laughing at this city slicker from the east who dressed as though he would be starting his local radio career in Siberia. After a good laugh, Wayne guided me to his apartment and I began my first Montana night there.

The next morning, Thanksgiving, 1957, I awakened to see the beautiful hills and lower reaches of the Helena Valley, as well as the more formidable mountains to the west. It was a great first day to begin a new phase of my life, scared to death, but trusting all would be okay.

In a nutshell, and to make a long story mercifully much shorter for you, I got a wonderful apartment on the second floor of a home owned by an elderly couple whose last name was Lovely, reflecting how they really were. It cost 40 dollars a month, and I still had more than a little bit of my 55 dollar a week salary left to cover expenses and a bit of living. I didn't know news directors, newscasters and disc jockey announcers had to run their own control boards at smaller stations. I was used to engineers doing all the control room technical work for the announcers (in New York and even Pittsburgh) with announcers simply talking or reading copy. Because I was (and still am) technologically challenged, Lou Torok told me he knew I had a ton of talent but radio control boards were sapping me of what I could really do and elected to fire me because of it, but gently. Lou called a man named Art Mosby who owned television station KMSO-

TV, Channel 13, in Missoula and urged Art to meet me, asap, for a possible job there. Mosby agreed. (I later learned Art's daughter, Aileen Mosby, was AP's Paris, France, Bureau Chief and writer for the International Herald-Tribune.)

On my way to meet Mr. Mosby a couple days later, I had to drive over McDonald Pass, just west of Helena, which housed the Continental Divide on its peak. My brakes snapped on the western side of the pass as I started down a very long hill. The road was mostly ice and snow covered. All I could do was pray and hope I'd not run into any other cars or trucks (literally) in either direction. God was at my side that morning (as has been the case so many times in my life) because, after going down that hill at breakneck speed, I reached a flat spot at the bottom of the Pass and coasted slowly enough into a little spot in the road where I could turn into a gas station and actually stop with my emergency brake literally five feet before I would hit the gas station's garage door. I had to wait for about an hour for the brakes to be fixed and called Mr. Mosby from the gas station's pay phone to tell him I'd be late, and why. He said my being late wouldn't be a problem. When I arrived at the station, I met Mr. Mosby and he said I could be a switcher-director-announcer-film shipper and kids show host as "Shorty, Foreman of The Circle 13 Ranch Gang." The pay would be 60 dollars a week. I was moving up in the world of finance. I went back to Helena, collected my worldly belongings (all of which fit into my little 1946 four-door Ford sedan) and got an apartment on Front Street, above a restaurant named The Shack, about three short blocks from the station.

The most important career "happening" at Channel 13 shaped my life for decades to come: We were a CBS-TV affiliate and Douglas Edwards was anchoring the CBS Evening News. In those days, it was a 15-minute program. I was called into General Manager S. (for Sylvester) John Schile's office, thinking I was on my way to being fired again, but for what reason I wouldn't know, since I was doing the job there diligently and correctly. Instead, he asked if I knew anything about the weather. Eureka! I told him about my Air Force training and he was delighted. He said CBS was now going to have its affiliates fill a full half hour with news, i.e., Douglas Edwards with the national/international news for the first 15 minutes and local affiliates filling the last 15 minutes with local news, sports and weather. This would all begin in less than a week.

There were no camera people to person the two cameras in the studio, thus I had to walk into my own weather set which was a green chalkboard with a U.S. map outline. The boss had told me to do the weather report any way I wished, so I began explaining things and writing, with chalk, on the board. However, I remembered a person is supposed to look at one's audience thus I turned back around toward the camera, which had been positioned a bit lower than eye level. In order to get my full face into the camera to maintain eye contact with the audience, I looked into the camera at somewhat an oblique angle, somewhat "peek-a-boo" style. I heard our news anchorman laughing quietly across the studio from where I was positioned and thought, "Well, time to get fired again." (Our anchorman was a wonderful non-egotistical pro named Ron Richards, who also did radio news in Missoula.)

When I got off the air from my first weathercast, the phone rang in the control room and I was summoned to take the call. It was from the boss, stating, "You keep looking around into the camera and that'll be your meal ticket for a long time." He liked it and I became "Barry ZeVan, the Peek-A-Boo Weatherman" from then until the mid 1980s, with only a few breaks in between.

I would be very ungrateful and remiss if I didn't acknowledge those who took the time to teach me what I needed to know about running a television station control board, as well as proper pronunciations of words like "news", pronounced "nyews" with a "liquid" U sound, instead of "nooz". My primary tutor there in that regard was Gerald (Gerry) Grisham. He and his wife, Gail, were wonderful to me. *Once, when I had a date with a girl named Millie Enebo in nearby Stevensville, Gerry and Gail loaned me their almost new 1955 Chevy station wagon lest Millie have me pick her up in my boiling-over 1946 Ford. Millie was impressed with Gerry and Gail's car, but that was the only date we had. Her father owned an insurance company in Stevensville and I was just a poor kid trying to make it. I don't blame her for wanting to raise the bar in regard to whom she dated. She was a very sweet girl, a class act and later moved to Lake Merritt in Oakland, California, which she told me during that one date she'd be doing. Why I remember or know these things, I don't know, but there they are. Sorry!* In later years I was told Gerry and Gail spent most of the remainder of their lives heading a stage play theater in their native Sacramento, California. Bob Conger, a San Jose, California, native, taught me how to run a camera and ship film. Bob was a great guy, too, and although he never knew it, a mentor regarding my ad libs, i.e., with me frequently saying, "My goodness" after I'd received a response from a kid of whom I'd asked a question on The Circle 13 Ranch Gang program. One day Bob came up to me after a show and said, "We're so tired of hearing about your goodness." I laughed, realized he was correct and I'm smiling as I type this, remembering his funny but wise comment. Program Director Ron Maines, Sales Manager Vi Thompson and truly dear office people Maida Gunther and Laurel (Laurie) Eichholz also probably never knew how much their niceness to me would stick in my mind for the remainder of my life.

After leaving Channel 13 in the summer of 1958, and with some radio station news and announcing/DJ gigs in between, or simultaneously, my television weathercasts would have me delivering them on the air in Kalispell, Montana (for nine months, because the station transmitter burned down while I was on the air), Lethbridge, Alberta, Canada (one year), Idaho Falls, Idaho (five years), Seattle-Tacoma, Washington (one year, also as Program Director, and working for a boss whose son would become the inventor of cell phones, more about which will be chronicled later), Las Vegas, Nevada (four years), Minneapolis–St. Paul (four years), Washington. D.C. (three years), Detroit, Michigan (four years) and weekends on ABC-TV's Satellite News Channels based on Shippan Point, east of Stamford, Connecticut (one year, simultaneously with Detroit) then back to Minneapolis–St. Paul (four years on air, again).

CHAPTER EIGHT

Rungs on Other Ladders

Success is not final, failure is not fatal: it is the courage to continue that counts.

—Sir Winston Churchill

When I quit Channel 13 in Missoula in the summer of 1958, I moved to a radio announcing job in Butte, again to try to advance financially because I'd become engaged to my first wife, a rancher's daughter named Dorothy Johns, the youngest of ten children, from Montana's Mission Valley near the town of St. Ignatius. During part of one summer, her folks actually had me branding cattle for a couple days. As was stated in the Prologue and Stories Preview, I've experienced almost everything, not all of it pleasant, but all of it definitely an education, building an encyclopedic reservoir and eidetic events repository from which to draw when necessary. Following are some of my strongest memories of those places and times, aside from doing television weather:

Missoula, Montana—I also hosted a talk show on Channel 13 and my first two guests were U.S. Senator Mike Mansfield and magnificent singer William (Bill) Warfield. I had actually met Warfield during my teenage acting days in New York, thus we reminisced about those days. Bill was in Missoula to do a concert. Although eventually divorced, he was also married to another magnificent singer, Leontyne Price, who I "covered" when she was the opening performer at The Ordway Center for the Performing Arts in St. Paul, Minnesota, circa January 1, 1984. That was also the day Willard Scott and I were on *The Today Show* together with me as Willard's "guest" describing the theater on its opening day. Willard and I were great friends during my TV weathercasting days in D.C., but much more about that later. Connie Chung was doing the news on *Today* that morning and was wide-eyed when we tossed it back to her in New York because she and I had also been friends during my D.C. TV days. Senator

Mansfield also taught guest classes occasionally at then Montana State University (now The University of Montana). A bit of fun trivia: Senator Mansfield was born in Gloversville, New York. So was George "Gabby" Hayes, who I referenced earlier, and also knew during my *Peepers* days. (I used part of my GI Bill to take Liberal Arts and Humanities courses at "the U" while on TV in Missoula.)

Perhaps the most unusual occurrence at Channel 13 happened when our new Program Director, Stan Deck, who later went on to amass fortune without fame, told me he'd received a call from an actor named Steven Geray. Stan told me Geray had just moved to Missoula with his wife, Roanne, a Missoula native who wanted to end their married lives in her hometown. Because Stan knew my show business background, he wanted me to go to Geray's house to listen to what Mr. Geray had to say regarding establishing a weekly television variety show on Channel 13, for which I could direct and co-produce, if it ever happened. In case you don't know who Steven (Steve, as he told me to call him) Geray was, just watch any movie from *Spellbound* to *Gilda* to *All About Eve* to *To Catch A Thief* and dozens more, and you'll see Steven. We had three wonderful visits at his Missoula house, with him frequently reminiscing about how theater was in Hungary during his early acting days prior to coming to the U.S. in the 1930s. We aired only one of his planned series of shows. The show was too high-maintenance for the station, long before videotape was invented, but every time I see him on TCM I remember those gentle times with that truly gentle man and his wonderful wife.

Butte, Montana—I had the morning shift at KXLF, the flagship station of Montana's "XL" radio network that was owned by a broadcast pioneer named Ed Craney. Between keeping all his other stations "fed", doing newscasts and babysitting the equipment, it was still overwhelming for me to have to deal with the technologic side of the business, thus I called a radio station in Anaconda to learn if they had any simple shift openings for an announcer/DJ/newscaster. Happily they did, thus I quit the Butte station after being there only one month. I also wanted to stay in Montana because of my engagement. In Anaconda I was making 75 dollars a week, a fortune.

Anaconda, Montana—It was home of the world's tallest smokestack and only mountain (behind the town) I ever climbed. What I remember most was during a newscast I was delivering, on a very high stool on which we announcer/DJs sat, I was in the middle of saying President Eisenhower's name when the playful station manager goosed me from behind (I hadn't seen him enter the studio) and the name Eisenhower exited my voice as Eisenhoooooooo. The manager was laughing uproariously when he heard me say that, but, being a "serious" newscaster, I didn't think it was too funny at the time. He was a wonderful boss named Mike, but whose last name I sadly can't remember.

Kalispell, Montana—Kalispell was nearer to my fiancée, thus I landed a job at the local television station whose call letters were KULR-TV and owned by a nice man named Norman Penwell and his family. It was also close to The Big Mountain in Whitefish, where I'd developed strong relationships with the owners of the then fledgling ski resort, and maintained the relationships until their deaths in the early 2000s. One night about nine months into my work there as announcer/director/weatherman, I had just signed off the 10 o'clock news and began to roll the film of *Bat Masterson* as the late night fare it was, Monday through Friday. A couple minutes into *Bat*, I smelled smoke and also saw the film burning, visible on people's TV sets. I made a hasty announcement stating Channel 9 was signing off the air, got out of the announce booth and to the fire extinguisher. I sprayed as much as possible, but the major components in the transmitter had burned to a crisp and the station signed off for at least a year. I was out of a job, thus back to Missoula, where some more fun memories that affected my life many years later, prevail.

Missoula, Montana (again)—In order to keep my finger in the broadcast pie, I was lucky enough to get a part-time announcing/DJ/baseball play-by-play re-creation announcer job at radio station KBTK. I remember the film *Raintree County* was playing in the theater next door to our station and co-starred Eva Marie Saint, who I would get to know very well in later years, and about which will be described later. Regardless, the most fun was doing the baseball play-by-play re-creations when the Missoula Timberjacks baseball team was on the road and we'd get the play results from the teletype machine, then pretend we were broadcasting from where the team was playing out-of-town. I had a little stick that hung from the ceiling that I could hit with a pencil to make it sound like a bat hitting a ball (very near my microphone) as well as continuous low-level crowd noise playing in the background. My play-by-play partner was a great kid named Gene Marianetti. Gene later became in charge of all of NASA's astronauts publicity. When I appeared on the air for the first time in D.C., Gene called the station and we saw each other a lot during my TV days there, more than 25 years after our Missoula days. He also got all the astronauts to sign great NASA photos for me, which hang on one of my walls to this day. Neil Armstrong is the most prized, since he was not only the first human to step on the moon but we also shared the same birth date, August 5th. (Ronald Reagan also used to do play-by-play baseball re-creations in Des Moines on WHO radio there, as did the broadcasters in my hometown, Pittsburgh. Their names were Al "Rosey" Rosewell and Bob Prince. I remembered how they did it, which helped my delivery knowledge for the Missoula broadcasts. We also had a record that lasted almost five minutes if we wanted to pretend there was a "rain delay" in the out-of-town ballpark, so we could go to the bathroom. Happened during almost every game! I'm laughing while keying this.) In addition to the KBTK radio work I also painted signs at a gas station (I knew how to do that fairly well, intuitively, and had dabbled in it in the past at a sign shop in Pittsburgh just prior to my teenage years) and also worked, simultaneously, as a "tailer" at the White Pine Lumber Mill just west of downtown Missoula, "tailing" the long pieces of pine that would come from a rip saw and load the boards onto flatbed carriers. I wore gloves, a lot. One night, I also brought some pure pitch from the leavings at the mill into my little cabin west of Missoula, knowing it would be good "firewood". The little potbelly stove I had near my bed almost turned red that night, the pitch was burning so hot, thus it was the last time I ever did *that*. Truly could have burned the cabin down. Live and learn. One of the better things for me from that time onward: My landlady, named

Betty Otto, taught me how to properly iron dress shirts. In my opinion, some of *those* occurrences or lessons are what *really* matter most in life.

Lethbridge, Alberta, Canada—Because my first wedding was a bit more than a year hence, I wanted to make even more headway financially. I'd heard of a great announcing and on-camera weather/ movie-hosting job in Lethbridge, Alberta, Canada, and only four hours drive from my fiancée's family's ranch. It was at a CBC-TV affiliate with the call letters CJLH-TV. My boss was a man named Sam Pitt. He had the voice of ten Gods and was the most professional broadcaster for whom anyone could ever work. Before coming to Lethbridge as Production Manager, he had been Lorne Greene's understudy as Chief Announcer for The Canadian Broadcasting Corporation in Toronto and told me he prayed Lorne would fall ill every night! Sam lived in Hamilton, Ontario, during his CBC-TV understudying days, but because of the commute to Toronto every day and not knowing Lorne would soon leave to begin acting and starring in *Bonanza* in the U.S., Sam left the CBC for Lethbridge. (During my D.C. TV days, I was with Lorne at a social function and told him about Sam hoping Lorne would get ill. Lorne laughed heartily and felt badly Sam didn't stay with that CBC position long enough to replace Lorne as Chief Announcer. For our sakes at CJLH-TV, I'm glad Sam didn't stay in Toronto. He was a perfectionist and his tutelage became the foundation for all future broadcasting I did, even to this day. One of the special times there was seeing Robert Goulet sign off from a CBC-TV show on which he'd appeared regularly in order to go to the states to seek his fortune as an actor/ singer on Broadway. His first play, of course, was *Camelot*, which my wife and I saw while he was still in it, two years hence. Robert became one of my very best friends beginning in 1968 in Las Vegas, much more about which I'll be relating later. To know *he's* no longer with us is also difficult to accept. Our private and public times together were a "hoot", a couple of them even available to see on Google.

Idaho Falls, Idaho—Dorothy and I were married June 4, 1960, in St. Ignatius, Montana. Our first home was in Lethbridge, Alberta, above-referenced. On May 31st, and preparing to leave Lethbridge for the wedding, my mother called me from Pittsburgh to let me know my grandfather had died. I told her I was deeply saddened, of course, but couldn't postpone the wedding. She understood. (Because of financial ignorance, it took me almost 50 years to buy a proper headstone for my grandfather, buried in Pittsburgh's Homewood cemetery. That headstone is firmly placed there now, although I've never seen it in person, but have pictures of it sent me by the cemetery's overseer. Seeing it in person is definitely on my "bucket list".) My mother had nowhere to go, so she sold everything in the Pittsburgh apartment for $500 after Dorothy agreed it would be okay for my mother to live with us. A month later she arrived in Lethbridge by train. A month later, she decided she wanted to move to Las Vegas, since "Aunt" Ora was there and Lethbridge was definitely not my mother's "cup of tea".

Dorothy and I drove my mother to Salt Lake City to catch the train to Las Vegas. She boarded the train in the late afternoon. That night was the night we *know* Dorothy became pregnant with our first child during our overnight stay there. We drove back to Lethbridge the next morning to continue my on-air work at the television station.

A few weeks later, in September, Dorothy told me she was pregnant. I'd heard about dual-citizenship if a child is born to American parents in another country, thus, in my non-infinite wisdom (in retrospect) I told Dorothy I thought I should try to get a television job, asap, back in the U.S. because dual-citizenship might prove a problem for our child in later life. I was incorrect, of course, but, at age 23, one knows *everything*, right? Not!

Regardless, unknown to us at the time, while watching television with Dorothy in Lethbridge on September 26, 1960, I observed one of the many threads that would interweave in my future broadcasting life, i.e., Howard K. Smith moderating the first-ever televised Presidential-candidate debate, which, of course, was between John F. Kennedy and Richard M. Nixon, the latter with whom I'd have three very strong connections in later years and which will be chronicled later in this book. The thread with Howard K. Smith blossomed in 1974 when I began working for WJLA-TV, the ABC-TV affiliate in Washington, D.C., and had the privilege to not only have Mr. Smith's friendship, but also, several years later, actually tap him to host a ten-hour documentary for which I was consulting producer, entitled *The Remarkable 20th Century*. Howard's daughter, Catherine, was also one of our producers at WJLA-TV and we've remained friends ever since. Howard's son, Jack, had become a superb correspondent for ABC for 26 years and hosted me in Paris when he was ABC-TV's Bureau Chief there in the mid-1970s while I was producing my first documentary, about the French Alps. Jack died at age 58 of pancreatic cancer in 2004 at his post-broadcasting home in Mill Valley, California. His untimely death is still difficult to accept. Because Howard and Walter Cronkite had been former colleagues at CBS, I convinced both of them to interview each other at Howard's home in Bethesda, Maryland. Prior to that shoot I also mentioned they had been World War Two colleagues of my second cousin, Cecil Brown (earlier referenced) who was, with them one of Edward R. Murrow's "boys" in London. That information triggered some nice interaction between the three of us. *No* degrees of separation continued.

With all our worldly possessions jammed into a sturdy and like-new 1948 Dodge four-door sedan I'd purchased from the grandparents of one of the Missoula television station's secretaries, named Laurel (Laurie) Eichholz (previously referenced), Dorothy and I left Lethbridge, headed back into the U.S. I had made some calls to stations I thought might hire me, but we truly were headed into the unknown as we crossed the border into Montana. By late afternoon, we'd reached Idaho Falls, Idaho. It was early enough to still reach any of the television station executives who might have still been at work. As Divine Intervention would have it, at then KID-TV, a CBS affiliate, I reached the General Manager whose name was "Rosey" Lane. I told him I was looking for a job as announcer/director/control room person, whatever. He told me to meet him at the studio at 7 that evening. We met and he, at 8 p.m., actually had me do a live unscripted "audition" on the air promoting the upcoming program. I got the job as all described, eventually becoming Promotion Manager and full-time weatherman, afternoon talk show host on a program called *Telescope* (among those I interviewed were ventriloquist/actor/comedian Edgar Bergen, who also had his "dummy", Charlie

McCarthy on his lap; Louis Armstrong, as wonderful, warm, gentle, first-class and humble as any human being could ever be; and Clarence "Ducky" Nash, the voice of Donald Duck for 50 years) and children's show host as Kedso, the Clown. I thought I'd be there six weeks. I was there five years, during which time both my daughters (Shaunda and Lisa) were born, in 1961 and 1963, respectively. That station also opened the doors for "magic time" to start again, beginning the first parade of unforgettable friendships and stories that are unabashedly unique and I'm happy to share.

CHAPTER NINE

Unique Stories, Nuggets—Part I

Great spirits have always encountered violent opposition from mediocre minds.
—Albert Einstein

S ome revelatory Idaho Falls-years stories, some of which I hope evoke a smile, or trigger other thoughts akin to what you might also remember, especially regarding the assassination of JFK:

Sun Valley and Ketchum, Idaho's hot water: Wait until you read the "punch line"!—In 1962, well after I'd become established as "The Conoco Weatherman, Barry ZeVan" on KID-TV, blessed with the highest ratings in the state for weathercasts, I received a phone call from a viewer named Dave Brandt. He said he and his family lived in Sun Valley and would like to have me visit them for dinner and even overnight at their place in Warm Springs, a "suburb" of Ketchum, adjacent to Sun Valley. (Author Ernest Hemingway . . . a fellow Leo . . . was buried years later in the Ketchum cemetery, a gravesite I visited often in later years during ski and filming trips there.) I accepted Dave Brandt's offer and drove to their home on a Saturday afternoon. It was a very comfortable and well-appointed home near the base of "Baldy", one of Sun Valley's more notorious ski mountains and at the end of a Warm Springs road.

When I looked out the window, I saw a labyrinth of very large pipes, elevated about ten feet above the terrain. Since it was winter, there was abundant snow on the ground, but not in the Brandt's backyard, replete with very green grass and an abundance of flowers blooming. I asked Dave about what all this was. His father was listening with pride as Dave told me the story: His father, a native Swede, retired from being a J.C. Penney store manager in Twin Falls, Idaho, in 1935. He had heard that W. Averill Harriman, then Board Chairman of the Union Pacific Railroad, was planning to build North America's first ski resort adjacent to Ketchum. Mr. Brandt, being an enterprising chap, thought it might be good to buy some land and build a house near Ketchum since property values would probably increase after the ski resort (Sun Valley) opened.

The punch line: When contractors started digging to build the foundation for the house, nothing but very hot water kept springing up all over, thus they had to build the house on a slab. However, Mr. Brandt looked carefully at the deed for the land and found he had purchased the rights to Idaho's Thousand Lost Springs, an almost inexhaustible supply of boiling hot water, similar to Yellowstone National Park's thermal "Paint Pots". He brilliantly had the idea to propose to the town of Ketchum the town use his hot water to heat the sidewalks with pipes underneath the concrete or asphalt and also propose to the Sun Valley hierarchy they use his hot water to create heated swimming pools as well as heat the hotels and other buildings that would be part of Sun Valley's infrastructure. Both the town of Ketchum and the Union Pacific Railroad said "Yes" to Mr. Brandt's idea and the rest is history. Ketchum boasts the world's first heated sidewalks, thanks to Mr. Brandt's ingenuity. Mr. Brandt's modest retirement pension from J.C. Penney blossomed into millions of dollars from those unsightly (but nicely painted) large pipes running from his backyard to where they'd provide indefinite blessed heat to those who visited and lived in Ketchum and Sun Valley. (In later years, I produced, filmed and narrated a documentary about how Sun Valley was founded, literally by an accident of nature, by an Austrian Count named Felix Schaffgotsch, a friend of Harriman's, but that's another story for another time.)

Art Linkletter and family—In the winter of 1962, I got a phone call at KID-TV from a friend of mine in Los Angeles who worked for John Guedel Productions, producers of *Art Linkletter's House Party* which aired on CBS-TV and our station. He said Art and his family were friends of Bill Janss, CEO of The Janss Corporation, which had recently purchased Sun Valley from the Union Pacific Railroad and the afore-mentioned W. Averill Harriman (who by that time had already been Governor of New York and even glared at me years earlier from his limo as I was admittedly driving too fast going south on Manhattan's West Side Highway, actually fairly close to Jerry and Anne's neighborhood. I'll never forget that encounter, or Governor Harriman's look!). That aside, my friend told me Art wanted someone to film him and his family, sans Art's son Jack, learning how to ski at "The Valley", and I'd been chosen to produce and interview as long as I could also supply a photographer. The station let me have Quincy Jensen, the station's chief photographer, do the filming. It was almost two years before videotape was "born", or at least installed, at KID-TV.

Quincy and I spent four days with the Linkletters in many very private moments. The first time I met Diane, then aged 16, Art's younger daughter and youngest child, I got into the car that was to take us to Dollar Mountain to begin filming Art and his family that morning. Diane was seated on the front seat. I sat beside her because the back seat was loaded with Quincy and his camera equipment, far from compact in those days. The very first thing Diane said to me, with an intense look in her eyes and an unhappy face, was, "My father won't let me doing anything." I was taken aback and wanting to be respectful, I said, "Well, with a last name like yours, you shouldn't have any trouble getting to do what you want." She said, "That's what everybody thinks, and they're wrong." I didn't respond and we were silent the entire remainder of the drive, although not combative in any way. I really felt sorry for her because, in essence, one would think she shouldn't have a care in the world.

Art had us take ski lessons with him and the family when we weren't filming. I had skied once, in 1954, on Berthoud Pass, Colorado, during my Air Force time in Denver, but wasn't very good at it, thus was happy to get the real lessons. Our instructor was a native Austrian named Sigi Engl who had taught every imaginable movie star and head-of-state how to downhill (Alpine) ski. Sigi was the best instructor in the world at that time and I appreciated Art's largesse to allow us to take lessons on his "dime".

It had been raining and snowing in Sun Valley during the next to the last day of shooting. Art, his wife Lois, daughters Sharon and Diane and Quincy and I were shielded from the rain on one of the hotel porches when Jimmy Stewart and his wife, Gloria, appeared on the porch and walked up to Art to exchange complaints about the rain the Stewarts had just experienced in Aspen and the rain that was raining in Sun Valley at that moment. The Stewarts chose to come to Sun Valley for possibly better weather and Art jokingly told them they brought the rain with them. While Jimmy was just standing there, I asked for his autograph. He gave it to me on a little slip of cardboard I had found in my pocket. He didn't say a word either before or after he signed it, but I was glad to get it and still have it. He was always one of my heroes since we were both native Pennsylvanians and he was, of course, a great actor I admired in every film he ever made. Again, as fate would have it, in later years, Frank Capra's son, Tom Capra, would be both a broadcasting colleague and boss of mine in both D.C. and Connecticut. Frank Capra, of course, directed Jimmy in *Mr. Smith Goes To Washington* and *It's A Wonderful Life*.

Sun Valley's Boiler Room nightclub was considered one of the most "in" spots at the time and was frequented by a lot of the celebrities who came to Sun Valley to ski. One of them was actress Ann Sothern, a Minnesota-born actress who, as most people reading this book will know, became a major film star. Ann and I were sitting at adjacent tables, smiled at each other and I asked her to dance. She said, "Yes" and we danced one dance. It was a modified jitterbug/lindy, played by a DJ (with records!) and I silently thanked Patty Baumholz (Dore Schary's niece, previously referenced) for teaching me so well how to do that dance. Ann and I weren't tipsy, but for the fun of it, we affixed our names in crayon to one of the walls, which read, surrounded by a heart, "Ann + Barry".

Writing wholesome sayings or names on the walls of The Boiler Room was a standard practice in those days. I have no idea if The Boiler Room still exists, but if it does, I could identify the exact spot where we wrote that playful saying. Every time I see Ann in one of her movies, that fun memory certainly presents itself immediately.

The final day of shooting it was still raining and snowing, but, regardless, I did a fun interview with Art for my local television talk show in Idaho Falls (called *Telescope*) and it can now be seen on a Google piece about my television career (TC Media Now is the site). Near the conclusion of the black-and-white interview, Art said, "Now since you're the weatherman, do something about this bad weather". I said, "We'll try." And I smiled. Art then turned to me on camera and teasingly said, "That's the weatherman for ya: We'll try." Concluding with a close-up big grin on his face while delivering that line to me. It was fun. Lois, Art's wife and daughters Sharon and Diane were in parts of the piece. It's now very sad to watch it, knowing Diane committed suicide six years later. Apparently her unhappiness, expressed to me the first time I met her, as previously mentioned, was too perpetually deep-seated and prevalent. Her death was tragic and a travesty, to say the least.

Art Linkletter (additional fascinating stories about, and told to me by, him, including Walt Disney being broke and that "broke" connection with Art), Maureen O'Hara, Henry Fonda, James MacArthur and Delmer Daves—My next time with Art was in Jackson Hole, Wyoming, in mid-May, 1963, covering the entire premiere week of the film, *Spencer's Mountain*, as Warner Bros. director/writer/producer Delmer Daves's driver and gatekeeper for the media, which hadn't been planned. I had been sent to the premiere week event by KID-TV's sister station, KID-AM radio, to cover the premiere week and garner as many interviews as possible, since I was also a guest invited by Warner Bros. The interviews evolved into years-long friendships and acquaintances, as follows:

When I got into the ranch house pressroom in the shadow of The Grand Tetons, no one was there except Mr. Daves and me. He asked if I'd consider being "His Man Friday" for the week and I said, "Yes", to say the least. It began a 14- year very strong friendship, including thrice visiting him and his wife, Mary Lou, at their home in West Los Angeles at 107 North Bentley Avenue, just two houses north of Sunset Boulevard. He had converted his garage behind the house into his massive offices. The numerous file cabinets therein contained, among other reference materials, renderings of every costume or piece of clothing ever worn in every year since human attire began. Mr. Daves had used those to apply to the many films he directed and wrote, based in different periods of history. Among those films were, *Demetrius And The Gladiators*, the sequel to *The Robe*, both of which starred Victor Mature (who Mr. Daves told me he considered a "sissy" because Mr. Mature wouldn't go anywhere near the lions cages during filming) and *Destination Tokyo*. He also wrote the screenplay for *An Affair To Remember* and directed or was screenplay writer for countless other major films.

Mr. Daves had also given a lot of stars their first film parts, including John Forsythe, Suzanne Pleshette (who would in later years marry a dear friend to me, actor Tom Poston), Troy Donahue, Debra Paget (who he told me was "Little Debbie Paget") and Jeff Chandler. Chandler starred in Mr. Daves's film, *Broken Arrow*. The title of the film, seen on screen, was painted on a stretched tanned deerskin canvas and that stretched canvas with the title hung above Mr. Daves's fireplace in his office. Seeing it evoked a big smile, knowing how many millions of people worldwide had seen it on screen and here I was, lucky again, seeing it in person affixed to his fireplace wall.

Being immersed in hours-long conversations with him there, and which had commenced in Jackson Hole, was a continual film industry history lesson. Some more fascinating trivia: Del (he insisted I call him that) also told me he and actor Ward Bond, in their fledgling acting years, were always auditioning for the same parts, thus one day they flipped a coin deciding who would be the actor and who would be the director. We now know the results of that coin flip. During my last visit to his North Bentley Avenue house, Del said he felt I merited a screen test at Warner Bros. and would arrange it when possible. That was in June, 1977. The test was scheduled for September that year, and I was to portray a sinister Middle Eastern type. Del died in August, 1977, at his and Mary Lou's La Jolla home and the test was canceled. To say I was devastated about his death, and not the screen test cancellation, would be a major understatement.

The time with Art Linkletter during that week was similar to the Sun Valley time, although the time with him alone in Jackson Hole was only twice, once at a ranch house party (see Maureen O'Hara story, forthcoming) and once at a lavish exclusive party at Laurance Rockefeller's house (see Henry Fonda story, also forthcoming), when we discussed our Sun Valley filming, which aired on *House Party* shortly after the filming in February, 1962. In later years, here are some other stories Art told me, which I think are among the most fascinating and hopefully meriting a big "Wow!" from you after reading the "punch lines". Here we go.

Walt Disney being "broke" and Art eventually becoming happy for that twist of fate—While speaking with Art for another documentary I was producing and writing in 1998 about television's first fifty years, and him being one of the interviewees, he told me some stories that always tickled *his* fancy. One of the most fascinating, in Art's words, was Walt Disney called Art to ask him to emcee the opening of Disneyland in 1955, but told Art he couldn't pay him. He said Walt told him he didn't even have enough pocket change, until Disneyland opened, to live month-to-month. He said Walt knew everything would be just the opposite after Disneyland opened, but that was the case pre-opening. Art said Walt asked him to figure something regarding deferred compensation for the opening emcee work. Art said he told Walt he'd think about it and get back to him in an hour or two. Art said he called Walt and told him . . . this is verbatim . . . ."I know you're probably going to sell a lot of rolls of film there, so why don't you just give me ten percent of the retail sales price of each roll of film you sell, in perpetuity, and that can be my compensation." Art told me Disney said "Yes", and told me he made almost as much money from those rolls-of-film sales as he did from broadcasting. With that money, he told me he bought 4,000 acres of tomatoes in Oceanside, California, and, knowing the President of Hunt's Ketchup, he made a deal to sell all his tomatoes to Hunt's, also in perpetuity.

For Art, regardless of fame or success, sometimes one doesn't always get what one wants: I once asked Art if he hadn't done anything he might have always wanted to do. He told me it was a very pertinent question, saying, "Yes, unfortunately. After *House Party* and *Kids Say The Darnedest Things* ended their runs, I told Bill Paley (Founder and Board Chairman of CBS) I wanted to be a *60 Minutes* correspondent, joining Mike Wallace and the others. Paley turned me down three times, stating people perceive me as being lighthearted and warm, the opposite of the *60 Minutes* persona required. Art said he literally

begged Paley to reconsider, but the answer was a third and final, No."
(I think in later years, Art may have won the argument by reminding
Paley that an actor who starred in a lighthearted movie entitled *Bedtime
For Bonzo* would be twice elected President of the United States,
proving people can change their perceptions and levels of acceptance.
The actor referenced, was, of course, Ronald Reagan. I also developed
strong relations with Reagan's "kingmaker" and one of Reagan's
daughters in later years, those stories still to be related in this book.)

Henry Fonda—The party at Laurance Rockefeller's house, almost
literally in the shadow of the Grand Tetons, to which I was invited
because of my relationship with Delmer Daves, was one of the most
beyond-special gatherings anyone could imagine. Even though I'd
been blessed to know and do some actual living with the "iconic
glitterati" in my childhood and teenage years, the guest list for this
party was just about as exclusive as that word intones. The guests
were, en toto, Delmer Daves, Henry Fonda, Maureen O'Hara,
James MacArthur and his wife, actress Joyce Bulifant, actress
Mimsy Farmer, Bronwyn FitzSimons (Maureen's daughter), Art
Linkletter, Jack Slattery (Art's CBS announcer for *House Party*),
Fonda's companion, named Marjean (last name omitted on
purpose) and me. (The reason I've omitted Marjean's last name, to
save her embarrassment here, was because she pulled me aside during
a lull in the party and said, verbatim, "I know you from television.
I'm from Idaho Falls. You and I can get together after I ditch Fonda
this week." I thanked her for the "offer" but told her I didn't think
that would be a good idea and we never did see each other again after
the festivities that week. Even if I'd been single at the time, I would
have had no interest in her proposed liaison.) Marjean and I were the
only "outsiders" there, but ironically, I didn't feel uncomfortable in
the illustrious group. The schmoozing was "natural" since I'd had the
luxury to be around those sorts of people from almost birth. I also
knew it was not a "given", but rather a privilege to be accepted in that
rarified circle and have never taken those sorts of times for granted.

The food and beverage offerings were as delightfully decadent as
one would expect at a private late afternoon gathering such as this,

from caviar and champagne, to seafood and meats of the highest caliber and a four-foot high American Indian bust, complete with war bonnet, carved out of butter, as the food table's centerpiece. I've never since seen anything like it.

After exchanging pleasantries with others, I went up to Fonda and told him I'd worked with Wally Cox for two years on *Peepers*. I thought it would be a good "ice breaker" since Wally was in *Spencer's Mountain*, too, but couldn't make it to that festive premiere week in Jackson Hole. I actually called Wally after the party to ask if he was okay, because a party like this would have been very memorable to attend. He told me, verbatim, "No, I'm a peach farmer and this is the time of year I have to pay attention to the peaches." Wally's farm was in Connecticut. He told me he and Marilyn had been divorced for about three years, also stating verbatim, "Seventeen years is long enough." It was sad to hear him say that, since I remembered all those pieces of paper in Wally's and Brando's apartment with Marilyn's name affixed dozens of times (previously referenced).

Fonda was as charming and "himself" off screen as on. He told me he and Wally did a lot of fishing during breaks in shooting the film. He also said, verbatim, "I'll tell you a story about Wally, and since you know him, I'll make it longer." It was one of those comments always cemented in my brain. I can't remember the story he told me, but I definitely remember he said what he did regarding the length of the story. He was a charming person. When I was with Jane Fonda and Ted Turner during that New York gathering I previously mentioned, I told her that story and she was delighted, also eager to hear as much more as possible about her Dad. There's also another story related to Mr. Fonda and Marjean when all of us who attended the Rockefeller party had supper at Jackson's Wort Hotel dining room later that night, but I think it's best left untold.

Maureen O'Hara—At a separate ranch party the night preceding the Rockefeller party, I asked Ms. O'Hara if I could interview her for the Idaho Falls radio station. I had a full-size Webcor reel-to-reel tape recorder (all anyone had at that time), plugged it in and began recording. She described the fun she had learning how to bake bread with "the Mormon ladies" in the Teton Valley, as well as how World War Two had determined her career choices and fate (previously described). She then used a few choice words about a person in the cast who was "after" her beautiful daughter, the aforementioned Bronwyn FitzSimons, She then named the person (I won't) but said her efforts in her daughter's behalf were successful. She also said her marriage to Bronwyn's father wasn't pleasant, but she had now married a man who ran an airline in the Caribbean, where he and she lived. She eventually became President and Chairperson of that airline. Then we began talking about show business in general. As was stated early in this book, she said talent means nothing unless a person gets the breaks. She also said she knew so many people who had all the talent and never got breaks and those who had no talent and got all the breaks. That comment was somewhat discouraging for so many, but so very true. For her own career, she said Tyrone Power was her favorite leading man, "such a gentleman" and John Wayne a close "second". (I interviewed Tyrone Power's son for a film in the 1990s and he was the spitting imageof his father.) She also sensed things weren't exactly stellar for my roller-coaster career at that time and told me to "never, ever give up." I've heard her words ringing in my ears more often than not from that night to the present.

The next time I saw her was in Chicago for a formal interview for a syndicated television show I was hosting. I interviewed her and John Candy, the latter for his last film. She remembered our time in Jackson Hole and seemed happy to remember it.

James MacArthur—Jim and I were born the same year, 1937. I was four months older than Jim, so we got along well as "contemporaries" in age and thinking. Jim and I were together privately only twice during the *Spencer's Mountain* festivities week, once at the previously described Rockefeller party, but also again in my car during a torrential downpour when I was driving Jim to another ranch house gathering for the cast. It was raining so heavily it would have been dangerous to keep driving, so I pulled over for a few minutes until the rain subsided enough to continue the drive. One of the things I said to Jim, respectfully, was how blessed he'd been to have been born into a famous family. (Jim was the adopted son of mega-star Helen Hayes while she was married to playwright Charles MacArthur who fathered Jim during an affair, which has been public knowledge for many years.) Jim said, "Yeah, but I got to where I am on my own." I nodded my head, changed the subject and we drove on to the destination. We maintained an occasional correspondence for several years thereafter. I was glad to see his future success on the original *Hawaii Five-O* series, but very saddened when he passed away.

With Dr. Vincent Schaefer for the world's first on-the-ground snowmaking experiments and successes—I received a call in 1963 from the Science Department at the State University of New York (SUNY) in Schenectady telling me one of their professors, Dr. Vincent Schaefer, would be conducting the world's first on-the-ground snowmaking experiments in Yellowstone National Park in January, 1964. They asked if I'd interview him and have the interview and his experiments filmed, for posterity (I still have the 16mm film) and also to use as I wished for my television weathercasts as a feature. I said, "Yes", of course, thus the aforementioned photographer, Quincy Jensen and I trouped up to Yellowstone, driving through thunder-snow that dark January morning. What occurred thereafter, and also filmed by us the following January, was truly breathtaking, as follows: I interviewed Dr. Schaefer standing in front of one of Yellowstone's "Paint Pots". They were, and are, thermal pools of water that perpetually emit steam. When that steam rises and hits zero or below zero Fahrenheit temperatures, Dr. Schaefer wanted to prove it was the perfect formula and simulation of what occurs in the clouds to create snow, but wanted to prove it on the ground instead of from an airplane. The ground temperature had to be "just right" to make it happen. Here's how he did it, with that black-and-white film fascinating to watch: He flailed/twirled a bag full of dust over the "Paint Pots". The dust was the condensation nuclei around which moisture would form, the same natural occurrence for snowflakes to form in clouds. Within literally five seconds, an abundance of snow formed over the "Paint Pots" and, Eureka!, he had proven his theory about the ability of snow to form at the Earth's surface when proper temperatures and condensation nuclei "meet". He explained everything to me (and the television audience via that film) after the first dust-bag "flailing". Dr. Schaefer I and I kept in touch for many years after those experiments, reaching him mostly at General Electric's headquarters where he was one of GE's top scientists in addition to his professorial duties at SUNY. Indeed, I've been a lucky boy.

President Truman—KID-TV was located in Idaho Falls, but had offices and a satellite station in Pocatello. The Pocatello-based sales manager, Jim Tyne, also had a side-job as one of Idaho's U.S. Senator Frank Church's speechwriters. Jim had introduced me to Senator Church and his wife, Bethine (whose father had been an Idaho Governor), on more than one occasion and, thanks to Jim, I got to know the Church's socially throughout an almost five year period of time. Jim also knew I'd had family members in Pennsylvania involved in politics (previously referenced), thus he allowed me to read a couple of the speeches he had written for Frank for the pending 1963 re-election campaign and suggest edits for them ("speech doctoring", he called it), if necessary. Being as urbane and brilliant as Jim was, my input was hardly necessary. It was a compliment to have Jim give me the chance to use the sometimes-irritating trait of "wordsmithing" at a very respectable level. (Jim told me he at one time during his post-teen youth had occasionally dated singer Peggy Lee, but that's definitely another story for another time . . . maybe! Ironically I got to know Peggy, briefly, during my Las Vegas broadcasting years, but never told her I knew Jim. Jim told me Peggy and he apparently had a very tempestuous parting of the ways, thus mentioning Jim's name might not have been the wisest thing to say to her. Only once in a while have I employed common sense!) *Jim also once playfully, but semi-seriously, told me I live in a time warp. That's frequently correct, as an actually sub-conscious mechanism to preserve some individual peacefulness and sanity in an increasingly insane world. Thank goodness, in my opinion, for the brain's ability to transport us back to happier times, available instantly.*

Jim told me President Truman was coming to both Idaho Falls and Pocatello in October that year (1963) to stump for Frank's re-election. I had told him I'd seen Mr. Truman in 1948 when I was 11

years old at a huge Pittsburgh Democratic rally for him when he
was running for President that year. My grandfather and mother
took me there to let me have the opportunity to see him in person.
We were positioned far back in the arena where he was speaking.
It was the election wherein the Chicago Tribune had printed that
infamous banner headline, *Dewey Defeats Truman*. The picture of
President Truman holding a copy of that newspaper, and smiling
broadly after he'd defeated Governor Dewey, is, of course, one of
the all time classics. I asked Jim if he thought Senator Church could
arrange for me to be part of a media interview session I knew had
been planned for the former President, as well as a photo with Mr.
Truman. Long story short, it was approved, for what turned out to be
almost 20 minutes to hear him tell his favorite personal stories about
his presidency, followed by a photo taken of him and me after he
honored us with that special time at KID-TV. The photo, taken by the
aforementioned Quincy Jensen, is one of my most prized possessions,
which Mr. Truman kindly signed to me and seen on the second
page of this book. Excerpts from the filmed interview session and a
subsequent Pocatello gathering for Mr. Truman aired the next evening
on KID-TV. That was a year before videotape existed at our station.

He signed the photo to me via my mother's visit to him (with 8x10
photo in hand) in his suite at the Carlyle Hotel in New York, where he
often stayed. Jim told me to just send the photo to my mother (because
she lived and worked in New York) and then have her reach Mr.
Truman at the Carlyle number supplied by Jim and Frank. My mother
said she almost fell over when Mr. Truman answered the phone. He
told her to come to his suite and he'd be glad to sign the photo. That
was January 15, 1964. She said when he was signing it, he looked up
at her, smiling, and said, "Good thing the last name isn't Goldwater,
right?" He was of course referring to my first name being the same as
Senator Barry Goldwater's. He signed it *Kind regards to Barry N. ZeVan
from Harry Truman. 1-15-64*. Those few moments alone with him were
the highlight of her life and I could never thank Senator Church or
Jim Tyne enough for making that magic time happen for her, or me. I
visited the Truman home and Presidential Library in Independence,
Missouri in the 1980s and purposely . . . and proudly . . . brought the

framed photo to show the home and Library personnel. They agreed it was, and is, something for which I should be very proud, and grateful, both of which I will always be for that great honor. Every time I see a historic television feature or documentary about his presidential years, and all he accomplished, from ending World War Two to signing the U.N. Charter to rebuilding Europe via The Marshall Plan, and so much more, I just shake my head in appreciative wonderment for that time with him. His take on deciding to drop the atomic bombs on Japan to end the Pacific war is described in his recollections, which follow this paragraph. *During my D.C. television days, I was invited to take the inaugural ride on the D.C. subway. My seat partners were Margaret Truman, her husband Clifton Daniel and their two sons. I told Margaret about my time with her father and she expressed delight at the coincidence she and I were assigned to sit next to each other. She later gave me the book she wrote about her father, but that was the only other time I was with her. That book, too, is a prized possession.*

His recollections: Having Mr. Truman recall these stories was like listening to . . . and watching . . . a history book talking to you (me) just a few feet away. The first story he told was, verbatim, "I was sitting on the edge of my bed in a room at The Muehlebach Hotel in Kansas City with a couple of my Senatorial staff in the room. I'd heard President Roosevelt was thinking of choosing me to be his running mate and I kept looking at the phone, hoping it wouldn't ring. I didn't want to be Vice President, but sure enough, the phone rang and it was the President. All I kept saying was 'Yes, Mr. President', several times and hung up. You just don't say 'No' to The President of the United States." He said because the convention that year (1944) was in Chicago, he took the train to be on the convention floor in time for the next evening's final convention business, was accepted as the nominee there, and Roosevelt was elected for a fourth term that November, with Mr. Truman becoming his Vice President.

The next story he told was the most chilling. The date was April 12, 1945. He said he was sitting in his Senate building office when then Speaker of the House, Sam Rayburn, came rushing into his office saying "Harry, we have to get over to The White House right away.

Something's happened and I'll tell you about it in the car, but get Bess and Margaret over to The White House, too, as fast as they can get there." He said he thought this was obviously serious and called them at a house party where he knew they were. He said Bess gave him some "guff" about leaving the party and he told her he'd send the Secret Service over to get them if she and Margaret didn't leave "right away". He said Bess agreed.

He said when he and Rayburn got into the car on the way to The White House, Rayburn said, "Harry, the President's dead." Mr. Truman, verbatim, said "I would much rather, *much* rather, have been hit square across the face full force with a baseball bat than to have heard that news". I can still see his face as he told that. The grimness, I guess, always stuck with him, understandably. He said when they got to the Pennsylvania Avenue side of The White House, Mrs. Roosevelt was standing on the steps waiting for them to arrive. Mr. Truman said he got out of the car and said, "Oh, Mrs. Roosevelt, I'm so sorry. What can I do for you?" He said Mrs. Roosevelt replied, "Oh, Harry, it's not what you can do for me. You're the boy who's in trouble now." He said if anyone recalled the somber look on his face in the photos of him taking the oath of office that late afternoon in April, it wasn't there only because he knew he had two theaters of war on his hands, but her words, "You're the boy who's in trouble now" kept ringing in his ears, not only that day, but until the entire war ended in August that year.

He said he called a cabinet meeting the next morning, since the government had to go on with its business regardless of the tragedy of President Roosevelt's death. He said toward the end of the meeting, the then Secretary of War, Henry Stimson, told Mr. Truman there was something the new President hadn't been told by Mr. Roosevelt. Mr. Truman said he asked what it was. Stimson then told him about The Manhattan Project, i.e., the development of the atomic bomb. Mr. Truman asked why he hadn't been informed, and was told President Roosevelt didn't think Truman was "smart enough" to understand it. Upon hearing that, Mr. Truman said his emotions ran the gamut from feeling badly about the President's death to also being furious with Roosevelt for thinking Truman wasn't "smart enough" to handle The Manhattan Project information.

Mr. Truman said he immediately asked for all the details. After
receiving all the information, he said he told Mr. Stimson to schedule
the first atomic bomb test, which was eventually named Trinity, at
Alamogordo, New Mexico's White Sands Proving Grounds, July 16,
1945. (I drove near there in 2005. Those sands are definitely white.)
The test, which I remember vividly from the newsreels, showed the
signature mushroom cloud that had never been seen, no one knowing
the world would see two similar mushroom clouds over Japan the
following month.

Mr. Truman said he ordered the first atomic bomb to be dropped
on Hiroshima August 5, 1945 (my eighth birthday, previously
referenced), which was August 6, 1945 in Japan. He said everyone was
surprised the Japanese didn't surrender immediately. Thus, the next
bomb was dropped on Nagasaki three days later, and that sealed the
end of the war in the Pacific. V-J Day was declared August 14, 1945,
when the Japanese officially surrendered. Mr. Truman said he had no
hesitation whatever in regard to ending the war with the dropping of
those bombs. He said, again verbatim, "It was them or us. If (General)
MacArthur had gone through with his wanting to do a land invasion
of Japan, we would have lost many more American lives than the
Japanese lives lost in the bomb drops over Japan." Mr. Truman also
smiled about V-E Day, the day the war ended in Europe. It was on
May 8, 1945, his 61st birthday, coincidentally or not. I didn't ask.

I asked him about the firing of General MacArthur. He said, "If
you'll recall the picture of us smiling at each other before our meeting
on Wake Island, it was ten minutes before I fired (him). He thought
he was the Commander-In-Chief and I let him know he wasn't." That
was all he said and the interview ended.

JFK'S assassination—Since I was one of the charter members of The
Broadcast Promotion Association (BPA), thanks to one of my duties
at KID-TV as their Promotion Manager (previously referenced),
I was invited to speak to the national convention as a CBS affiliate
spokesperson at San Francisco's Jack Tar Hotel, November 20th, 1963.
I drove to the convention from Idaho Falls. Among those with whom
I got to schmooze a lot, and maintain friendships afterward, were Ray

Walston and Bill Bixby (*My Favorite Martian*), Bea Benaderet and Edgar Buchanan (*Petticoat Junction*). Benaderet and Buchanan were my dinner partners on one of the convention nights. Buchanan told me he had been a dentist in Oregon and switched to acting at a fairly advanced age. It certainly paid off for him, and us, as the loveable Uncle Joe on *Petticoat* and so many other roles he portrayed in films and on television.

I gave my speech the evening of the 20th and decided, because I had the entire week off, to visit friends in Yuma, Arizona, not too long a drive from San Francisco, relatively speaking, since any drive under ten hours in the U.S. west is considered to be no big deal. I left the Jack Tar at 6 in the morning on November 21st and arrived in Yuma in the late afternoon. My friends there suggested we walk across the border into San Luis, Mexico, for a light dinner. We did so, returned to Yuma for catch-up conversations and then turned in for the night. The next morning, I left Yuma around 10:00 to begin my drive back to Idaho Falls. I crossed the Colorado River near Quartzsite, into California, briefly, then drove northward toward Searchlight, Nevada, which would years later become famous as U.S. Senate Majority/Minority leader Harry Reid's hometown. I hadn't had the radio on, so I decided to listen to whatever news I could find in that remote location. When I turned it on, around 1 p.m., Pacific Time, I heard Fulton Lewis, Jr., one of that era's more respected newscasters, discussing "Presidential succession" and what it would mean for this country. I thought that was a strange subject to be discussing. Five minutes later, I heard the announcement that President Kennedy had been assassinated. I screamed and nearly went off the road. As was the case with almost everyone in the world, I became numb and in disbelief. To say it was difficult to maintain any sort of driving composure would be an understatement, but I made it to Las Vegas around 5 p.m. Fittingly, to add to the gloom of that day's news, it was snowing and raining. The local stations said, for the first time in Las Vegas's history, all the signs on The Strip and on Fremont Street wouldn't be lighted that night, to pay homage to JFK.

I called Dorothy from a pay phone and told her I'd be driving all night, urged her to be calm during this crisis and I'd see her in the early morning. I did drive all night, mostly through snowfall from about Pioche, Nevada, almost all the way into Idaho Falls.

About 4 a.m., near Twin Falls, Idaho, I turned the radio on again and listened to the calming voices of Senators Hubert Humphrey and John Pastore, trying to comfort the nation. It was the first time I'd ever heard HHH speak, not knowing he would become a truly wonderful friend to me in later years, which will be fully-addressed in the Seattle-Tacoma-Wenatchee and D.C. chapters (see photos section).

I arrived home at about 8:30 the morning of November 23rd. Dorothy and I were still in shock, as was everyone, of course. Around noon, I went out to shovel snow off the sidewalk when, a few minutes later, Dorothy came rushing out of the house saying someone else had been shot. I thought the world had grown even more insane than it already had the preceding day. The shooting casualty was, of course, Lee Harvey Oswald and the shooter Jack Ruby. In later years, I would get to know now retired CBS News Anchor and *Face The Nation* moderator, Bob Schieffer and his wife, the latter of whom had me give a couple school talks about weather to her D.C., students when she was a school teacher there in the mid-1970s. The significance of mentioning Bob here is he actually drove Lee Harvey Oswald's mother from Fort Worth to the Dallas jail to see her son, not knowing Oswald would be shot by Jack Ruby shortly after she and Bob arrived. I'll relate Bob's complete story about that day, as he told an audience of us many years hence (in Bismarck, North Dakota), later in this tome.

CHAPTER TEN

Aloha and "Goodbye-Ha"

No good deed goes unpunished.
Oscar Wilde, Billy Wilder, Andrew W. Mellon, Letitia Baldrige
and Claire Boothe Luce!

The broadcasting business and even a modicum of fame in any arena or discipline often takes its toll on domestic life, either because of the immaturity of the person "on stage", ego or grueling schedules. I was guilty of all three, and it took me decades to "grow up", a "mea culpa" I have no qualms admitting. In that regard, and in a nutshell, Dorothy and I divorced in early1964. The divorce was granted in person to me, solo, by a judge in Sun Valley, as Dorothy had already moved back to Montana with Shaunda and Lisa. Sitting waiting for her divorce to be granted . . . I was next in line after her . . . was "Happy" Rockefeller, who was divorcing Nelson Rockefeller. She and I exchanged some small talk before she went in to get her signed divorce decree papers. When I went in, the judge said he recognized me from television and said, verbatim, "You damned celebrities are all alike with your six-week quickie divorces." Although the occasion was not a happy one . . . no pun intended . . . I'm smiling remembering his almost cartoon-like delivery of that comment, since he'd just finished with the former Mrs. Rockefeller a couple minutes earlier. In case you didn't know, Idaho and Nevada have the same waiting period: six weeks from filing to divorce finalization.

In August, 1965, I'd heard about a job opening in Hawaii, and even though I'd become very established with the highest ratings for weathercasting, talk show and kids show hosting in the Idaho Falls-Pocatello market, I thought, after five years there, it might be time to "spread my wings" and move farther up the ladder. Being single, the Hawaiian opportunity also meant I could move without inconveniencing a wife and children.

I accepted the job as Promotion Manager for the television station (KGMB-TV, a CBS affiliate) and comedy writer for the then world's highest paid disc jockey (one-million dollars a year), whose radio name was Aku. Lengthened, it was J. Akuhead Pupule, part of it meaning "Fish-head", because Aku's face really did look like a fish! He was a superb talent whose real name was Hal Levinson, then changed to Hal Lewis, then Aku when he landed the DJ radio job in Honolulu on KGMB radio. Hal had been a violinist with The San Francisco Symphony prior to moving to Hawaii.

The moving van took my houseful of furniture and other belongings for the move to Hawaii, paid for by KGMB-TV. When I got to San Francisco prior to boarding the second leg of the flight to Honolulu, I was notified there was a SeaLand storage strike and my belongings would remain in storage on a dock in San Francisco until the strike was over. That should have been my first clue the decision to take the Hawaiian job wasn't the best decision I ever made. Regardless, I arrived in Honolulu (my first time there) and rented a house from one of the radio station's popular DJs, whose radio name was "Granny Goose". His real name was George Groves, a native Hawaiian who passed away not too many years ago, I'm saddened to state. George was a great friend and a very popular talent there for many years. The address of the house I rented from George is my favorite of all the addresses I've ever had: 1281 Ulu Pii Street, Pohakupu, Kailua, Hawaii. Makes me smile to just read it, let alone say it.

Something that didn't make me smile was I was actually hired to help break a strike and was told that the day after I arrived. The person who told me was the man who hired me, the station's general manager and owner, Cecil Heftel. Heftel had married well, into Utah's Hatch family (Senator Orrin Hatch being the most famous and justifiably revered) and Heftel became a congressman from Hawaii in the mid-1970s. I exchanged a few words with him on a Capitol Hill street corner in D.C. one afternoon during my D.C. television days (1974-1977). He didn't have much to say, knowing I still remembered the strike-breaking reason for my hire in 1965 and his duplicity to not have told me before I left the Mainland.

Regardless, I still did the work I was hired to do: Writing and voicing promotional announcements for both stations and writing comedy lines for Aku's morning program. To say I was unhappy would be putting it mildly. Heftel had even asked me why I was so livid upon learning the news about why I was hired. I just looked at him, as opposed to having a verbal meltdown.

Most all my co-workers were more than enjoyable with whom to work. The television news anchor was a fellow named Jim Topping. (Jim and I kept in touch occasionally through the years and he eventually became News Director at ABC's flagship local station in New York, WABC-TV. He now has a documentary production company based in Tucson, Arizona. More about Jim and me later.)

Aside from the unhappiness about the reason for my hire at KGMB-TV and the nightly torrential rains, like clockwork between 2 and 4 a.m. leaving assorted fruit from the fruit trees and lizards on my borrowed (from George) car every morning, there was one dominant factor that determined my decision to quit the station and go back to the Mainland: Every evening when I'd drive back to Pohakupu, I'd have to drive over the Nuuana Pali (the pass) that separated the south and north sides of Oahu. When I'd reach the crest of that hill and start downward, all I could see, of course, was the vast expanse of the Pacific Ocean and I got "Rock Fever", which was the feeling some people get there, i.e., being "trapped", surrounded only by thousands of miles of water.

To make this long episode as short as possible, I quit the station, caught a flight back to San Francisco and, because there were no jetways then, I walked down the stairs from the airplane and literally kissed the tarmac. I took a cab to the SeaLand docks and was able to get my car (by then a 1960 black and white Cadillac, with fins), but not everything else in storage, for which there would not be a "home" until almost two years later. I didn't return to Hawaii until 2009 when my wife and I hosted a promotional cruise of all the islands, even though Hawaii's magnificent Senator, Daniel Inouye, became a good friend to me during my D.C. television years until the time of his passing, often jokingly angry with me for not going back, one time on live television in D.C. (More about my times with Senator Inouye later.)

Two wonderful people who had befriended me during my Idaho Falls years were Art and Kerry McGinn. Art was Bureau Chief for the Associated Press in Idaho Falls. They were two of the most delightful people one could ever hope to know and as of this writing are still alive and well in their native Spokane, Washington. When I landed from my Hawaiian adventure, I knew Art and Kerry then lived in Sacramento, as he had become AP Bureau Chief there. I called and asked if they had room at the inn while I got my act together again to get back on the air somewhere. They said "Yes", thank goodness. I stayed with Art and Kerry for almost a month, tried to get hired at a couple Sacramento stations to no avail, and then heard about a possible job in Seattle-Tacoma, via one of the broadcasting business's station "reps" there, named Art Moore. I bade farewell to Art and Kerry and started northwest toward Seattle-Tacoma and never saw Art or Kerry again, although I found, spoke with and emailed with them as recently as last year. Thank you, Internet.

CHAPTER ELEVEN

Unique Stories, Nuggets—Part II

He who trims himself to suit everybody will soon whittle himself away
—Anonymous, but brilliant

Art Moore, previously referenced, told me a fellow named Jim Agostino was running one of Seattle-Tacoma's independent stations (then KTVW, Channel 13, "The Independent Site on Puget Sound") and he felt Jim would hire me to be that station's Program Director. Jim and I met and he, God bless him, hired me on the spot, to not only be Program Director but to also create and host a talk show, as well as do the weather reports. It was October, 1965 and the station was owned by a man named J. Elroy MacCaw (sometimes spelled McCaw), about whom I'll relate later in this chapter. Please don't skip that story. It has more than one powerful "punch line".

Our studios were near Point Defiance Park in Tacoma, very near where "Galloping Gertie", the bridge seen in 1940s newsreels swinging and swaying in high winds, then collapsing, was situated. Our headquarters offices were in The Northern Life Tower in Seattle, then the tallest building in that city. I split my time between each venue, but was mostly planted in the Tacoma studios.

The most memorable times in those cities and Wenatchee, Washington, both good and bad, were as follows:

For my Channel 13 talk show, interviewing Norwegian explorer Thor Heyerdahl, describing how he felt his Kon-Tiki expedition didn't really achieve what he wished to prove, i.e., the South Pacific islands could have been populated by South Americans who had the made their own raft journeys thousands of years before he made his famous journey on the raft he built himself, i.e., the Kon-Tiki. At the time of the interview, he told me he planned to construct other boats in future years to prove other migrations from Africa and elsewhere. He indeed built those boats, the Ra and Ra II in 1969 and 1970, respectively. He was a very soft-spoken man for one who had endured the roughest conditions during the Kon-Tiki voyage. It was another unexpected honor.

Oscar Peterson, Quincy Jones, et al: One of the most influential
people in my life was an African-American named Bob Gill, sadly
not still alive. He hosted a ski program on our station, for which I was
his producer and was the world's first Black ski instructor, teaching
weekends at Snoqualmie Summit Ski Area at the top of Washington
state's Snoqualmie Pass. Bob taught me how to use my first (and only)
16mm film camera that I had been given during my Idaho Falls years
by one of our photographers at KID-TV's Pocatello satellite station
when he upgraded to a better model. I wish I could remember his
name. I still have that Bolex H16 hand-wind camera that provided
me with more joy than for which one could ever wish, shooting
documentaries and ski films literally all over the world. My friend,
filmmaker Dick Barrymore, called it a "coffee grinder". Lots more
about Dick and me and our exploits in Iran, circa early 1977, later in
the book. Thanks to Bob, that wonderful professional colleague and
true friend, learning how to use that camera provided me with more
life-experiences, globally, than I could ever have wished or imagined.

Bob told me he became the world's first Black ski instructor
because he was standing on the Snoqualmie Summit Ski Area
slopes one afternoon and a non-Black passed by him on skis saying,
"N****r's don't belong on ski hills." Just remembering and writing
this makes me as incensed as it must have made Bob. Bob's legs
were so strong he could already literally ski *up* hill (I saw him do it
often). After Bob heard that horrendous insult, he met with Webb
Moffett, legendary founder and owner of that Snoqualmie Pass ski
hill, told him what the person had said and asked if he could
become an instructor. Webb said "Yes", Bob took and passed his ski
instructor certification courses and did become the world's first
Black ski instructor. Bob was great at it, too, teaching me additional
"tricks" Sigi Engl had not taught me at Sun Valley, but not in any
way here minimizing Sigi's deserved fame as "the best ski instructor
in the world".

Bob Gill's brother, Elmer, was a prolific jazz pianist who was
based in Vancouver, British Columbia. Bob and Elmer had a Seattle
high-school relationship with jazz giants Quincy Jones (Quincy
was born in Chicago, but spent his high school years in Seattle)

and Oscar Peterson. The first time I met Quincy was at Bob's house during a weekend party. The same was true for Oscar, although he was more frequently at Bob's house for weekend parties when he was playing occasional "gigs" in the Seattle-Tacoma area. I'm honored to say Quincy has remained a wonderful friend from those days to the present. His Bel Air, California, home is a tribute to the richness of his talents and life, and yet, during one social visit in 2000 to his smaller home across the street, prior to construction of the larger facility in which he now lives and also has offices, we met with him paddling around in cut-offs and flip-flops, displaying the "down to Earth" and truly loveable humility that is really "him". He once told me when Frank Sinatra tapped him to be Frank's conductor, "It was like a lightning bolt coming down from Heaven and striking me. I never expected something like that would ever happen." Quincy also revered the now late Leigh Kamman, a Minnesotan who in the 1950s was a disc jockey on a New York radio station based in Harlem. He was the only non-Black DJ to ever be hired at that station because his knowledge and love of jazz made Leigh the eventual jazz radio legend he became, nationally, on Minnesota and National Public Radio. I met him at broadcast functions through the years, as he and I also worked for the same employer in the Twin Cities, but not at the same time. Quincy has always given Leigh credit for Quincy's eventual decision to "spread his wings" and become the giant he's become. Leigh passed away in 2014. (See photos section for part of a wonderful note Quincy spontaneously emailed me December 30, 2008, about missing seeing both Leigh and me. That note is a treasure, as is Quincy, as almost everyone is aware.)

There's only one remembrance of Bob that's bittersweet: Every time I see, or have been to, Seattle's Pike Place area, I remember one Thanksgiving Eve when Channel 13 had given each of us a frozen turkey as a Thanksgiving present. I told Bob I'd be happy to give him mine so we could all eat Thanksgiving Dinner, 1965, together at his house, since I was living in a rented hovel near the television station in Tacoma. He liked the idea and told me to meet him at a club near Pike Place at 11:00 that Thanksgiving Eve. I stood outside in the mist and light rain for about 45 minutes. Bob never showed, and those were the days before cell phones existed, thus I couldn't call to ask where he was, nor could he reach me. Somewhat dejected, I saw a bar across the street and walked in with the bagged turkey under my arm. There were very few people in the bar, but the barkeep was an older lady who looked like she might be able to put that turkey to good use. I told her it had been a gift to me from my employer but I didn't have the facilities to cook it and asked her if she wanted it. She said, "Yes", and that was that. I exited into that Sherlock Holmes-like night thinking perhaps the turkey had found a home that might have been more special. Bob called me the next day to apologize for not showing up, saying he had stayed at a party that evening longer than he expected. No problem and life went on. Bob eventually became an executive with Bonneville Broadcasting's affiliate, KIRO-TV in Seattle and then moved on to own his own television station in that market. He and I kept in touch through the years until he passed in the 1990s.

J. Elroy McCaw, Craig McCaw (sometimes spelled MacCaw by them), The Highlands, i.e., The Boeing Estate and Manhattan Cablevision—As Channel 13's Program Director and part-time talent, Mr. McCaw had me sometimes get my programming "marching orders" from him in person. In person was at The Highlands, the estate Bill Boeing (Yes, that Boeing) had sold to Mr. McCaw and where Mr. McCaw, his wife Marion and sons lived with their dog, Duke. In order to enter the estate's grounds, I had to press buttons outside the tall iron gate leading into the long uphill driveway, which also had electric "eyes" on several trees along that route. There were three living rooms, and a long hallway connecting each.

A couple of the times I visited with Mr. McCaw, always alone, I used to see one of his and Marion's sons riding a very large tricycle up and down the hallway. He was one of the sons, along with his brother Craig and two other brothers, who would eventually sell their cell phone company, McCaw Communications to AT&T for 11.1 billion dollars. That company became AT&T Wireless. Craig also became a partner of Bill Gates in a venture other than Microsoft. Craig's second wife, Susan, was U.S. Ambassador (correctly Ambassadress) to Austria for two years during the George W. Bush presidency.

The punch line: Mr. McCaw had no idea how shabbily I was living, but during one visit with him at The Highlands in March, 1966, he told me I was the best "idea man" he'd ever known and offered me the job as President of a New York City-based cable company (Manhattan Cablevision services), which he'd recently purchased and of which he was eventually Board Chairman. Cable was in its infancy. Mr. McCaw remembered I'd lived my teenage years in New York, knew the "territory" and had been deeply immersed with the best talent and production people in television, thus the job offer. I thanked him and immediately said, "Yes". He said he wasn't certain when I could start, but we'd "keep in touch". Unfortunately, the "keeping in touch" didn't happen because there was a "power struggle" shake-up at Channel 13, thus I and some other employees there were out of work. Mr. McCaw died in 1969, very deeply in debt, which is, sadly, longtime public knowledge. He helped a lot of people up the career ladder.

Tammy Wynette's future husband, et al—To make more income, I landed a weekend job (even during my six month tenure at Channel 13) as an all-night DJ on Country KAYO, a 50,000 watt powerhouse that scoured the Pacific Northwest. The Seattle Symphony and a major chorus even created KAYO's station break music and lyrics, with violins prominent in the "song". A part of the lyrics were, "From the Cascade Mountains, to the blue Pacific (then strings), etc.", then identifying the call letters. I hated country music (at that time) but one has to do what one has to do to survive. Our station manager was a DJ, too. His name was George Richey. In later years, he became Tammy Wynette's husband. Our Program Director, and also a DJ, was named "Bashful" Bobby Wooten. At that time, and continuously until Buck Owens's passing, Bobby was Buck's manager. *In later years, during my Las Vegas life, I had a one-time dinner date with one of the girls Buck would eventually date, an actress/singer named Gunilla Hutton, who became one of the stars on Buck's successful television series,* Hee-Haw. *Gunilla was a sweet and beautiful girl, as anyone who ever watched* Hee-Haw *would remember.*

During the weekend days in Seattle, I was also a taxicab driver, again trying to supplement income. My reason to want (and need) to make as much money as possible was to never miss monthly child-support payments, which I never did, for all 16½ years they were due. That doesn't make me a saint, but it was my first priority, always.

Wenatchee blues—I needed to not have to work two or three part-time jobs in order to survive, as well as preserve a modicum of sanity and dignity, thus heard about a full-time radio announcing/DJ/newscasting/account executive position in Wenatchee, Washington, only a two-plus hour drive from Seattle-Tacoma. I got the job. My first boss there was named Roy Robinson. He had been a professional singer with Charlie Barnet's big band. Roy's wife, Annette, was born in Paris, France. They were a fun and easy-going couple and I enjoyed practicing my French with Annette whenever possible.

The station's call letters were KUEN, owned by a man named Miller Robertson. Robertson lived in Anchorage, Alaska and owned a radio station there, too. I "DeeJayed", hosted a daily noontime music half hour show called "Western Roundup Time" and sold ads for a dollar a holler (as they used to say) in the afternoons. I also hosted a news-oriented program every Sunday, but taped during the week. Some of my frequent guests included a local Councilman, later Congressman, named Tom Foley, who later became Speaker of the U.S. House of Representatives and Ambassador to Japan. Mr. Foley and I kept in touch through the years, and thanks to former Vice President, Walter Mondale (previously referenced and to be more referenced later) I was able to re-unite with Tom in Minneapolis at the Marquette Hotel in the early 2000s, prior to a speech Tom was giving the next evening (see photos section). Also a frequent guest on the program was one of Washington state's most respected U.S. Senators, Henry "Scoop" Jackson. "Scoop" once told me, on the air, I asked him better questions than they asked him on "Face the Nation". I thanked him, wishing someday I'd get to host something similar on a national scale, which, of course, never happened. It was an honor to have him say that and I still have that audiotape.

Roy Robinson left the station to "pursue other interests" and was succeeded by an energetic and very sales-focused station manager named Bob Sumbardo. Bob was delightful but had a very intense personality. He also had managed a radio station in Ellensburg, Washington. In later years, a co-anchor team member with me in the Twin Cities, now anchoring in Chicago, told me Bob had been his first boss in broadcasting. It's often a small business.

After a little over a year, I decided my career had to start back up the ladder, thus began to contact friends I'd known during my Idaho Falls life to begin the job-hunting networking process. One of them was a former Filmways and CBS executive named Don Garrett. (Garrett, in later years, oversaw Spokane, Washington's World's Fair). The others were KID-TV's Art Director named Melissa Daw and an NBC-TV publicist named Joe Bleeden, who was Johnny Carson's personal publicist for many years. After contacting all of them, Melisssa and Joe urged me to move to Las Vegas. Don Garrett invited me to visit him and his wife in L.A., stating if nothing worked out there, I could then easily drive the four hours to Las Vegas and see what was available. Made sense to me, since my mother was already living in Las Vegas (as previously noted) so I packed the little red Triumph Herald I'd bought in Wenatchee and headed south toward L.A., with all my furniture and belongings still in storage on the SeaLand docks in San Francisco. *As part of the time I'm writing this (June, 2015), major forest fires have just destroyed homes and even some downtown Wenatchee businesses, including a fruit warehouse. Wenatchee prides itself on being "The Apple Capital of The World". The Golden Delicious orchards are prevalent there.*

CHAPTER TWELVE

The Unexpected Next Life

You must live the life you were born to live.
—Mother Superior's admonition to Maria in *The Sound Of Music*

I arrived at Don Garrett's house in Beverly Hills two days after leaving Wenatchee and, kind person he was, one of those with "my back", he said he'd been sleuthing about possible work for me in L.A. His connections at CBS told him there was a Promotion Writer's job open. Knowing I had been a Promotion Manager for the CBS affiliate in Idaho Falls, and asked to do occasional special projects for the network by CBS's two highest-level promotion execs at that time, named Alex Kennedy and Leonard Broome (the latter a native New Zealander), Don arranged for me to meet with the decision-maker at Television City to do a writing audition for the job. Long story short, I got the job, but the day I was to start work, a union actors strike began that year (1967) and The Writers Guild honored the picket lines, thus I wasn't able to get to work. Ah, fate.

Not knowing how long that strike would last, I decided to explore the possible Las Vegas work. I thanked Don, called Joe Bleeden in Las Vegas (who, after working for Carson was now PR Director for The Desert Inn) and asked him what thoughts he had for my possible re-emergence into broadcasting work at a possibly higher level than I'd been experiencing in Wenatchee and Seattle-Tacoma. Joe reminded me he and I both knew Hank Greenspun from the BPA days. Greenspun owned *The Las Vegas Sun* newspaper and KLAS-TV, Channel 8, the CBS affiliate. Joe said he'd call Hank to learn if Hank would entertain a meeting with me to discuss working for Hank. Hank remembered me and told Joe to have me meet Hank and his station manager, Mark Smith (a former ABC-TV executive) to discuss any possibilities. The meeting occurred and I was hired as the station's weathercaster and promotion/sales service manager.

The first clue I had some of the stars who lived in Las Vegas were watching my weathercasts as "fans" was receiving a postcard addressed to me at Channel 8 from the singing duo, Art and Dotty Todd (of "Chanson d'Amour" fame, one of music's iconic hits). They wrote, "You are wonderful" and signed it with both their names. I still have that treasured postcard (please see photos section). I'm sorry to state I never had the pleasure and honor to meet them, because they initiated the beginning of developing self-confidence for one who truly never had much of that. They never had any idea of how very much that meant to me. I sent them a note thanking them, but any words would have been inadequate to express my gratitude. Seemingly "small" and innocent happenings of that nature are, in my opinion, the biggest happenings in our lives. Someone or "someones" validate you. Je me souvien, toujours, Art and Dotty.

Only a few months after I started on the air and in Channel 8's offices, Greenspun sold KLAS-TV to Howard Hughes. Hughes had been welcomed to Nevada by newly elected Governor Paul Laxalt (who became a lifelong friend to me, more about whom later, and still alive as of this writing. Paul was Ronald Reagan's "kingmaker", too.). Hughes bought six hotels and Channel 8.

From this point, some of my favorite Las Vegas-related memories:

Howard Hughes: Programming the station—When Mr. Hughes took over the station, doing business as Summa Corporation and Hughes Tool Company, no one knew what to expect, of course, since his eccentric reputation preceded him. There was no reason to worry. Our paychecks came from the Hughes Tool Company and he let Mark Smith and Program Director Jack Reynolds (as nice a human being as could ever be) continue business as usual, except for contacting Mark via one of Mr. Hughes's aides, or in writing, requesting *The Outlaw*, or any other films Mr. Hughes had produced or financed, be shown instead of what was scheduled for late-night fare. (Years later, during my Minnesota life, it was fun to learn the female star of *The Outlaw*, Jane Russell, was a native of Bemidji, Minnesota, and of which that town is very proud. I did some public relations work there in 2014 and those of an older age remembered her fondly, along with Hughes proudly media-touting his "discovery". Indeed, *The Outlaw* catapulted Jane to international fame, although, in those days, the character she portrayed was considered very controversial because of the "sexiness" the part conveyed. These days, the film and her character would be rated PG, maybe even borderline G.)

Monitoring an atomic bomb test—Three weeks before it occurred, Mr. Hughes and everyone who lived in Nevada were informed by the media the AEC had scheduled the largest underground atomic bomb test in history would take place beneath Yucca Flats (The Las Vegas Bombing and Gunnery Range about 70 miles NNW of Las Vegas). Mark Smith got a call from Peter Maheu. Peter was the nephew of Bob Maheu, Mr. Hughes's top executive for his Las Vegas operations and a former FBI agent. Peter asked Mark if I could accompany him or one of Mr. Hughes's aides to photograph every wall of every room and the walls of all the casinos and hotel lobbies before that atomic bomb test, then after the test, take photos of the same locations to determine whether or not the bomb did damage to any parts of the hotels, casinos (including even the hard and soft count rooms in the casino "cages"). Mark gave me permission to take the photos. It took almost a week (eight hour-plus days) to accomplish what the boss (Mr. Hughes) requested.

After the bomb was tested (I felt it shake my house, 70 miles away), I repeated the photo taking, and, indeed, Mr. Hughes's suspicions were correct: there were cracks in the walls of some of the hotel rooms, but fewer in the lobbies, casinos and casino "count rooms". Mr. Hughes sued the U.S. government (for which he didn't have much fondness anyway) for property damages (an embarrassment to Governor Laxalt) and won a hefty settlement. Although he didn't pay me a bonus for taking the revelatory photos, he did something I consider more special, as follows:

Wishing death away—After finally being able to afford retrieving my furniture and belongings from two years of their "captivity" in the San Francisco SeaLand storage units previously described, I lived in a ground floor rented apartment in a building immediately adjacent to Las Vegas's Sunrise Hospital. One Sunday morning in early July, 1968, I felt my forehead. It was unusually hot. I walked into the Sunrise emergency room and one of the nurses on duty took my temperature.

A doctor named Norman Venger was on duty, thank God, literally. Although I didn't know what I had (until just before I was discharged a month later), Dr. Venger did, and took the first of many spinal taps. I was admitted to the hospital, treated well in a private room and all that occurred every other day were those spinal taps. The punch line(s) will, I think, be worth reading, coming soon to a paragraph not far away. In fact, it's next!

Around ten o'clock, August 4, 1968, the night before my 31st birthday, I laid my head on my pillow and prepared to go to sleep. I'd never thought about death, but when I closed my eyes, I saw an almost blinding white light surrounding a long tunnel. At the end of the tunnel I saw human figures, all in dark gray shadows, beckoning me with their hands to join them. There were no faces, just dark gray silhouettes. As I stated, I had never thought about death, but to myself I said, "No, not now. I'm not ready to die. No, no, no." I kept repeating it. As I did, the figures and light began to fade, and I went to sleep. The next morning, my 31st birthday, a nurse did another spinal tap. About a half-hour later, Dr. Venger came into the room and told me I'd be discharged the next day. He then told me what I had: "Valley Fever" (Coccidiomycosis, medical term for "Valley Fever"), which is 97 percent fatal; meningitis and encephalitis, all at the same time. "Valley Fever" is indigenous to newly developed agricultural areas in the western U.S. and most prevalent in California's San Joaquin Valley and Arizona's Salt River Valley. Migrant workers have been its primary victims. I contracted it by breathing normally while driving through a dust storm near Modesto (in the San Joaquin Valley) on a trip from Las Vegas to San Francisco in late June that year.

Mr. Hughes's medical insurance for us was via Aetna, but when I went to the cashier to pay my hospital bill, the cashier said, "Oh no. That won't be necessary. Mr. Hughes has taken care of everything." There are no words, now almost 47 years since then, that could sufficiently express my perpetual gratitude to that man. I was also later told by Dr. Venger prayers were being said for me daily at St. Viator's Catholic Church, a half-block from both the station and The Desert Inn, wherein Mr. Hughes occupied the entire ninth (top) floor. More about that floor, soon!

When I went to see Dr. Venger for a final post-hospital checkup, I told him about my near-death experience. He then told me, "I've heard of people wishing it away. Apparently, that's what you did." Thank you, God.

Mr. Hughes was a "fan"!—Two months after the "Valley Fever" episode, I received a phone call from a man named Keith Dare. He was General Manager of Las Vegas's ABC-TV affiliate, Channel 13, then with the call letters KSHO-TV and owned by a man named John Ettlinger, whose grandfather was one of the co-founders of Hertz Car Rentals. Keith, a former ABC-TV Vice President who was a close friend of ABC-TV President, Elton Rule, offered me a job as weatherman and eventually talk show host, as well as morning news anchor. The pay was sufficiently more than what I was earning at Channel 8, and his enthusiasm for hiring me was infectious. Much as I had sincere gratitude for all Mr. Hughes had done for me, I decided it was time to move ahead, thus took the job, but not without temporary mockery from Channel 8's news anchor, who later apologized and wished me luck at Channel 13. He had asked, "Hah! Where are you going to go from there?" In later years, he visited his daughter in Minneapolis, met with me at KSTP-TV and saw where I "went from there". I truly believe in that old saying, paraphrased, "Be careful how you treat people when you're on your way up, as you'll certainly meet them when you're on your way down."

About a month after I started at Channel 13, I was having a mid-afternoon iced tea break in the nearby Frontier Hotel's lounge with that hotel's orchestra leader, Al Alvarez. During our conversation, Al asked me, "Did you know Hughes was a big fan of yours?" I told him I didn't and asked how he knew that. He asked, "Do you remember getting a call in the Channel 8 control room one night with someone asking you if you were changing your style of weather presentation?" I told Al I actually did remember that call because it wasn't that long ago prior to Al asking me that question and the person questioning me on the phone sounded above average articulate and polite. I also told Al my response to the caller was I just didn't feel well that night and wasn't up to doing my "personality" weathercast. I told Al

I remembered the person said, "Thank you. That's all we wanted to know." "We", Al told me, was Howard Hughes, who had asked one of his aides to call me to ask if I was changing my style. Mr. Hughes ran an empire and yet was interested to learn if I was changing my style of presentation. That was one of the more mind-boggling, and humbly flattering, events in my life. (Al told me the aide had quit about three weeks before Al's and my conversation that day and told Al that story.)

During my Channel 8 and Channel 13 days in Las Vegas, I also did weekend morning deejay work at KLAV, the CBS radio affiliate there. The owner/manager of the station was a man named Maury Stevens, originally from Philadelphia, who later became Merv Griffin's producer for The Merv Griffin Show. *Merv's announcer/sidekick, as many may recall, was Arthur Treacher, the man who lifted me above his head when I was two-years old and announced from* The Stanley Theater stage to *the 1939 Pittsburgh audience, "This child was born for the footlights!" as earlier referenced. I wish I had told Maury about that, but just didn't. Maury's wife, Muriel, was a cuisine media personality who also wrote for* The Las Vegas Sun. *"If you love to cook, they'll love your cooking" was Muriel's signature slogan. Maury's and Muriel's daughter, Robin, eventually married one of Hank Greenspun's sons, named Danny. Robin and Danny, in later years, produced some feature films, one with Reese Witherspoon. KLAV's secretary was a lady . . . with the accent on lady . . . named Ruth Irwin. Her husband, Stan, was Johnny Carson's agent. I met him only once. Thanks to the blessing of being popular in the market, I was lucky enough to convince a lot of the A-list people who either performed on* The Strip *or downtown, or were in town for other work, to do free station-break promo announcements for the station, recorded on a portable reel-to-reel tape recorder I carried to wherever they were. They included Sarah Vaughan, Robert Goulet, Peter Nero, Peggy Lee, Wayne Newton, Pearl Bailey, Ella Fitzgerald, Helen Reddy, Matt Munro, Howard Keel, Kathryn Grayson, Don Rickles, Donald O'Connor, Louis Prima, Jack E. Leonard, Pete Fountain, Joe Williams, Jack Jones, Pete Barbutti, Marty Allen, Steve Rossi, Tony Bennett, Harry Belafonte, Gregory Peck, Eva Marie Saint and several others. Their line was: "This is (name). You're tuned to* The Station of the Stars, *KLAV, 1230 on your dial, Las Vegas". Most of them allowed me to become one of their social*

friends for the almost four years I worked there, and several of them,
for many years thereafter. Sarah Vaughan and Pete Fountain later told
me they used to delay opening their late night shows at The Tropicana
for twenty minutes so they could watch my weathercasts at 11:15. Pearl
Bailey and I shared several early morning times hitting buckets of balls at
The Dunes Hotel's driving range. She was delightful, laughing much of the
time, not just at my bad drives. And, speaking of hitting balls, although
different kinds of balls, via an introduction from a mutual friend and
colleague named Chuck Hull, I was MGM owner Kirk Kerkorian's mid-
morning tennis partner on one of the pre-MGM-site tennis courts that
existed at the time. He was a very serious tennis player, but endured our
couple of matches pleasantly. In later years, during my D.C. television
days, one of my regular tennis partners was Minnesota Senator Eugene
McCarthy, along with the Mayor of San Juan, Puerto Rico's D.C. office
secretary and her friend. I have been a very lucky boy.

Harry Belafonte—Dennis Belafonte, Harry's brother, was one of
our high school contemporaries in New York, a student at PCS. One
Saturday afternoon I was scheduled to be at Channel 8 for some
additional voice recording and saw Harry sitting alone on a riser in
the studio. He was looking out at the non-descript landscape the open
studio garage door afforded, with the very bright sun almost masking
what anyone could really identify outside. I'm painting this visual
picture because the cosmetics married themselves to the wistful look
in Harry's eyes. He seemed very contemplative as if definitely mentally
somewhere else. After I said hello to him, he said, "I hate Las Vegas."

I told him I was sorry to learn that, as if whatever I said mattered.
Harry picked up on it, though, stating, "Oh, I know the money I'm
getting is good, but it's just this town, not the people." I acknowledged
what he said, then told him about my high school-years friendship
with his brother, Dennis. He smiled, said that was nice to know, and
that was that. Harry was headlining at Caesars Palace at that time.

Woody Allen: "Saving his life"!—Caesars Palace's main showroom
was also one of the last major venues wherein Woody performed
standup comedy. The year was 1968. During that time, I directed

Woody in a local television show at Channel 8, with then *Las Vegas Sun* columnist Ralph Pearl hosting. After the taping, a major afternoon thunderstorm had dumped enough rain on Las Vegas to create significant flooding. Woody asked me how he was going to get back to Caesars, which was about a mile up The Strip from where Channel 8 was located, only a block north of The Strip. I told Woody I'd very gladly drive him back to Caesars. He said okay, then looked at my car, that little red Triumph Herald convertible I previously referenced. The top was up and the windows closed, but he noticed the flood's water was almost reaching the running board. (If you're too young to remember running boards, just look them up on Wikipedia!) He asked if I was "sure" I could do this safely and I replied in the affirmative, knowing I could.

Woody very gently got into the car from the driver's side, since I was parked at a spot in front of the station's two or three steps that led into the station, thus allowing him to step into the car without stepping into any water. Because of the flood's waters, and the passenger I had, I pulled away from the Channel 8 steps very slowly, continued slowly driving the one block to The Strip, turned left and headed toward Caesars. Since The Strip very slowly rises in elevation the farther one drives in that particular direction, the less the flood waters accumulate, thus when Woody and I reached the point to turn right into the long entryway driveway to get to Caesars' main entrance, there was no flood water on the ground. Bringing a smile to my face as I type this, Woody turned to me and, with his signature smile on his face, said, "Gee, you really did it." I said, "Yes, I had very precious cargo." He didn't respond, but when we got to the main entrance, he thanked me and that was that. Woody had been visibly slightly nervous for the entire drive until we reached that driveway. I saw him again in early 1971 when he kindly agreed to tape a television promotion for me prior to my coming to The Twin Cities to begin another phase of my television career there, for which I was very grateful (please see photos section).

Elvis and Priscilla Presley—During my Channel 8 tenure, one of the people I didn't know was one of my weather "fans" was a then well-known comedian named Irv Benson. Irv had been a regular cast member on Milton Berle's *Texaco Star Theater* during television 's Golden Era in the late 1940s and 1950s. Irv called the station one late afternoon and invited me to be his guest during a performance he was headlining at The Silver Slipper (also a property Mr. Hughes owned) located on the south side of The Strip only two blocks from the station. When I got to the late night performance (11 o'clock), Irv did his show, and immediately afterward, still on stage, he introduced me to the audience as his guest. Another guest there, at the next table to me, fewer than five feet away, looking at me "intently", was Johnny Carson, introduced to the audience by Irv after Irv had introduced me. Johnny was tapping his fingers rapidly and wasn't smiling. It was the one and only time I was ever with Johnny in person, but was blessed to get to know Johnny's producer, Fred de Cordova, very well in later years. I never told Fred that story. (Prior to *The Tonight Show Starring Johnny Carson*, Fred de Cordova had also produced that delightful television series, *My Three Sons*, starring Fred MacMurray, with whom I also had a delightful meeting, including with MacMurray's wife, June Haver, in Las Vegas, a few years later. But I digress . . . for a change. Now to Elvis and Priscilla Presley.) Irv told me Elvis had just gotten married the day before at The Aladdin. It was big news the preceding day, but I thanked him for the reminder. Irv had known Elvis very well, and told me Elvis told him to stop by and say "Hello" after Irv's show the night after the wedding. Elvis also told him where Irv could find him. Irv kindly invited me to go along, to say "Hello" to Elvis, for which I, of course, thanked him, thus we hopped in a cab and arrived at The Aladdin. Irv took me directly to the blackjack table where Elvis was playing on the left side of the table (when one was facing the table) at the second position, with Priscilla, not playing but looking, seated in the first position, to Elvis's left.

There was no crowd, nor even a few people, watching Elvis play, which was, to me, a shock, but also a blessing regarding the ability to meet him as not part of a crowd. Irv had me stand next to the seated Elvis, while Irv was standing at my right and said to Elvis, "This is my friend, Barry ZeVan, who does the weather on Channel 8 here." Elvis looked up and said "Pleased to meet you", with a very warm, genuine smile. I told him it was my honor to meet him and congratulated him and Priscilla on their nuptials. I also told him how much I enjoyed his talent. He thanked me and said, I'd swear on a stack of Bibles, "I've watched you. I enjoy you, too." I thanked him and said I was honored he had watched. He smiled again, Irv said our goodbyes, and that was that, except to let you know Priscilla was looking somewhat un-pleased at Elvis, obviously not happy he was playing Blackjack the night after they got married. In later years, I had the honor to interview Priscilla a couple times for my *Hollywood Update* syndicated television series, which focused on new films and their stars. The first time I interviewed her, I good-naturedly reminded her of the night at The Aladdin I just described and she said she didn't remember me, but definitely remembered that night, and smiled.

Carol Lawrence, Robert Goulet, Juliet Prowse, Redd Foxx, Joan Rivers, Bob Newhart, George Carlin, Steve Allen, Peter Nero, Howard Keel, Duke Ellington, Stein Eriksen, Joe Delaney and more:
 Carol Lawrence—One afternoon, while preparing my weatherboard for the early evening newscast, I was told I had a call in our Channel 13 newsroom office. I got on the phone and heard, "Hi, Barry. This is Carol Lawrence." I gulped and said, "Hello, Carol. To what do I owe the honor of your call?" She said, verbatim, "Bobby and I love your weather show and he'd like to come to the station and have some fun with you on the air as part of your show." I told her that would be wonderful, to say the least. She said she'd have "Bobby" call me in less than an hour. Robert Goulet did call me and we arranged he'd appear on my show the following late afternoon. Thanks to the Internet, you can watch that first appearance (and many other's guest appearances) if you Google my name. You'll see Bob joking around with me, the first of several times for at least 20 years in different television markets, with his first appearance playfully stating he was Eddie Fisher (who I would also get to know in later years). For whatever very blessed reason, Bob and Carol became wonderful and warm friends to me, continuing even after their divorce. Once, while they were still married, I was walking through one of the Las Vegas hotel lobbies and spotted Carol seated on the route I was headed. I told her it was wonderful to see her

again, and she said, "*You're* wonderful." I thanked her and said I hoped we would see each other again sometime, with her nodding approval in response. To have people of her caliber state something like that was beyond heartwarming to this recipient, especially as I've always felt I was not anyone special, with no false humility here, I assure you. *In the 1980s, I reconnected with Carol to interview her for my* Hollywood Update *syndicated show. It was several years after she and Bob had been divorced. She told me to come to what had been her and Bob's hilltop home to do the interview. That house was positioned literally beneath a television transmission tower near Mulholland Drive. What was supposed to be a 30-minute visit turned into almost two hours, talking about everything from the time I was "this close" to acting with her in* West Side Story *on Broadway, which she hadn't known until that visit (to which I previously alluded regarding Jerome Robbins's reaction to my non-tough speech pattern), to just everyday events in both our lives. We had most of our conversation (after the interview taping) simply walking slowly around her huge backyard. It was a memorable day, to say the least. During that time period, Carol had recently married an L.A. real estate developer whose first name was Greg. She introduced me to him when the cameraman and I arrived, but that was the last time I ever saw him. Carol and he divorced after only one year. I never saw Carol again, but if she's still in good health and able to re-connect after this book is published, will definitely hope to see her again, since she started the parade of more mega-stars marching into my professional and personal life. Thank you, Carol.*

Joe Delaney—Joe, whose ashes were scattered over Ireland many years ago by his now widow, Roberta, was one of my strongest life and career champions. He really cared that I climb back to the top of the career and recognition ladder again and did everything possible to help me in that regard. "Help me" is an understatement. He was a constant cheerleader for me and I'll always be more than grateful to him for what he did, to say the least.

Joe was a justifiably revered and well-established entertainment columnist for *The Las Vegas Sun*. Joe had also, in his deep show business career, been the A & R man for a major record label and manager of *The Dukes Of Dixieland*. Joe also hosted his own one-hour celebrity television interview show on Channel 13 that aired from 4 to 5 p.m., just prior to our early evening newscast at 5.

After Carol Lawrence started the celebrity ball rolling with Bob being the first to join me to have fun on my weathercasts, Joe made certain every world-class celebrity he had as a guest on his talk show would also have some fun with me on my weathercasts. Among the most fun were Juliet Prowse and Redd Foxx (the latter two who appeared on my same weathercast one night, which you can watch if you access Google to see that "episode"). The next morning, *The Las Vegas Review-Journal* said I had as many guests on my weather show that night as Ed Sullivan, which, of course, was stated facetiously. During the course of one week, though, the R-J's assessment was close to correct, thanks to Joe Delaney. None of their appearances on my weather show were scripted, all spontaneous and stream-of-consciousness dialogue. *You can watch the following bit on the Internet's placement of* Comedy Central's Daily Show's *tongue-in-cheek satirical anthology of my career or* Twin Cities Media Now's *placement of the same excerpt: Juliet, on the air, came onto my set asking which way it was to The Joe Delaney Show. I pointed in the proper direction and then she said, "You're awful cute", and walked out of the picture. I resumed doing the weather after giving her a one-line reference to her then current gig at The International. Then Redd came rushing in about 30 seconds later, asking if I knew where Juliet Prowse went. I pointed in the proper direction for him, too. He exited the picture. I then looked at the camera feigning disbelief, and resumed doing the weathercast. After Joe's show, I thanked Ms. Prowse for her kind comment and bravely asked if I could have the honor to take her to lunch or dinner sometime. She very warmly said that would be "enjoyable". We went to lunch the following day at one of the restaurants in The International (which later became the Las Vegas Hilton), where she was performing, and discussed her South African roots, being born in Bombay, India, to South African parents and being reared in South Africa, show business and Las Vegas itself, which she said she enjoyed as a city, as well as my career, briefly, but wherein she strongly encouraged me to keep climbing back up the ladder, knowing I'd started at the top of the ladder during my teenage acting and singing years in New York. We didn't discuss her former engagement to Frank Sinatra. I wanted to, since I had the good fortune to have Frank, Jr.'s friendship/acquaintance during those Las Vegas years (which I'm happy to say I still have, although I haven't been with him since 2003. See photos section), but thought it wouldn't be very classy, since their breakup wasn't pleasant. After lunch, she gave me her best phone contact number, which I never used. The next time she was in town she was performing at The Frontier. I called and she said I could come backstage to see her before her performance, but when she answered the door . . . she had recently become engaged to her first husband, Eddie Frazier . . . she said he was nearby and might not understand my visiting. She apologized with an understandably panicked look on her face. I told her no apology was necessary and I understood. We said a fast but cordial "adieu" and that was the last time I ever saw her. Her premature death was another very difficult to accept.*

Redd became a close acquaintance and "fan", God bless him. My daughters always remember the time they were both with me in the gift shop of The International and Redd happened to be in there when we entered. I went up to say hello, and he said, in front of my daughters, "You're the best damn weatherman anywhere!" Again, I was very grateful for words like that from one who had more than made it to the top of the entertainment ladder. My daughters had big grins on their faces after he said it, as do I while typing this, remembering that warm moment. Redd's friend, and sometimes guest actor on Sanford And Son, *comedian Slappy White, also became a friend to me, thanks to Redd, during those halcyon years.*

Others who Joe kindly suggested should be on my weathercasts included former iconic MGM musical stars Kathryn Grayson and Howard Keel. Kathryn had as sweet a personality as came across on screen and always called me "cutie". The "Howard Keel story" is one of my all-time indelible memories, to wit: I was preparing my totally glass weatherboard for that late afternoon's newscast when I saw this gigantic human figure coming toward me from behind. I thought it was Howard Keel, as I'd heard he was going to be a guest on Joe's show (sans Kathryn Grayson that time), but wasn't. Then, less than two feet away from me, he said his first words to me in that booming voice of his. Those words were, verbatim, "You're the best f***in' weatherman

in the world." I turned around and looked up at him (he *was* Howard
Keel), somewhat taken aback, but appreciatively so, and meekly
said, "Thank you." He smiled, put his hand on my shoulder and
continued with one or two additional kind compliments about my
work. I thanked him again and that was that, until the next time he
was at the station with Kathryn (they were appearing at The Fremont,
downtown). He saw me before my weathercast and said he and
Kathryn would enjoy having me join them for dinner some evening
while they were in town, which was at least three times a year, for
two to three weeks each time. I told him that would be wonderful
and thanked him. I was their guest for dinner once during the
ensuing year. Every time I see them on TCM's movies, I pinch myself
remembering how they were as human beings, warm, welcoming and
so much fun with whom to be, resurrecting memories galore from
both their stellar careers. It was truly "magic time" again. It reminded
me of a comment I recently read about that magnificent actress, Amy
Adams, who was quoted as saying, "I don't belong with these people!"
when she attended her first Academy Awards show. "BTW", as they
say these days, Ms. Adams and I share the same birthday, August 5th.
Same birth date for Charlize Theron and my longtime friend, Loni
Anderson. I look nothing like them. I thought you should know that.

One of my very favorite stories during those fun days at Channel
13: Another who appeared on Joe's show (on tape) during a time I
wasn't in the studio was Duke Ellington. I had no idea Duke was even
in the building or scheduled to tape a segment for Joe. I was sitting
at my Promotion Manager desk (I had that job, too, at 13) when all
of a sudden Duke walked in to my office clad in a big fur coat (it gets
cold in Las Vegas in the winter) accompanied by an entourage of at
least three others. He was an imposing figure, marching straight to
the front of my desk and leaning over, cupped my cheeks between
his hands and gave me a big wet kiss on the lips, then smiled, looked
at my astonished face and warmly laughed. All he said was, "I love
you, man.", still with that big smile on his face, then turned around
and walked out of my office. Sitting across the room from me was a
fellow named Kent Harman, our Program Director, who witnessed
the entire event, and had a wide-eyed big smile on his face, too. Kent

asked me, "What was that?" wiping his glasses from happy tears. I told him I had no idea, and to this day, I don't. Joe might have put Duke up to it, but I never asked and Joe, nor anyone else, ever told me, even after I told them what happened, and with Kent as a witness. I'm sad to say I never saw Duke again, but I also have never washed my lips since that day, either!

One of those who regularly visited Joe's show was the dear and now tragically late Joan Rivers. I first met her in the studio when she was pregnant with Melissa, her now very grown daughter. I also met and chatted with Edgar, her husband, who later committed suicide, as most people are aware. Joan was a delight. In those fledgling career days, she mostly appeared at The Riviera or The Sahara. During my D.C. television years (1974–1977) she was booked to be a guest on my weathercast (yes, the weather guest appearances carried over there, too, which will later be fully described) but there was a flood and she couldn't get to the station, thus sent me the note you'll see she inscribed on her picture, in the pictures section of this book. In 2014, thank goodness, I was able to have some semi-private time with Joan backstage at one of the casinos near the Twin Cities where she was appearing. We reminisced about the old days, and especially Joe, and she said, "Oh, I loved that man. Joe, Joe, Joe. (shaking her head from side to side.) And I also loved those days in Vegas when all us headliners would actually have coffee at a little coffee shop somewhere and just talk. Those days are so gone." She said it very wistfully, and I agreed. A picture was taken with her, my older granddaughter Maritsa, her husband Gunnar and me (see photos section). My granddaughter was one of her biggest fans, thus the reason I secured the booking. When Joan unexpectedly died, all who knew and loved her and her work were devastated and angered, because it shouldn't have happened. Joan's death was a true travesty, to say the least. Joan was also a close friend of Jerry and Anne, the latter two with whom I corresponded about that very sad occurrence. Jerry wrote he and Anne were in disbelief, too.

Thanks to Carol Lawrence and Robert Goulet ("Bobby" as Carol called him and he didn't object to my calling him "Bob"), not only did Joe Delaney pick up on the idea to have the celebs visiting his show be on my weather show, too, the station decided I should host a morning talk show because our ratings were climbing fast. The show was politically correctly, in those days, called *13 Women's Magazine With Barry ZeVan*. The boss's reasoning was the morning audience would be mostly women watching. Our new owners (who bought the station in 1969, six months after I started working there,) were an attorney named John Laxalt (Nevada Governor Paul Laxalt's younger brother) and Alan Abner, along with a fellow named Arthur Powell Williams, who owned P & O Orient Lines (passenger and cargo ships) and who lived in Santa Barbara. Alan Abner, who co-managed the station with Keith Dare after the purchase, was disrespectfully considered a "bag boy" for Richard Nixon throughout Nixon's career, but he was much more than that: He was a decorated World War Two fighter pilot and one of the classiest people I ever met. He also was a broadcaster who knew what attracted audiences and what didn't, thus felt creating *13 Women's Magazine With Barry ZeVan* would piggyback successfully in concert with our strong evening ratings. He was right.

My guests on that show, which lasted for almost a year, until I quit for greener pastures (story upcoming), included almost everyone performing in town and on The Strip. They included Steve Allen, Louis Nye, George Carlin, Maureen Reagan (Ronald Reagan and Jane Wyman's daughter, who also died at a very premature age), Francesca Gabor (Zsa Zsa's daughter), my aforementioned friends Charlie Brill and Mitzi McCall, Irv Benson, Pete Barbutti, Peter Nero (we're friends to this day, honored to say) Louis Prima and Bob Newhart, among many others. Following are remembrances of the preceding and subsequent relationships with them thereafter:

Steve Allen—What an honor it was for him to say, "Yes", to be a guest on *Magazine*. You can see a glimpse of that appearance on the aforementioned *Comedy Central Daily Show* feature about yours truly, which aired when Criag Kilborn was still hosting that show. When he got to the studio he said he enjoyed my weathercasts. He had just released an album for children and about which we also talked. I noticed one of the songs he wrote for the album was entitled "You're a mugwump!". I teasingly asked him if that was supposed to be an insult and he laughed, good-naturedly, knowing my question was tongue-in-cheek. From that time on, whenever fate allowed our paths to cross, for either interviews or just socially, he was always welcoming to me. I told him after that first interview how us Lodge and PCS kids would occasionally go to the NBC-TV theater near Columbus Circle on Friday nights to watch him host *The Steve Allen Show*, which eventually became *The Tonight Show*, which Steve continued to host. I told him one of the more memorable moments was being in the live audience the night Steve had both Eydie Gorme and Steve Lawrence as guests on the show, which was the first time they'd ever met and, as most people of a certain age know, eventually got married. I also told Steve one of my part-time jobs aside from acting in New York was to park and watch over Eydie's car at her apartment building garage in The Bronx prior to her and Steve's marriage (previously mentioned. Sorry!).

The last time I was with Steve was three months before he died. It was at his offices in Van Nuys to interview him for a documentary I wrote and produced called *Television: The First 50 Years*. We discussed everything regarding television. His take on the 1950s sitcoms was, verbatim, "They were written for morons!". Steve was not only a genius in comedy, but also a great pianist and songwriter. He wrote over 7,000 songs, and most of the album covers lined the walls of his very large offices in a building he owned. I told him I remembered he'd written the lyrics to the song *Picnic*. Steve told me he was very impressed I knew that and he wrote those lyrics in 20 minutes in the back of a taxicab taking him from his Van Nuys offices to the Burbank Airport. At the conclusion of the interview, and as I was walking out the door, Steve kindly said, "It's a pleasure to work with you." I thanked him and told him the pleasure and honor were mine. Hearing about the car accident that eventually killed him three months later was another death more difficult to handle than most.

One of the most fascinating stories connected to Steve was I was blessed to meet and interview the person responsible for Steve's ascension to national prominence. To me, it's an illustration of any of the following: There are no coincidences. There are coincidences. The best things happen by accident. Divine intervention is always there. Here's how it happened and what that dear person responsible for

Steve's rise to national fame told me: Regardless of what one believes
regarding fate, I was getting a haircut during my two-year tenure
working as Vice President of Program Development for a now-defunct
documentary production company based in North Hollywood,
near the Toluca Lake city limits on Magnolia Boulevard. I found an
excellent barber nearby, in Toluca Lake, not far from Bob and Dolores
Hope's primary residence. My female barber asked me what I did for
a living. I told her I produced documentaries and the current subject
was the history of television, of which I'd been a part in New York City
two years before U.S. television was hooked up nationally (previously
referenced). She said that was very interesting because one of the
ladies whose hair she cut regularly was named Madelyn Pugh Davis,
one of the two original writers of *I Love Lucy*'s scripts. She asked if
I'd be interested in her contacting Madelyn to see if she'd give me an
interview. If I could have, I would have kissed her feet when she kindly
volunteered to make the contact. I, of course, said, "Yes" (possibly in
six different languages at that magic moment). She called Madelyn
immediately after finishing my haircut. Luckily she was home. The
barber put me on the line and Ms. Davis agreed to have the interview,
telling me she was certain her former *Lucy* writing partner, Bob
Carroll, Jr., would also agree. After another phone call later that day,
the interviews were set. A week later, my cameraman and I arrived
at Madelyn's house on an east side frontage road of the 405 Freeway.
Madelyn's name appears on early *Lucy* credits as simply Madelyn
Pugh, but she got married and added her husband's last name, Davis,
to the credits. Mr. Davis was also present at the historic interview.
You'll soon know why it was historic, for more than one reason.

Madelyn told me she and Bob were both originally from the
Indianapolis area and had been copywriters for ad agencies and radio
stations there. She said she and Bob were kind of a romantic "item"
there but decided if they were ever going to work together sometime
in the future, a combination of work and romance would never work
out, so they just decided to be friends. Bob said he was the first to
move from Indiana to Los Angeles to try his luck, and Madelyn said
she and her family moved to Phoenix because of health problems that
would be fixed in a drier climate.

Not long after Madelyn became established in Phoenix, she said a friend called her from L.A. stating an actress named Marie Wilson needed a writer for her radio show called *My Friend Irma* and it might eventually develop into a television show, too. This was in the mid-1940s, when rumblings of television's emergence were being heard and prior to the 1946 local New York City television show on which I was "talent", as previously referenced. Madelyn took the job and became established as one of national radio's premiere comedy writers, with *Irma* the catalyst. (I used to listen to that program religiously on CBS radio when I was a pre-teen in Pittsburgh.)

Punch line number one: When Madelyn became "accepted" in Hollywood, she remembered a brilliant young disc jockey in Phoenix to whom she listened on KOY radio there and always thought if she had the clout, she would hope to help his career become as strong as it could be. The disc jockey's name was Steve Allen. She told me without telling Steve, she told the General Manager of KNX, the CBS radio powerhouse in L.A., that he would be missing the boat if he didn't hire Steve. The General Manager went to Phoenix to listen (no easy Internet access in those days) and hired Steve, who then skyrocketed to deserved national fame. A bit more trivia about Steve: Steve was born in Chicago, into a show business family. The only reason the family moved to Phoenix was because Steve had asthma, ironically the same reason Madelyn's family had moved to Phoenix, because someone in Madelyn's family also had asthma.

Punch line number two: I asked Madelyn and Bob how they ever came up with the candy factory scene on *I Love Lucy*, voted by audiences the all-time most popular and memorable scene ever seen on television. Madelyn said Desi (Desi Arnaz, of course, Lucille Ball's husband in real life) told her and Bob he wanted Lucy and Ethel's characters to get a job, thus anything Madelyn and Bob decided would be the job, would be what Lucy and Ethel did on the following week's show. Madelyn and Bob said they decided to look in The Yellow Pages and whatever page to which they first turned would determine what the "job" would be for Lucy and Ethel. The page to which they turned stated Candy Manufacturing at the top of the page, and the rest became real history. (A bit more trivia: Madelyn told me Desi pronounced his first name as Dessi, not "Dezzy".)

George Carlin: George was a guest on *Magazine* because, when I called him at The Frontier, where he was performing, to ask if he'd agree to do so, he said he was only doing it because he really liked my "shtick". He also told me, in addition to performing as Al Sleet, the Hippy-Dippy Weatherman in his stand-up routines (and a classic on one of his comedy albums), he also told his Las Vegas audiences about my weathercasts and urged them to tune in, and also, he told me, peeking around at his audiences when he told them about my show. (Peeking around at the camera to keep eye contact with the audience was my trademark, as earlier mentioned) I was humbly flabbergasted, thanked him (profusely) and he was on my show the following week. We learned we had both spent at least three of our teenage years in New York living just three blocks from each other after my mom and I moved into Manhattan from Rego Park, Queens. My mom and I lived on 100th near West End Avenue and George lived at 103rd and Riverside Drive. He and I also joined the Air Force at around the same time, so the common bonds became strong and lasted until George's untimely death. We both met socially many times, in different locales, the last time being in Detroit in the early 1980s, but that will be related later.

George's appearance with me on *Magazine* that morning opened a new chapter in his life the next day. He was always refreshingly outspoken, but that morning, he was especially so, referring to Las Vegas audiences as "mostly hicks from Iowa", in somewhat of a small rant. I felt badly that perhaps he might have had a bad morning, but didn't think much of it until the next morning when I read George had been fired from The Frontier because of his remarks on my show. I was devastated, because he'd been genuinely friendly to me during our first in-person meeting, as well as kindly plugging and imitating my weathercasts in his shows at The Frontier. During his appearance the preceding morning, he touched on how life in a commune might be. A newspaper interview with him the day he was fired claimed George and his family decided they were going to move to British Columbia to live in a commune. He later told me that firing actually was okay with him, but I still felt badly its reason for happening was because of his appearance on my show.

Peter Nero: Peter is, in my opinion, and the opinion of many others, the greatest pianist and conductor of modern times. His genius was noticed when he entered Juilliard on a scholarship at age fourteen, with seven years of other distinguished piano studies, and prodigious talent, already in his quiver. The first time I was with Peter was when he agreed to be a guest on *Magazine*. He was headlining at The Tropicana at that time. He said he would enjoy being a guest on the show because he always watched my weathercasts when he was playing Vegas. Having been a major fan of Peter's unmatched talents since I did some occasional disc jockeying, in addition to my television work, in Idaho Falls in the early 1960s when his first RCA albums were released, I was almost shaking because I'd finally get to meet him face-to-face. His and my relationship, for whatever blessed reason, immediately "clicked" and has never "un-clicked" to this day, sharing a lot of personal stories about "real life" throughout. He told me, during several social times together, about issues he had with contractors building a house he had helped design for him and his family on Long Island, but on the upside, how proud he was of his children, Beverly and Jedd, as well as his parents and their humble backgrounds. During my D.C. television days, Peter told me he'd be doing a concert at The Kennedy Center. He invited me to be his guest, seated next to his mother and father. It was a very special night, to say the least. During my Detroit television years, from 1978 to 1983, Peter told me he was bringing his orchestra, The Philly Pops, to East Lansing, Michigan, and said I'd be welcome to be his guest. I went. The concert included some of my favorite Gershwin compositions (Peter's favorite composer, too). The orchestra was magnificent, along of course, with Peter's prolific piano. When I went back to meet him in his dressing room, I entered the door and he was literally shaking. "They were so tight", he said, meaning the excellence of the orchestra. I told him I'd never heard those pieces (*Rhapsody In Blue* and *An American In Paris*) played so superbly. He said, "Yeah, that's why I'm shaking. They were great." Peter also has a great sense of humor. He often said he always played the music from *Hair* on a Steinway because you can't get hair out of a

*Bald*win." To have the privilege to still keep in touch with him privately is another major honor with which I've been blessed.

Louis Nye: Lou's friendship and his kindnesses to me were so complete and varied, it could almost make another chapter or book (see photos section), but I'll do my best to impart how special he was in as succinct a manner as possible, including some Lou stories I think you'll enjoy, especially if a fan of that brilliant actor/comedian.

I, as millions of others, first saw Lou (as he preferred being called by friends, as well as his wonderful wife, Anita) on *The Steve Allen Show* when he portrayed one of the "men in the street" whose character's name was Gordon Hathaway, the Man from Manhattan. The other "men" on the "Man In the Street" segment were Don Knotts, Bill Dana and Tom Poston, the latter of whom would also become a very, very close lifelong friend (previously referenced in the Prologue and my times with Tom also to be amplified later, including in the photos section). Each week, Lou's opening line to Steve on the segment was the classic, "Hi-ho, Steverino!" *Lou told me the first time he ever worked with Sammy Davis, Jr., he walked into the studio and said, jokingly, of course, "Hi-ho, Negro!" He said Sammy fell on the floor laughing. I'm proud and honored to say Sammy also became a very close friend and champion for me from 1971 until his death, the most memorable times about which will be described later.*

I first met Lou when he was performing at The Tropicana, alternating stage time with Marlene Dietrich. His comedy albums were beyond classics and we discussed them and his brilliant ideas for the subjects of the albums when he was a guest on *Magazine.* We kept in touch, and visited often at his and Anita's home on Corsica Drive in Pacific Palisades, California, from 1968 until his passing, the memorial service to which I was invited, which took place in the backyard of his home, December 1, 2005. Among the other invited guests were Karl Malden, composer/conductor John Williams, Carl Reiner, Peter and Laurie Marshall, Don Knotts, Tom Poston, Suzanne Pleshette, Jayne Meadows, Henry Gibson, Dom and Carol DeLuise and others (see photos section). Lou's and Anita's house was just two blocks from Dom and Carol DeLuise's house. More about my blessed friendship with them, and some of the other invited guests, later.)

During two of the three times I lived in L.A., Lou used to invite me to the house at least every two weeks to just talk about "the business" and we'd always go to Zucky's, a delicatessen on Santa Monica Boulevard, for lunch. Lou would always preface that delicatessen visit with "Do you want to go to Zucky's for soup today?", followed by that infectious grin, because he knew anyplace he chose would be fine with me. The staff at Zucky's did everything but genuflect every time Lou and I entered, and while we were there. He always picked up the tab, for which I was appreciative.

One of the more memorable times with him was when he asked me to drive him to the downtown L.A. Brooks Brothers store. He had an older Benz, but in very good condition, and told me he hated driving in thick traffic, thus asked me if I would mind being his driver that day. I happily told him I'd be glad to, thus our adventure to Brooks Brothers commenced. After we arrived, we got on the elevator. The chief salesperson must have known Lou was coming, because when the door opened, that very tall and distinguished older man literally bowed when Lou and I exited the elevator. He then, I swear, got on his knees, again bowing. I'm laughing out loud as I write this, because it was a classic sight as Lou reacted "in kind", with his left hand beckoning the salesperson to rise, then both smiling and laughing appreciatively. I just smiled. Still am.

Another "fun" time (they were always fun with him, and Anita, too, when she would be there) was when the three of us spent literally five hours in the sun porch adjacent to their living room, just laughing and reminiscing even more than usual about the business and all the truly iconic friends we were blessed to have, Lou among them, of course, but truly too humble to trumpet himself as an icon. He told me his father was a grocery store owner in Hartford, Connecticut. Their real family name was Nizer, which Carl Reiner brought up at Lou's memorial service. Lou changed it to Nye when he got into show business, laughingly saying it was not only easier to pronounce, but would also fit better on a marquee. Lou also told me he started his show business career as a radio announcer on a Hartford station. Ironically, it was the same station on which Tony Randall started announcing just after Tony got out of the service in

1945. I always wondered if Tony and Lou ever compared notes about that, since they both worked together in later years, more than once, in popular feature films.

On the grand piano in their living room, on an appropriate stand to hold it upright, was a platinum record, honoring Anita for writing the lyrics to *A Sunday Kind Of Love*. That song, for those who remember, was, and is, an all-time classic standard. Anita was a prolific lyricist, deeply into the professional music industry. Her depth in the industry was one of the reasons John Williams attended Lou's memorial service, previously referenced.

During one of the taping days for my *Television: The First 50 Years* documentary, Lou chased me around his backyard, pausing to pick lemons from the trees there, then playfully throwing them at me, with him pretending to be a monster, growling much of the time, then afterward both of us almost collapsing in laughter. I still have that unedited tape.

Lou also used to call our house occasionally. Many times, my wife Ellen would answer the phone and talk to him at great length about their mutual love for Shih-Tzus. He would sometimes bark like a dog (one of his multiple brilliant "shticks") during the conversations with both her and me. Watching him on re-runs of feature films and television shows is difficult to do, especially remembering all the private times and his genuine friendship and caring.

When I walked up the driveway to go into the house for Lou's backyard memorial service, Lou's son, Peter, met me halfway down the driveway. I'm not embarrassed to tell you I broke into almost uncontrollable tears when I saw him. When Peter saw that, approaching me, he hugged me and said some comforting words as I repeated how sorry I was his Dad was gone. Peter was (and is) a wonderful son, of whom Lou and Anita always spoke with pride. He's a cartoonist, married to a lovely Oriental lady who, of course, was also there that sad day. Peter and his wife reside in San Francisco.

Dom and Carol DeLuise: Two of the most wonderful, loveable people anyone could ever hope to know. We discovered during our first meeting in January, 2002, we were also fellow Leos, with their birthdays each falling within two days of mine. I don't really know why those sorts of things matter to me, but, hey, we all have our idiosyncrasies, eh?

That first meeting was in early 2002 when Dom and Carol came to visit their longtime friend, Dick Van Patten, at the L.A.-area's Cerritos Center for the Performing Arts Theater where Dick, Frank Gorshin, several others and I were acting in a national tour of *The Sunshine Boys* (see photos section). I was also double-understudying Dick and Frank, the latter a Pittsburgh grade school mate of mine (three years older than I, although we used to walk together to school) before we moved to New York, and Dick, as earlier mentioned, a friend since my teenage acting years in New York when his mother, Jo, was one of my agents.

Dom, Carol and I immediately clicked (see photos section). They were both filled with life and energy that would light the sky. We compared notes about our respective teenage years in New York (although Carol was still a New Jersey girl in the 1950s). The next time we met was at Lou's memorial services, December 1, 2005. I was saddened to see Dom walking with a cane. I sat down next to him and Carol to recall our previous time together and they both kindly remembered. I also mentioned to Dom I had a potential Italian restaurant-owner client in The Twin Cities to whom I mentioned Dom would be a great spokesperson as well as chef when he was available to cook on site. Dom sweetly said, "Oh, I love food." I told him I thought that was the case, although I noticed he'd lost a lot of weight in the three years since I'd last been with him and Carol. Unfortunately, the restaurant owner in The Twin Cities (Saint Paul, specifically) decided to not have Dom be his spokesperson, which, in my opinion, wasn't a very smart decision. We began to exchange Christmas cards from 2002, and still do, although Carol sadly became a widow in 2009. We all lost when Dom passed.

John Williams: When I arrived at Lou's memorial service, I saw those gathered to honor him personified a "Who's Who" of show business giants, except for yours truly. One of them was composer/conductor John Williams (*Superman, E.T., Star Wars, Harry Potter, Indiana Jones, The NBC Nightly News Theme*, ad infinitum). After I'd sampled some hors d'oeuvres and had exchanged re-acquaintances

with Tom Poston, Karl Malden and Carl Reiner, and making new
acquaintances with Henry Gibson, Peter and Laurie Marshall and
Jayne Meadows, I spotted this very tall, distinguished-looking man
just outside the house in the backyard where the services would take
place. I thought he was John Williams, but wasn't sure. Regardless,
I went up to him and asked if he was whom I thought he was. He
said, "Yes", and gently smiled. I said, "Mr. Williams, thank you for
everything you've done for this world." His response was, "Well,
thank *you* for just saying hello." There are no sufficient words to
follow his response. After composing myself (no pun intended) I
mentioned a television "special" I wanted to create for him and the
then still alive composer, John Barry, whom I'd met years earlier while
interviewing him for *Dances With Wolves*. I described the project
to Mr. Williams. He said he liked it and said, "We'll see." Then a
wonderful guest at the services took the photo of Mr. Williams and
me you'll see in the photos section. The special I conceived for them
was to be entitled "What were you thinking, John?" regarding what
each was thinking when they composed such iconic movie theme
music, each asking the other in front of a live audience at a prominent
orchestral venue. Sadly, I couldn't find sponsors, but Mr. Williams
accepted a couple calls I made in regard to the project for a couple
years hence.

Karl Malden: In late 1953, during my teenage acting years in New
York, I was urged to see if an agent named Charles Feldman might
take me under his wing to get better parts. Mr. Feldman had offices in
one of the smaller buildings in Rockefeller Center and was the agent
for Burt Lancaster, Howard Hawks, John Wayne, George Stevens,
Claudette Colbert, Irene Dunne, Charles Boyer, Lauren Bacall, Kirk
Douglas, Ava Gardner, Tyrone Power and . . . Karl Malden. I meekly
walked into the reception area of Mr. Feldman's dark mahogany
paneled office and told the receptionist I had an appointment with
Mr. Feldman. After not too long a wait, I was told to enter his office.
It was stereotypically everything a mega-mogul's office should be,
although almost too intimidating, as the dark walls surrounded
several lighted table lamps in the office. Bright it wasn't. He kindly
welcomed me, gave me the once over, visually, had me leave my

pathetic head shot and resume and told me if he felt I would be right for anything he'd give me a call. Not long after, thanks to him, I was given a token background extra part in a scene right next to Marilyn Monroe in *The Seven Year Itch*, which Mr. Feldman produced. He was also a lawyer. That was definitely a "power" office.

When I went to the elevator to go downstairs and the elevator door opened, who was standing there but Karl Malden, but he didn't get off, which I expected he would. Instead, he rode down to the ground floor with me, and asked where I'd been. I told him it was to Mr. Feldman's office. He said, "Charlie's a good agent. *you* look like a good kid, and I hope he helps you. I'll suggest that to him." He smiled down at me, patted me on the shoulder when I got off the elevator, we both walked out and that was the last time I saw him until Louis Nye's memorial service.

When I saw him there, he was seated against one of the walls of Lou and Anita's dining room. He was hunched over his cane. I said "Hello" and reminded him he'd been very nice to me that day in the elevator and how I'd never forgotten it and how it may have resulted in my getting that bit in *The Seven Year Itch*. He smiled, and said, "I'm glad." I then told him I wished he was still acting in films and on television. He smiled and said, "I had my time". He then told me he was 92 years old. We shook hands and that was that. Mr. Malden passed away four years later.

Carl Reiner: After composing myself after that tearful meeting with Peter Nye on Lou and Anita's driveway, one of those already gathered in the dining room prior to the outdoor service was Carl Reiner. Carl had also visited Dick Van Patten and all of us in the cast before and after one of *The Sunshine Boys* performances at the L.A.-area's Cerritos Center for the Performing Arts Theater in early 2002, earlier referenced regarding Dom and Carol DeLuise's visit there, too. I reminded Carl of his visit and also our having acted on the same stage, one night apart, during his *Your Show Of Shows* and my *Mister Peepers* telecasts at the RKO Center Theater in the early 1950s. He remembered we'd discussed that at Cerritos. Carl then looked at the top of my head, which had a small bandage covering some skin cancer surgery, saying, "Let's compare heads!" He then showed me scars he'd had from skin cancer removal on the top of his head, asking, "I wonder who has the biggest scars?" We had a good laugh and he then said, "You're the best dressed man here." I wanted to be respectfully attired for the somber occasion, so apparently it was noticed (see photos section). I thanked him. Carl presided over the ceremony. *One who also visited us at Cerritos was Valerie Perrine, best known to global audiences for portraying the character Lex Luthor's girlfriend in* Superman, *Luthor portrayed by Gene Hackman, in case you might not have remembered. I remembered Valerie had been a showgirl at The Stardust in Las Vegas during the years I was on television there, and I decided to ask if she remembered me. She paused for a second, then her eyes got as big as saucers, saying, "Yes!", loudly enough anyone in the large backstage area could hear and with a giant smile on her face. It was very gratifying and I'm glad I asked, telling her I appreciated her remembering. She asked, "How could anyone forget?" I again felt validated by her enthusiastic and kind recognition, with insecurities always lurking much of my life. No pity party here, just a fact.*

Peter and Laurie Marshall: Also at Lou's memorial service were Peter Marshall, of *Hollywood Squares* hosting fame, and his wife Laurie. We also "clicked" and I'm blessed Peter and Laurie have become wonderful friends ever since. The first time I visited Peter and Laurie at their Encino home, Peter showed me a very special letter he'd received from John Wayne, framed, and hanging on one of the kitchen walls. To reveal its contents would be inappropriate, but let's just say what Mr. Wayne wrote was "powerful" and definitely worth Peter's having saved it. Peter built and designed his wonderful home. One of his sons-in-law is a *60 Minutes* producer and Peter's late sister was film actress Joanne Dru. Peter, now aged 89, is still professionally singing and even dancing, having also starred on Broadway more than once during his great career. Peter, Laurie and I had a delightful private post-birthday lunch together at an Encino restaurant in May this year (2015) to celebrate both their April birthdays, belatedly. Once again, I've been very blessed.

Gregory Peck and Eva Marie Saint: In May, 1968, during my weekend DJ and interviews tenure at KLAV radio, previously

referenced, I received a call from a publicist for a film producer/
director named Robert Mulligan. He told me if I was available, I
would be the only one in Las Vegas to interview Gregory Peck and
Eva Marie Saint (for radio) while they were shooting a film called
The Stalking Moon on The Spring Mountain Ranch, about 25 miles
west of Las Vegas. I drove to the site where the interviews would take
place and was introduced to perhaps the classiest of all actors and
genuine gentlemen, Gregory Peck. He bade me a cordial and warm
greeting, then said, "Let's go over here into the bullrushes" to do the
interview. We did so, near his trailer, and then the publicist shot the
classic signed photo you'll see in the photos section, signed by Greg
to me about a month after the shoot, calling me his "podner". It and
my picture with President Truman are my two most cherished. One
can't do much better than that. More about Mr. Peck's kindness to me,
working together in 1974, one-on-one, later.

Then I was led to Eva Marie Saint's trailer, only about 20 feet from
where Mr. Peck and I had done his interview. She was expecting me
and gave me a friendly greeting with that great (and genuine) smile
and said she wanted to do the interview inside, thus we both climbed
up the couple steps into the little dining table area. Eva had become
the "mommy" to a large turtle she found on the desert, thus the turtle,
who was sitting on that table, became the catalyst for a lot of laughter
during the interview as though it wanted to be interviewed, too. This
is another story that makes me smile as I type this. It was a fun twenty
minutes. After the interview, she voluntarily said she'd give me her
home phone number if I needed to keep in touch. I thanked her, and
then, about a minute later, before she found a pen and some paper on
which to write that number, she changed her mind and said, "Maybe
that might not be such a good idea." She said it was nothing personal
but just might be construed by her then husband as something not
appropriate. Indeed, better to keep peace, so I never got the number.
In 1998, while producing the documentary, *Television: The First
50 Years* (previously referenced), I called the agency handling Eva
Marie's acting career and asked if she'd do another interview, this
time for television. A couple days later, the agent told me she refused,
but "fondly" remembered our time on the desert west of Las Vegas

and wished me the best luck regarding the documentary. *The Spring Mountain Ranch was purchased by the Hughes Tool Company (my former boss, Howard Hughes), in 1967, from wealthy heiress, Vera Krupp. It was later sold to Fletcher Jones, a very successful Las Vegas and Southern California Cadillac dealer, whose wife, Jan Jones, would eventually become Mayor of Las Vegas, and became a good friend to me then and later in my life. I'm blessed to say she still is.*

Dwayne Hickman: Again, amazed at how the fates placed me into "living it" with entertainment icons as friends, I got a call at Channel 13 from Dwayne Hickman after I'd quit Howard Hughes's employ at Channel 8. I had heard Dwayne had been hired by Hughes to be an entertainment and publicity executive at Mr. Hughes's Landmark Hotel (now imploded), but never expected I'd meet him, let alone have his genuine (and very caring) friendship. About what he called I can't remember but I do know we shared the respectful bemusement we'd both worked for Hughes, with him still in his employ when he called. He told me he liked my television weathercasts and regularly watched them, for which I was, and will always be, very appreciative. We talked a lot on the phone during our Las Vegas days, but never met in person until the 1980s when I was seeking to resurrect my acting career and had the luxury of some time to do so. Dwayne had then become a major programming executive with CBS-TV in Hollywood and kindly welcomed me to have some personal time with him.

Dwayne graciously treated me to lunch at Musso & Frank's (officially the Musso & Frank Grill), a Hollywood mainstay eatery since it opened in 1919, and where Dwayne and his brother Darryl used to eat even when they were youngsters growing up in the film industry. One of the celebrities eating at a nearby table was the iconic Ralph Edwards, whose *Truth or Consequences* radio program was so popular in the 1940s a town in New Mexico was named Truth or Consequences and remains so to this day. Ralph also conceived *This Is Your Life*, a great television series that brought famous people and special people from their past lives together for live reunions. He walked by Dwayne's and my table but we didn't make any attempted encounters. Mr. Edwards was very distinguished with thinning dyed red hair. I think he was already evidently well into his 80s when we saw him that day. He was a classic and seeing him evoked many warm childhood radio-listening days memories.

Among other things related to our show business and television lives, Dwayne was bemused at the fact I'd shared high school days in New York with Tuesday (Weld) and amused for the coincidence she played his character's girlfriend on *The Many Loves Of Dobie Gillis* years after I'd respectfully declined to be her date at a party when she was 11 and I was 17 (previously described).

Through the years, I'm honored to report Dwayne remained a friend, even to the point of meeting me one very early morning at his and his wife's condo when he was actually very ill with a cold. There was a document or package I needed, which he handed me in his bathrobe, even coming out the door briefly, to give it to me. Talk about a "real" person.

In later years, I had been promised an assignment to produce a television special and had told Dwayne about it, wanting him to star and be executive producer. Sadly, those who promised the special never came through and it tainted Dwayne's feelings toward me in the 1990s, for which I don't blame him, as I was promised the production was "a sure thing" and had assured him it was, believing in those who had sold me a "bill of goods". Sadly, there are a myriad of occurrences like that in that crazy business and I'm sorry it had hurt him emotionally, which was never deserved.

When we were walking down a street in Hollywood one day, Dwayne gave me the smartest advice ever, wishing I had known it in years past, i.e., "When you're established somewhere, stay there". He was referring to the precariousness of the broadcasting industry, as talent, and I wish I'd heard years before I ever made some very bad career decisions. He and his wife, Joan Roberts, were also among the truly nicest people anyone could ever have the privilege to know. The last time I spoke with them was in the late 1990s during a time Dwayne and Joan were traveling around the U.S. displaying his great paintings at art shows focused on his work. I think of them often and with gratitude.

Henny Youngman: During my Channel 8 days, I used to eat lunch occasionally at the nearest lunch counter situated in a gift shop named Mr. Sy's. It was about as basic as lunch counters can get, but good for satisfying one's hunger when nature called. I ate there at least three days a week, and who would be sitting on a lunch stool, sans his violin, but Henny Youngman. Henny was one of the funniest, most beloved and famous comedians in modern history. His one-liners, especially, "Take my wife. Please.", has been one of the most quoted classic lines ever. For whatever reason, there was always an empty stool next to his, and always to his left, thus I decided to begin sitting next to him. He was mostly very quiet and soft-spoken, but told me he recognized me from the weathercasts and enjoyed them, for which I thanked him and was flattered, because Henny almost invented standup comedy. He would always eat either a grilled cheese sandwich or a BLT, drinking either just water or a Coke. Without fail, though, he would repeat three or four of the classic one-liners from his repertoire while we were eating. What a treat. Henny usually was second on the bill at Caesars, but played all the major hotels in Las Vegas at one time or another. Our little lunch fests lasted for almost two years. A bit of trivia: Henny was born in London, England.

Russ Morgan and Freddie Martin: Often (very often) after my 11 p.m. weathercasts, I'd unwind and visit The Top Of The Dunes. It was a nightclub with a dance floor on the highest floor of the now longtime gone Dunes Hotel. The orchestras that played there alternated between Russ Morgan's and Freddie Martin's two of the most outstanding big bands of the 20th century. Both Russ and Freddie became social friends to me during all the years in Vegas and in later years, Russ's son, Jack, also became a good friend when he often played The Twin Cities after he took over The Russ Morgan Orchestra following Russ's death. Jack had watched me when he was a youngster living in Las Vegas while his Dad's orchestra was booked at The Dunes.

I idolized Freddie Martin's Orchestra when I was a kid listening to all his orchestra's hit songs on the radio in the 1940s. His pianist, Jack Fina, played the most iconic version of "Flight of the Bumble Bee" and Freddie's band singer was a kid named Merv Griffin, whose most memorable song was "Managua, Nicaragua". I sang it to Merv once on the phone, long after he'd established his huge empire, during a call to reminisce about the people we had in common. Merv seemed to love it, and howled, "Oh, my God!" then laughed, but not in a mocking vein. OMG, as they say these days: the memories.

Frank Sinatra, Jr.: As to which I alluded earlier, I had the pleasure to have Frank Sinatra, Jr.'s friendship during the four years I lived and worked on television and radio in LasVegas. Our first meeting was in his hotel room at The Frontier, where he always headlined in the lounge. Again it was to do a radio interview for KLAV. He was genuinely humble and soft-spoken. Following the interview, he told me how honored he was to have me do that interview. Honored to have me do the interview? I thanked him of course, but told him I was the one who was honored . . . and I was . . . as a lifelong devotee of anyone or anything Sinatra. Frank Jr.'s manager was named Tino Barzie. Tino had been with Frank, Sr., from almost the very beginning, during Frank's Tommy Dorsey days. Tino became a wonderful friend to me from 1967 until his passing. He told me I could always have unlimited "comps" to Frank, Jr.'s shows. One day, I was bombarded by calls from some out-of-town visiting broadcasters I'd known in previous years, asking if I could arrange any kind of show for them to see, free. I was blessed (and also felt embarrassed) to have a lot of "juice" with all the casinos and their showrooms in those days, but I knew getting a booking for 16 people with just a few hours notice would be impossible. I decided to call Tino and he "comped" all 16. I apologized for the number and he said it was no problem at all. In later years, Tino and I met in Minneapolis when he was then managing Pia Zadora (who had also gone to school at the aforementioned PCS, many years after I'd hung out with the PCS kids, previously described). We met for dinner at The Hyatt regency, where Pia was performing. He caught me up on a lot that had transpired for him during the years we hadn't seen each other. *Frank, Sr.: A longtime Las Vegas friend to me named Marjel deLauer, whose birthday we also shared, i.e., August 5th, although older than I, had a remarkably eclectic life, too. Must be an August 5th trait, or curse! We shared many friendships we didn't know we shared until close to the time of her death, including our friendship with producer Richard "Dick" Zanuck, son of Darryl F. Zanuck, who founded 20th Century Fox. Shortly after*

*Frank and Barbara Sinatra were married, Marjel told me she had been
the one who introduced Barbara to Frank, and the rest is history, as
the saying goes, except to say producer George Schlatter and I became
friends in later life. George created* Laugh-In *and* Real People *for
television. George once told me he and his wife, and Frank and Barbara
Sinatra were one another's best friends in private life. Once again, no
degrees of separation.*

Bob Newhart, a life-changer: The most significant memory related
to my Las Vegas years, and one that definitely changed my life for
the remainder of my life (mostly for the better) occurred because of
Bob Newhart being a "fan" of my weathercasts. He, as did George
Carlin, previously referenced, used to urge his Desert Inn audiences
to watch my weather show, always saying it was "truly very funny",
the latter his exact words. Bob had been a guest on *Magazine* more
than once. After one of his appearances, in mid-August, 1970, he
asked me if I could drive him back to the Desert Inn. I told him
I'd be delighted. On our way there, Bob said, verbatim, "You know,
Barry, you belong in a much bigger market. Why don't you look in
Broadcasting Magazine and see if there are any TV weather jobs out
there in a bigger market?" I thanked him for his confidence in me
and his suggestion, so the following day I looked in the most recent
issue of *Broadcasting* and, as the fates would have it, there was an ad
that read, "Upper Midwest major market television station wants
personality weatherman. Send resume and tape to Box (number),
c/o *Broadcasting.*" Always hating to hear the word, "No", I decided
to muster enough courage to try for a bigger market per Bob's
suggestion, and sent the two wildest tapes I could find. It featured
me on my weather set throwing a pie in the face of our sportscaster,
G.L. Vitto, with Jimmy "The Greek" Snyder, officiating regarding a bet
G.L. and I had about the origin of Daylight Saving Time. "The Greek"
was a great friend, too, to both G.L. and me. I also sent a second tape
with the Redd Foxx and Juliet Prowse fun appearances (previously
referenced). I purposely sent those most outrageous tapes thinking if
they like what they see, they'll actually consider me.

A week later, I received a call from a fellow named Ralph Dolan,
telling me he was with KSTP-TV in The Twin Cities, saying my

tapes "blew everyone away" and they wanted to fly me back for an interview. Now I knew the identity of the "Upper Midwest major market station" and it's whereabouts. I called Bob Newhart and told him where the station was. He said, "Oh, that's a great market and will be a great boost to your career, if they hire you." KSTP-TV booked me on a flight in late August that would only have me take two of my vacation days from Channel 13, with no one aware why I was taking only two days.

KSTP-TV paid all my expenses. I arrived on a very rainy, gloomy Thursday evening, displaying the antithesis of Las Vegas weather, but reminding me I was back close to my original home in the East where that kind of weather was normal. I met with Ralph Dolan the next morning and he told me my starting salary would be $17,000 a year. He also promised I'd make a lot more and they wanted me to be there for a very long time. With my perpetual insecurities present, I couldn't believe some organization in a larger market really wanted me "permanently" (even though I'd been born in Pittsburgh and lived my teenage years in New York City). In addition, I was making $12,000 a year in Las Vegas, which was the 120th market in those days, and Minneapolis-Saint Paul was the 12th largest market in the U.S., then. Even though the income disparity made me question whether taking the job was the right thing to do, I saw the quality of the operation and the caliber of people working there when Ralph took me on a tour of the gigantic and quality facility, and thought it was . . . and it really was . . . a first-class place. Thus, without a contract, which they didn't sign in those days, I said, "Yes", and they told me they'd pay my move to The Twin Cities for me to arrive in late November, i.e., three months hence.

CHAPTER THIRTEEN

Twin Cities, L.A., South Africa

When you can afford a steak dinner, everybody wants to buy you one. When you can't afford it, no one wants to.—Traditional, anonymous and sad

In my opinion, the choices one makes in life always make one wonder, "What if . . . ?" What follows is an example of what might make you wonder, too, especially about being "honorable":

When I returned to Las Vegas from the Twin Cities, I gave my notice to Channel 13, but asked if I could stay until mid-November. Alan Abner said, "Yes" and asked me if I'd reconsider the decision to leave. It was wonderful of him to ask, but I told him if I had this opportunity to spread my wings again, I think fate was telling me to do so. He understood and wished me luck. We, of course, saw each other, almost daily until the November day I left for the Twin Cities, privately scared to death of possible career failure there, even though I had the blessing of Bob Newhart's and KSTP-TV's confidence in me.

About a week after I returned to Las Vegas, I received a phone call at Channel 13 from a man named Steve Silverberg. He said he was an agent based in Beverly Hills and had been told by Nancy Sinatra and Dionne Warwick's husband I belonged in the L.A. market. I told him that was more than flattering, and then told him about my hire at KSTP-TV in The Twin Cities. He then said, "They don't sign contracts there." He was correct. He then said, "If I drive to Vegas, will you give me some demo tapes I can use to pitch you to stations here in L.A.?" I told him I thought it would be futile, but I appreciated his offer, and thought to myself, "What the heck. I'll never get hired in L.A. anyway.", thus told him it would be fine to meet him and give him some tapes to show. (Videotapes were, in those days, about three inches wide and on reel-to-reel spools).

About three or four days later, in early September, I met Steve in the lobby of Caesars Palace and gave him a paper shopping bag filled with five or six tapes. He thanked me (we didn't even have a glass of water together) and that was the last I ever saw him, or even heard from him.

However, in November, three days before I was to leave Las Vegas to move to the Twin Cities, I had just finished anchoring the morning newscast on Channel 13 when a phone rang in the news office. It was 7:35 a.m. I answered and the man at the other end of the line asked to whom he was speaking. I told him my name and he said, verbatim, "You're hired!" I asked, "Who are you and for what am I hired?" He said, "My name is Bill Fyffe and I'm news director at KTLA-TV, Channel 5, in Los Angeles and we want you to be our new weatherman. You'll be working with a new up and coming young news anchor named Tom Snyder and we'll start you at $40,000 a year." I thanked Mr. Fyffe, then told him the moving van was literally in my driveway, loading up to get everything to The Twin Cities because I'd already agreed to work there. He said, again verbatim, and echoing the agent, Steve Silverberg's, comment, "They don't sign contracts there, so we could fix it." I thanked him again, but then told him, "In good conscience I could never look in the mirror if I told KSTP-TV I wasn't coming", which would have not honored my commitment to begin work. Fyffe said, again verbatim, "Well, if you feel you have a moral obligation, go ahead and we'll catch up sometime in the future." My heart sank as I hung up the phone, but being "honorable" was probably the right thing to do.

Punch (in the face) line: I arrived at KSTP-TV a week later. I was made booth announcer until the station could find the remainder of the new news team of which I would be a part as weathercaster. I was still booth announcing in February, 1971, and getting impatient while waiting for our new news team to be selected (the news and sports anchors) so I decided to call Fyffe and ask if that KTLA-TV position was still open. Fyffe told me my timing to call him was perfect, as that was his last day at KTLA-TV, because he was hired as news director for KABC-TV, ABC's flagship station on the west coast. He said there weren't any weather openings at either station but wished me good luck saying we'd catch up in the future. The future for Fyffe was his becoming Vice President of ABC-TV's News Division, and based in New York, of course.

When I was visiting him in New York during my D.C. television days, vignettes of which will be described later, Bill told me if I'd hopped aboard his coattails at KTLA-TV, he would have kept me under his wing and made me *Good Morning, America's* first weatherman. Live and learn, but I was still glad I honored my commitment to KSTP-TV in 1970. *"Honorable" was the word Stanley S. Hubbard used when I told him that story at a KSTP-TV Pioneers Summer Party in 2013. As previously noted, "S.S." was one of the sons of Stanley E. Hubbard I, who founded Hubbard Broadcasting, Inc. (HBI) and, as I write this, HBI just provided distribution for The 2015 Miss USA Pageant to air on one of the Hubbard properties, The REELZ Channel, following Donald Trump's loss of an outlet for it because of controversial remarks Trump made during his 2016 presidential campaign bid. REELZ is under the leadership of Albuquerque-based Stanley E. Hubbard II, one of two of S.S. Hubbard's sons. The other son, Rob, heads the television division of Hubbard Broadcasting and S.S's daughter, Ginny, heads the radio division.*

During the booth announcing months, Mr. Hubbard (S.S.) called me in to his office and asked, "What about having your famous friends in Las Vegas do some promos for you?" I made some calls and, God bless them, they, without charge, did the promos for my pending and subsequent on-air work at KSTP-TV. KSTP-TV photographer Levi "Skip" Nelson, his wife Grace and I went to Las Vegas for the three-day "shoot". Among those who agreed were Jimmy Durante, Woody Allen and Sammy Davis, Jr., all of whom can be seen now when one Googles my name. I wrote the copy for each of them in the style I knew to be their trademarks (including a later one for Bob Hope, the shoot for which will be later described). Jimmy, God bless him, just before one of the shoots, asked Skip, "He's in the picture, isn't he?" Jimmy wanted to make sure I was in the shot, which started as a solo on Jimmy, then with the camera pulling back to include me. The lines I wrote for Jimmy were, *"I like Barry ZeVan, the Weatherman, because he's a real meat-headologist".* I then say, *"Jimmy, that's meteorologist."* Jimmy then says, *"That's what I said.",* in his typical mock-offended style. The other bit I wrote for Jimmy to say was, *"I like Barry ZeVan, the Weatherman, because he has a real nose for weather,* (then Jimmy grabs my nose and holds on through the end of the spot), *and who would know, better than me?"* then looks at the camera with that great hot-cha-cha smile, still holding my nose. (see photos section)

Since Woody had not too many years earlier hosted a great television series for young people with the name of *Hot Dog* (showing how everyday things or food items were manufactured), I wrote the following for him, and which he said: *"I think watching Barry ZeVan, The Weatherman, is better than eating a hot dog . . . a hot dog . . . a frankfurter."* (See photos section)

Sammy, who I had the blessing to get know in years past, was wonderful to me during our many private and public times together (more about which later) so for this shoot, he amplified what I had written, and it's a classic, featured on Comedy Central's *Daily Show* feature about my career which aired in the early 2000s and can also be seen on Google. He said, with a tight solo shot on Sammy, *"Ladies and gentlemen, having traveled around the world many times, I can say this honestly: I like Barry ZeVan, The Weatherman, because* (long pause and scratching his head, then the camera pulls back and I come into frame with Sammy, just looking jokingly anticipatory for what he might say) *. . . well, stay with me. I'll think of something"*, then grimaces to the camera, as do I (see photos section).

What an honor, again, to have had people of that caliber like me enough to try to help advance my career. Whenever I see any of them on television film re-runs, the memories are never-ending regarding how kind they were to me, to say the least.

The new KSTP-TV newscast finally debuted July 19, 1971, as *The World Today.* My co-anchors were news anchor, Ted O'Brien, a Twin Cities native and sports anchor, Tom Ryther, originally from St. Louis. Two months prior to our debut, Ted, Tom and I met for the very first time to have a soda (literally) at a drugstore across the street from KSTP-TV. Ted said, verbatim, "At this moment, we're the only three who believe in each other." Ted was very articulate, as was Tom, and with different personalities, but each with good track records in the broadcast industry. Another punch line, but not in the face: The drugstore in which we met was named Schneider Drugs and owned by a man named Tom SenGupta. Tom has remained a friend to all of us to this day, and in case Tom's last name may be familiar, one his daughters, Stephanie SenGupta, was an executive producer of all the *Law & Order* television series, and now in the same capacity for the newest version of *Hawaii Five-O* and other series, too. I always wanted to meet Stephanie, but never have. Brilliant lady, who her mother Janis told me recently, can bat out a script in two days.

I, especially, was the subject of ridicule and derision in the print media for the first few weeks of our new newscast because of the unorthodox and mostly uninhibited manner in which I delivered the weathercasts, but which had brought me the highest ratings everywhere else I'd worked. Mr. Hubbard, Sr., told me to not pay attention to the critics. He said the Hubbards believed in me and that's all that counted. He was correct, broadcast giant and pioneer he was.

Even though O'Brien, Ryther and I seemed to be popular during appearances at The 1971 Minnesota State Fair, the first three ratings books went down, down, down. The Hubbards, brilliant as they were, and via the continued advice of Frank Magid, their consultant, stuck with us and told us (O'Brien, Ryther and me) things would change for the better. Change they did. Our ratings began increasing and never stopped during the remainder of my time at KSTP-TV. In the July, 1974, Nielsen ratings book, Ryther's and my half of the newscast had a 51 percent share of the audience, still a United States record for a local news team. Those record-breaking ratings were documented in the Minneapolis *Star Tribune* that month. The record still holds, 41 years later.

Because I'd hosted a weekly television ski program in Las Vegas, the station felt it was a natural for me to host an already-established ski program on KSTP-TV. It was called *The Ski Scene*. The program's host was Johnny Morris, a class act who I also succeeded doing the weather at KS. When I came aboard to succeed Johnny, the Hubbards moved him and his family to Albuquerque for Johnny to begin doing the weather there on the Hubbard station KOB-TV. Johnny eventually moved on to anchor news there and then anchor at another station in Albuquerque. He and I still see each other at Hubbard summer parties and occasionally at monthly breakfasts for KS retirees during the summer months, when Johnny spends summers here in Minnesota.

The Ski Scene was blessed to be successful enough to allow KS to get permission from NBC to delay airing, for one half hour, the then very popular *Midnight Special With Wolfman Jack*. Those Friday night airings were one of three airings of each individual show, taped earlier in the week, and followed *The Tonight Show Starring Johnny Carson*. Sometimes I'd think of Johnny's and my one encounter, previously referenced, as well as my friend Joe Bleeden, also previously referenced, and wonder what Johnny might think of my following his lead-in. Truly, in retrospect, some of us learn that sort of thinking becomes minutiae and not worth it.

Among those I picked up at their hotels and drove to the studio to be interviewed on *The Ski Scene*, were the world's greatest skiers, all of whom became close friends (Billy Kidd and Suzy Chaffee almost like family, to be later described) who included Billy, Suzy, Stein Eriksen, Roger Staub, Wayne Wong, Rudi Wyrsch, Pepi Stiegler, Eddie Ferguson, Scott Brooksbank and many others. Also interviewed one time was Michael Landon, regarding his love for winter sports in general and Chet Huntley, who was not only my guest three times on the show, but who also became a social friend (see photos section). On one of the shows, Chet told me he got into the news business when he discovered he had "a modest flair for writing" and landed a job as a newspaper reporter at *The Salt Lake City Tribune*. He also told me his father was "a railroad man". Chet said he spent many summers in his youth riding in either the engine or caboose criss-crossing his native Montana. Chet described his birthplace, Cardwell, as some place no one could ever find. I drove past the Interstate exit to Cardwell in later years. Should have turned off to see it, and wish I had. Maybe someday, as I hope they have a monument in Cardwell, honoring Chet, truly one of the giants in television news history. He also told me he didn't miss being in television news because all the news was coming in such "big chunks" and he'd be overwhelmed by it. I don't know what he'd think of today's constant avalanche of news. After Chet's death, Tippi, his widow, with whom I'd visited at her and Chet's condo at Big Sky, sent me Chet's biography entitled *The Generous Years*, inscribing it, "To Barry, Chet's friend. Tippi Huntley." En toto, I produced and hosted 500 half-hour *Ski Scene* telecasts in the Twin Cities, D.C. and Detroit between 1970 and 1986. Those blessings were incessant.

One of those blessings involved my frequent *Ski Scene* guest who was the Director of Thunder Bay, Ontario, Tourism. His name was Paul Drombolis. I skied Thunder Bay's hills almost every winter during those KS years. Paul said the ski tourism traffic to Thunder Bay during those *Ski Scene* years, tracked to viewers of *The Ski Scene* was so dramatic, it resulted in awarding and presenting me my official Thunder Bay Honorary Citizen document, live on television in D.C., January 20, 1975, three months after I'd left the Twin Cities to begin my D.C. air work.

I was told I was only one of twelve individuals to be designated an Honorary Citizen of Thunder Bay, one of them being Britain's Prince Philip, Queen Elizabeth's husband, the Duke of Edinburgh (please see photos section). I have no illusions I don't belong in that rarified company, but very gratefully accepted the honor. Paul remained a friend until his passing in 2010 and his wife, Helen, remains a friend who Ellen and I often visit in Thunder Bay. Helen's a native of Wales and former head of nursing at Thunder Bay's McKellar Hospital, after having been a Canadian Army nurse just after World War Two and where she and Paul met, i.e., in the Canadian Army.

S.S. Hubbard treated me like family. Frequent Saturday morning and afternoon rides on his St. Croix River yacht, The Hub, were de rigeur. I felt very spoiled, and I was, but gratefully. The yacht parked next to Stan's was named the "Curt C" and it's owner Curt Carlson, whose Carlson Companies included (and still do) Radisson Hotels, Regent Seven Seas Cruise Lines, TGIFridays Restaurants, Country Inns and Suites, Country Kitchen restaurants and more, would also be there almost every Saturday morning to banter back and forth with S.S., Stan E. II, Rob, Ginny and even me. In later years, Curt and I would occasionally keep in touch. He even sent me a very heartfelt and kind letter concerned about my health when he'd heard I'd had a health scare while living in Detroit long after I'd left KS.

Curt's daughter, Marilyn, who became Carlson Companies Chair, as also remained a friend and has tried to help people I've recommended might be business assets to Carlson Companies. One of those especially sticks in my mind. His name is Vika Khumalo, now South Africa's Ambassador to Turkey and one of the most outstanding human beings I've ever had the pleasure and honor to call a close friend. I recommended Marilyn meet Vika after he served well at The South African Consulate in Chicago. Marilyn met with him and then had him meet with others in the Carlson organization, but to no avail. Sometimes that great saying, "When God closes a window, he opens a door." comes to mind. Proof of that is Vika's doing very well in Turkey, following his long assignment as South African Consul General at the South African Consulate in Beijing, China. I'm happy to state we keep in touch frequently. Vika also has a wonderful wife and two great children, the latter of whom Vika told me learned to speak and write Chinese while in their pre-teens. Our last time together in the U.S. was at The Mall of America in the latter 1990s. Our last time together was in February, 2007, in Pretoria, South Africa, at a local restaurant, during the time I was a "door opening" consultant for an American bio-ID firm named Veritec, based in Minneapolis. I think the duration of Vika's and my hug may have qualified for the Guinness Book of World Records, genuinely heartfelt.

The aforementioned South African days were precipitated by my visit to the Chicago-based South African Consul General named Yusuf Omar. CG Omar and I have been friends ever since. He had great possible business suggestions for Veritec in South Africa, later serving as South Africa's CG in Sao Paulo, Brazil, and now retired in Johannesburg. The South African trip allowed Van Tran, Veritec CEO, and me to meet with and be treated royally by two prospective business owners also deeply involved with bio-ID security. We were feted in Pretoria, Johannesburg and Cape Town, as well as driven for an overnight stay in government-supervised jungle "huts" in Kruger National Park on the Zimbabwe-Mozambique border. The huts had all the amenities but listening to the roar of lions and other animals overnight was somewhat disconcerting when trying to sleep.

Regardless, Shaun Melass and Paul Engelbrecht and their families were wonderful to us. Paul, I think, still does a lot of security work in the DRC and Minsk, Belarus and Shaun has moved on to other

work. Shaun and I still keep in touch frequently, and if I could be
the housekeeper or "butler" for him and his fantastic family it would
be the best position I'd ever hold, somewhat facetiously stated, but
not really. Shaun, Erika and their three brilliant children could be
the exemplars for how individual people and families should really
be. I have never met or known more wonderful people and hope,
before the bucket appears, I'll have the pleasure of being with them
again. They still live in Pretoria, South Africa's magnificent capital
city. *Shaun is also a pilot and has visited the Oshkosh, Wisconsin, air
shows twice. Cape Town, as previously referenced as a suggestion for
everyone's "bucket list", also provided a few wonderful surprises, not the
least of which were the following: Several first-class Kosher delicatessens,
a replica of San Francisco's Fisherman's Wharf, mountains to the north
of the city, rarely seen in tourism photos because of the iconic Table
Mountain south of the city and a Nigerian Muslim chauffeur who
praised the Jews who settled in Cape Town after World War Two.*

First, the Kosher delicatessens: *Van, Paul and I landed in Cape
Town on the South African Airways flight from Johannesburg in the
mid-evening. Flying into Cape Town from the east is like flying into
L.A. from the east. The city just keeps going and going and going until
one's plane lands just a bit east of the Atlantic Ocean. Cape Town's
population numbers surprised me: It's a city with four-and-a-half
million residents. When we got to our hotel, near the beach, it was
about 9:30 that night. I was hungry and asked the concierge if there
were restaurants nearby. He said there were a lot of them just two
blocks from the hotel and pointed me in the proper direction. I got to
a large thoroughfare and staring me in the face as I walked to the left
at the corner was a gigantic Star of David brightly lighted in light blue,
positioned at the edge atop the roof of a delicatessen. I was taken aback
and walked into the restaurant, which I considered an Epicurean gold
mine, since corned beef sandwiches and matzo ball soup are among
my favorite food indulgences. I sat down, told the waitress about this
being my first time in Cape Town, or South Africa, and asked her to
tell me the "story" of why I'd find a Kosher delicatessen there. She told
me a lot of Jewish people who had escaped Europe after World War*

Two migrated to South Africa and helped the economy, not only with infusions of monetary infrastructure assistance but also providing incomes for workers via their delicatessens. Question answered, and the food was as good as I'd ever enjoyed at The Carnegie Deli in New York, Art's Delicatessen in Studio City, CA or Mort's in Minneapolis.

Fisherman's Wharf replica: *When I got back to the hotel, I was told by the concierge it had been decided by Van and Paul we'd take a brief nighttime tour of the city. One of the most popular sights is Cape Town's replica of San Francisco's Fisherman's Wharf, which we visited for a few minutes. There were yachts and sailboats by the hundreds, moored to the docks. We were told it had been conceived by an American because he felt the topographic configuration matched San Francisco's harbor area. With the confluence of the Atlantic and Indian Oceans just a few miles south of Cape Town, it made sense there would be a lot of sailors wishing to berth at that site. (On the beaches just south of Cape Town, fuzzy-faced penguins are also a common sight.)*

The unexpected mountains: *The iconic postcard photos of Cape Town always show Table Mountain in the background. That's facing south. When one faces north, there's a mountain range within very easy sight that rivals a Rocky Mountain view. That view, and that reality, is very surprising to those, such as me, who never knew what existed to the north and east of that beautiful city.*

Our Nigerian Muslim chauffeur who praised Cape Town's World War Two's Jewish settlers: On the way to a meeting east of Cape Town's airport, our driver had to take a freeway route from our beach hotel through downtown, replete with respectably tall buildings and excellent architecture. It was not too many years after 9/11 and he said, verbatim, "Look at those beautiful buildings and downtown. It's all thanks to the Jews. Thank God for the Jews." I told him I wish I could have had a tape recording of what he had just said to us, as it would have made a lot of difference to those who think all Muslims aren't universal thinkers. If I'd had what he said recorded, I would have sent a dub to the U.N. for the entire world to possibly hear.

During the KS days, after becoming established in the Twin Cities market, I was tapped to do some acting at the now defunct Friars Dinner Theater in Minneapolis, owned by Jack Dow, a prolific tennis player well into his 90s, who also owned considerable stock in Republic Airlines. Republic's largest shareholder was actress Ethel Merman. For a month, in 1973, I played the lead character, Barney Cashman, in Neil Simon's *Last Of The Red Hot Lovers*.

Jack had an actress named Chris Black coach me on the 88 pages of dialogue I had to memorize prior to my Friars acting debut. *Chris was a dancer and actress who had performed in the original Broadway production of* Sweet Charity *for Bob Fosse and Neil Simon, also in* How To Succeed In Business Without Really Trying, *also on Broadway and in the Tokyo production of* West Side Story *for Jerome Robbins. One of the other cast members left the show and Chris was asked to replace her. Chris took over the role, we started dating and a few months later got married by a Justice of the Peace on the highway in Moose, Wyoming, a few miles north of Jackson Hole, with The Grand Tetons as the backdrop. Chris and I drove to Steamboat Springs, Colorado, just in time to accept Billy Kidd and his wife's invitation to cook us our first dinner as a married couple.* Jack allowed the show to start early, at 7:30 each evening, as I was on stage in that show between weathercasts on KS. I lost 17 pounds that month, running back and forth between KSTP-TV and The Friars, but it was fun, and also good publicity for KS. I replaced actor Milt Moss of "I can't believe I ate the whole thing" television commercial fame. During the last few days of the performances, Jack Dow told me the legendary Rudy Vallee would be taking over my dressing room because Jack had booked him for some performances in another part of the theater. I had no problem with that, of course, but was bemused that Vallee and I had the same birthday, years apart, of course. I didn't get to meet Vallee, but was stunned to learn via the newspapers he had become angry toward the Friars audience during one of his performances, spouting a lot of epithets about "Hicks", stormed off the stage and never returned. I later learned what he specifically said to that audience, but in deference to decorum, and post-mortem respect to Mr. Vallee, won't print it here. We all have our "moments". (He was also another fellow Leo! Of course, so were Mussolini, Napoleon and Fidel Castro, the latter still among us as I write this, thus, perhaps, not always a Zodiacal sign of which to be always a proud member!) As I stated, we all have our "moments", and if anyone can find my wings and halo somewhere, good luck. I am happy to reiterate what my American Indian friend once said to me, i.e., "You've experienced everything in life except being arrested or serving any time in jail or prison." And that's true, thank goodness. *I gave two motivational speeches at two Minnesota prisons to prisoners who were on the verge of being released. After the speeches, at each prison, a couple of them asked me if I could help them on the "outside". I told them I didn't know how I would be of any help, but listened to them with sincerity. Those speeches were at the invitation of the Wardens at Stillwater and Sandstone. The Stillwater Warden walked me a few steps into one of the cellblocks prior to the speech. I told him I didn't want to see any more. After that, I never jaywalked or did anything remotely warranting arrest or prison. Never had previously, either, but that visit reinforced my "proper" thinking. At Sandstone, the prisoners actually gave me a more menacing impression, again reinforcing my mandate to not ever do anything warranting imprisonment.*

In March, 1974, I received a call from a fellow named Phil Nye at WXYZ-TV in Detroit, owned and operated by ABC at that time, asking me to consider joining them as their primary weatherman. I was also courted by a man named Al Primo, ironically a fellow Pittsburgher, which I think Al never knew, who was the Vice President of ABC-TV News, to take the job. Unknown to the Hubbards, I thought I'd see what they were offering, as well as the station itself. I flew there on a Saturday and was back in The Twin Cities the next evening. They said I was like Sonny Elliott, Detroit's most popular television weatherman, but "you do it better". Ironically, in later years, Sonny would replace me during my eventual Detroit television years, more about which later.

Regardless, I decided to say, "Yes". Primo and Nye flew to Minneapolis to sign the deal, along with Don Keck, another ABC-TV executive whose wife was a Minnesotan and one of the Andersen Windows family members. We signed it in Percy Ross's offices in Edina, Minnesota. I hadn't noticed there was one signature missing on the contract, thus told the Hubbards I was quitting to go to Detroit. S.S. wasn't happy about it (nor was I, in my heart) thus the next morning

S.S. told me to meet him in S.E.'s office. S.E. showed me a tape of one of Sonny Elliott's Detroit weathercasts, afterward asking me, "Do you want to compete with that?" My answer was an immediate, and gulping, "No". He said, "Good. We'll take care of that contract and I want you to be here 20 years from now to dance on my grave". Without melodrama, but true, tears are welling up in my eyes as I remember that moment and Mr. Hubbard's wonderful words. In the interim, I had received a beautiful note from Al Primo stating how happy he was I'd be joining the ABC family and then predicting a large future for me with them. The day after I received that note, the Hubbards told them because one signature was inadvertently missing from the contract I'd signed, the contract was null and void. Primo was angry and so was Nye, at the Hubbards and me. That decision affected my career in a very negative way for a very long time. In retrospect, I wondered about that decision many times. *Percy Ross was a well-known philanthropist and solid friend to me almost from the day I arrived in the Twin Cities until his passing many years later. Also, many years later, he had a nationally syndicated column called* Thanks A Million *wherein his goal was to give all his money away to those in need. He achieved that goal. Percy was also responsible for introducing me to people who would become very significant and supportive friends in my later life, including future Vice President Walter "Fritz" Mondale (please see photos section).*

In the summer of 1974, because of the blessing of those record-breaking weathercast ratings, I began getting phone calls from stations in New York, Chicago and Los Angeles, asking me to quit KS and move "upward". I said, "No" to every call because I was more than happy at KS and the Hubbards treated me even more like gold after I reversed my decision, with their valid input, to move to Detroit. However, in late August, 1974, I got a call from the ABC-TV affiliate in D.C., whose call letters at that time were WMAL-TV. They said they'd more than double the salary I was making at KS. I told them I'd consider it. They said they'd fly me to D.C. to talk on the Saturday before Labor Day that year. The reason they'd made me the offer will be described in the next chapter, including a profound "punch line" involving David Letterman and an emotional punch in the stomach, but definitely not because of David.

The trappings that came with the trip to D.C. included a Kennedy Center show and lavish dinner with the station executives, plus a limo at my disposal. The station manager, Fred Barber, had a party for me. Among the guests were Linda Ellerbee and a man to whom she was married at the time who was one of WMAL-TV's reporters. In later years, Linda was very nice to me following her gigantic successes on NBC-TV and producing great documentaries with her Lucky Duck Productions firm in New York (see photos section). The welcome from Channel 7 was very impressive, but I sensed something disingenuous about it, which, unfortunately, proved to be correct and about which will be described later.

Bottom line, no pun intended, I signed a three-year contract to do the weather and a ski show, plus produce occasional documentaries, at the aforementioned WMAL-TV, Channel 7. The station's call letters, except for the W, were the initials of its founder, a D.C.-area dentist named Martin A. Lease. The station wanted me to start immediately, but when I returned, S.S. said he wanted me to stay through the end of the November ratings book. He said he'd tell that to Channel 7, too. They reluctantly agreed, but it did give them time to craft a very strong pre-arrival ad campaign regarding my joining their news team. It was somewhat odd to know I'd soon be well known in a place where I'd lived briefly when poorer than a church mouse in 1955.

I had a few days prior to leaving KS to search for a house in D.C. I found a very nice rental in Potomac, Maryland. Nearby neighbors were New York Congressman Jack Kemp, Colorado Senator Gary Hart, ABC morning anchor Steve Bell and then network reporter, prior to *Nightline*, Ted Koppel and Selma Wynn, mother of Las Vegas casino-resort mogul, Steve Wynn, but originally from the Baltimore area. They all became either very close friends or casual social acquaintances.

In September, 2013, thanks to my successful years at KSTP-TV and the kind recognition of Stanley S. Hubbard, I was inducted into The Minnesota Broadcasting Hall of Fame. That very precious award sits next to another broadcasting award I was honored to receive in 2010, i.e., as an inductee into The Montana Society of Broadcast Legends.

CHAPTER FOURTEEN

Unique Stories, Nuggets—Part III

I cannot believe Barry ZeVan has been in broadcasting for 60 years.
Oh, what secrets he must have.—Longtime close friend Peter Jennings during his kind
radio tribute to me on KYCR-AM in the Twin Cities, celebrating my 60th year in
broadcasting, February 23, 2003.

The man from whom I rented the Potomac house was a man
named Charlie Hu. Charlie was a Taiwanese businessman who
owned all the Greyhound buses in Taiwan. The realtor who showed
me the house was a Chinese-American lady named Loretta Hum.
They were both "class acts".

The WMAL-TV "offer"—Six days after I started at Channel 7, but
before I did my first weather broadcast, I was told they didn't want
me to do the weather as I'd done it in the Twin Cities, or anywhere
else, for that matter. I asked why they hired me. They said, "We only
hired you because WCCO-TV in the Twin Cities wanted to get you
out of town and we're consulted by the same consultants who consult
WCCO-TV. We already have a 'clown' with Willard Scott at WRC-TV,
thus we don't need two in this market." It was like sticking a knife in
my heart. I did the weather there with as much personality as possible
and did have occasional celebrities and politicians appear on my set
between weatherboards as I walked by them, but it wasn't the same.
I never made more and enjoyed it less, regarding the weathercasts,
but in all fairness, experienced other life-enriching personal and
professional times I never would have even remotely approached had
I not made the move, as I'll illustrate in this chapter, and beyond. That
was one of those instances, in my opinion, wherein the saying, "It's an
ill wind that doesn't blow some good", certainly applies.

Not long after I began writing this book, in April, 2015, I was
on a broadcasting panel and one of the other panelists was a man
who had been WCCO-TV's News Director in the early 1970s. He

was News Director at WCCO-TV when I was on KS. That night, he jovially and well-meaningly stated to the audience, but looking and smiling at me, "Now you can thank me for getting you to D.C." I then, respectfully, told him it didn't turn out so well and described to him, the panel and the audience the story I've just written. I didn't want to embarrass him, but I thought everyone should know. He then very candidly said, "I asked our consultants to please find you a job somewhere else." He then said he had no idea it would turn out that way for me. He also told me, "You were killing us in the ratings, but I really had no idea they'd do that to you." I thanked him and he actually came to the house to visit a few weeks later, kindly stating, "This is overwhelming.", referring to all the years of memorabilia he saw at my house "museum", involving so many disciplines in which I'd been involved in addition to broadcasting. He kindly stated he'd be happy to see my book. He truly is a class act and a devotee of quality broadcasting that used to be the norm. He is also the author of several successful novels, but I've chosen to not mention his name in order to afford him the respect and courtesy he deserves.

David Letterman—Years after I accepted the job in D.C. and was already back on the air at another station in the Twin Cities (KARE-TV, Channel 11), two of my then on-air colleagues named Randy Shaver and Jeff Passolt, both sportscasters at the time but now news anchors (Passolt now at a different station) called me into the sports office one day while we were preparing for that evening's early newscast. They asked me if I knew David Letterman's eventual career rise to national fame might have been because of me.

I told them I didn't know that story. Here's what they told me, with David later acknowledging it after an article had been written about it in the *Minneapolis Star Tribune*: They said a former KMSP-TV, Channel 9 (Twin Cities) sports anchor named Jim Gilleland told Randy and Jeff he received a call late at night the Friday before Labor Day weekend, 1974, from a guy named David Letterman. He said Letterman told Jim he was scheduled to come in the next day to audition to become Channel 9's weatherman, but he just watched "this guy on Channel 5" (me) and "I don't want to compete with him, so tell them I'm not coming in for the audition tomorrow and will just go back to Indianapolis and begin to do standup (comedy)". David had been a weatherman, at that time, on an Indianapolis station. As Paul Harvey used to say (and who I also got to know in later years), here's "the rest of the story": David had no idea, of course, I was flying to D.C. the next day to sign the contract that would take me out of the Twin Cities. Had he known, the *Star Tribune* article (by Noel Holston) surmised David would have been a hit in the Twin Cities and I would have become "national", which was fun about which to think. In later years, I met with David once, just briefly and socially, but not for an interview, when he was still at NBC, and then later interviewed him via satellite for Channel 11, in which he said, "You were a pretty big deal there." David subsequently sent me a handwritten note thanking me for the interview, along with another nice comment or two (see photos section). We were indirectly in touch just a few months before his retirement from *Late Night*.

The move to D.C. provided life experiences and rich memories I would never have had, nor paralleled, regardless of the chicanery involved to get me to D.C., had I decided to not make the move. One of the many wonderful experiences was writing, for three years, a weekly ski column for the *Washington Star* newspaper, the only daily in competition with *The Washington Post*. In retrospect, I do owe thanks to that WCCO-TV News Director for wanting WCCO-TV's consultants to "get me a job" away from the Twin Cities, even though my career "heart" will *always* be at KSTP-TV.

Regardless, what follows are some of my most favorite, profound and unique memories of those D.C. days and the special friends, colleagues and world leaders who made them so memorable, starting with the broadcasters and concluding with the political icons:

Peter Jennings—Shortly after moving to D.C., I decided it would be good to have a party at the house. Since Channel 7 was an ABC-TV affiliate, I decided to brazenly invite every on-air network person who worked at the D.C. bureau, in addition to whomever would come from our station. They included Peter Jennings, Ted Koppel, Steve Bell, Barrie (that's how it was spelled and not Barry) Dunsmore, Don

Farmer and his wife, Chris Curle (who was on air at our station and both of whom eventually became two of CNN"s first anchors), Bill Lord (a former ABC reporter who was then ABC-TV's D.C. Bureau Chief) and others I sadly can't remember.

The first one to arrive at our house, a half-hour early, was Peter Jennings with his then wife, Anouchka (Annie). Annie had been a producer for ABC-TV. Born in Egypt, much of her family, at that time, was trapped in the hills above Beirut during those wartime days in Lebanon. Peter brought a bottle of red wine. Peter and I discovered we were both Leos, which made our eventual relationship, from then until he passed away, even a bit more psychologically bonded and character simpatico. Peter had a wonderful sense of humor. My mother, who was living at the Potomac house at that time, came down to the basement party room in a colorful one-piece dress with a multi-vegetable design. After all the guests had arrived, I was nearby when Peter walked over to my mother who was standing in a corner and playfully asked, "Mrs. ZeVan, have you ever been in another profession?" My mother either pretended she didn't think that was funny or really didn't like what Peter had said, thus went on for a few minutes telling everyone she could about how Peter had insulted her. She also had a great sense of humor, so following her mock muted tirade, she got a big smile on her face and she and Peter actually became warm acquaintances whenever she'd be present at a gathering where he also was.

Peter and I kept in touch frequently. A couple years after I left D.C., I was doing weather and a ski program in Detroit at the then CBS affiliate there, WJBK-TV. I'd heard Peter had become ABC's Bureau Chief in London. I decided to take trip to England and Scotland for the pre-Christmas holidays and visited Peter at the London Bureau. He asked what I was doing that night and I told him I had no plans. He said that was good because he had a ticket he wasn't able to use that night to attend The London Philharmonic Orchestra and Chorus's production of Handel's *Messiah* at the Royal Albert Hall. I'd been to London previously, but never to The Albert Hall. In my opinion, it's the world's best theater. I attended the performance in a kilt I'd purchased several U.K. visits earlier, along with all the Scottish regalia (bonnet, sporran, proper knee high stockings, garters, a small dagger affixed inside the right leg stocking and dress jacket, all of which I still have and proudly wear as a member of the Minnesota St. Andrew's Society, for all interested in Scottish traditions). It was just fun to do and my own personal private homage to just being there, even though I knew and know the Scots aren't exactly enamored with the Brits. A year or two later, even though Peter could have bought the French ski resort of Avoriaz, I arranged for him to be treated to free skiing there for a week as a kind of quid pro quo for his Albert Hall kindness to me. Peter told me a couple weeks later, the resort actually "comped" him for his lodging, too. I was happy they did that, as Peter was one of the kindest and most generous people one could ever know, far from pretentious and a joy with whom to be. Avoriaz was one of seven French Alps ski areas I'd filmed for my first documentary during my D.C. days at Channel 7. It was nominated for an Emmy and Dan Rather read the nomination that night in 1976 with more about Dan later.

When my mother died, I tried to reach Peter by phone at his office. He by then was anchoring *World News Tonight With Peter Jennings*. I wanted to tell him the news. His gatekeeper was rude and condescending, stating, "How do I know you know Peter?" sneering so far down her nose it would be impossible to see the end of her nose, in my opinion. I told her to forget it, then called Bill Rice, the announcer for *World News Tonight With Peter Jennings*. Bill was a dear friend for years. I told him about what happened with Peter's imperious gatekeeper and wanted to get a note to Peter about my mother's death, and also about suggesting to him he meet a lady from the Twin Cities, a friend of mine who had been a very globally-successful businessperson and possibly a "match" for Peter at that time, which was when he was again single. I asked Bill if I sent the note to him if he'd be willing to give it to Peter. Bill agreed and the return letter I received from Peter is in the photos section of this book.

The last note I received from Peter was an email only three months before he passed. I've saved all of his messages, from his and wife Kayce's vacation spot in Quebec to a literal farewell message that was difficult to choke down, to say the least.

It was an honor to be invited to Peter's memorial service at Carnegie Hall (see photos section). Among the eulogizers were the afore-mentioned Alan Alda to Peter's and my close mutual friend and colleague, Ted Koppel. One of the things Ted stated was, "Peter loved all women, but he only married four of them." It was the only light spot in Ted's eulogy, which he, a few sentences later, stated he couldn't continue giving to its pre-prepared conclusion. It was a tribute to the fact Peter meant so very much to Ted as a human being as well as colleague.

I visited Kayce (Freed) Jennings, Peter's fourth wife, only once, about three years after Peter's death. She was a former ABC-TV producer who became an independent producer whose documentaries are still part of the ABC "family" of programming. We had a cordial visit and she has kindly always responded to my emails and phone calls. During my visit, we discussed our mutual friends. I had mentioned something about Barbara Walters (who I met only once, briefly, in the lobby of The Kennedy Center in D.C.) and Kayce told me her father gave Barbara her first job.

Ted Koppel memories—Ted, his wife Grace Ann and their children . . . Andrea, Andrew (Drew), Deirdre and Tara . . . were very nearby neighbors of ours in Potomac, Maryland (see photos section). We lived on Bells Mill Road and they lived on Glen Mill Road, but they've since moved. The first time I met Ted and Grace Ann was when we threw that get-acquainted party after I arrived at Channel 7 and they kindly accepted the invitation to be two of our guests. There are many great memories of times with Ted and Grace Ann, and with Ted, solo, which I think you'll enjoy reading, to wit:

New Year's Eve Rickshaw Ride on the Koppel porch—Ted had, and still has, a great sense of humor. While having the joy to be invited to the New Year's Eve party transitioning from 1975 to 1976 at the Koppel home, Ted told Chris he'd take her for a rickshaw ride on their very long back porch. When Chris and I accompanied him to the sliding glass doors that opened onto the porch, at the far end of the porch, to our left, was, indeed, an authentic Chinese rickshaw. Ted said he bought it and brought it back from Hong Kong after leaving his post as ABC-TV's Bureau Chief there. I'm smiling as I write this because the memory of that fun time comes very vividly to mind and was certainly pleasant, unusual and unexpected. I stood there as Chris and Ted walked to the end of the porch, he instructed her how to step into the rickshaw safely, then he became the "Coolie", pulling the rickshaw, with Chris as the passenger, from one end of that porch to the other. Not many people can state it's ever been their privilege and fun honor to have Ted Koppel be their "Coolie"!

The great caviar delivery (one of my all-time favorite stories)— Prior to leaving for my second documentary filming trip to Iran, coincidentally leaving the following New Year's Eve (1976 transitioning to 1977) after Chris's rickshaw ride, Ted told me about an Iranian government store in Tehran that sold Golden Beluga caviar for fifteen U.S. dollars per tin. He said when I returned to the U.S. he'd give me 30 dollars for two tins he asked me to buy for him. Ted told me they'd pack the tins in dry ice and they would keep for 24 hours. He said if I bought them just prior to leaving for Mehrabad, Tehran's airport, to board the plane back to the U.S., they would keep from spoiling until they reached our refrigerator in Potomac, ready to give to him when he picked them up.

I did what Ted suggested. I returned from Tehran to D.C. (Potomac) in the evening. The next morning at about 8, I awakened because of the ringing of the front doorbell. I opened the door and saw Ted standing there in the pouring rain in cut-off shorts, a polo shirt and tennis shoes with no socks on. He had 30 dollars in his hand and asked, semi-smiling, "Where's my caviar?" I'm smiling as I remember that sight. I smiled, too, invited him to step out of the rain, went to the fridge and brought him the bag holding the two ample-sized tins of caviar. He thanked me and I thanked him for my education about where to buy caviar inexpensively in Tehran. I'm certain that store and those days are now non-extant, but hopefully fun for you to know of their existence.

During part of the time we were neighbors and colleagues, Ted became a house-husband for a year so Grace Ann could get her law degree. One of Grace Ann's classmates was Greta Van Susteren. I've never met Greta. Not long after I left D.C. for Detroit, the Shah's Iran fell and U.S. hostages were held at the former U.S. Embassy in Tehran for those infamous 444 days. The hostage taking was how *Nightline* was "born", with Frank Reynolds anchoring. Unfortunately, Frank became ill only a month after *Nightline* started and Ted took over as anchor. Frank died shortly thereafter. More about Frank in the Steve Bell story, which follows these "Ted stories".

Ted has kindly helped me do some networking through the years, for which I'm more than grateful and we still keep in touch. One very, very sad note was to learn of Andrew's (Drew's) passing. To say it was a shock would be an understatement. To lose a child would be among the worst of life's experiences. We expressed our condolences to Ted and Grace Ann and received a kind follow-up note from Ted (which will not appear in the photos section for obvious reasons). During my D.C. weathercasting days, I had actually given a school talk about weather to one of Drew's grade school classes, with Drew present. I think Grace Ann was the person who suggested it to Drew's teacher. Thanks to Ted and Grace Ann for their friendship and the great, very special memories and kindnesses.

Steve Bell—During those days, Steve was *Good Morning America*'s news anchor. He and his wife Joyce also lived near us in Potomac. He and Joyce attended that first party I hosted at our house and the big deal to Steve was I was the only one in that ABC-TV "mix" who had a pool table. Steve jokingly said he'd be visiting us a lot because he loved to play pool. He and Joyce did visit again so Steve could shoot some pool with me (I'm not that good at it), but not a lot! When Steve and Joyce finally got their pool table, I went there to test it and didn't rip the felt covering, nor had he at our house!

Steve and Joyce were both "PKs", preacher's kids. Joyce taught piano. It had always been my dream to learn to play at least one song on the piano. I took weekly lessons from Joyce and learned how to play *White Christmas* (not knowing until years later my "Uncle" Lou was Irving Berlin's personal song-plugger, as referenced earlier in the book.). I felt (and probably acted) like a five-year-old kid, happily going to the Bell house once a week around 10 a.m. with my piano lessons book under my arm and dutifully learning. Now, at age 78, I've not only forgotten how to read music but also how to play that hallowed song. Joyce and Steve now live in Indiana, thus the weekly trek to learn how to play again would be a bit difficult. Chris taught the Bell's daughter, Allison, how to dance.

Steve and Joyce's house parties were warm and memorable. The only time I was ever with Frank Reynolds and his wife in person was at one of Steve's and Joyce's parties. Frank was, in my opinion, one of the best prime time news anchors ever. He was from Hammond, Indiana and his son, Dean Reynolds, later became a network reporter based in Chicago, not far from Hammond. I was surprised to see Frank was exactly my height (5′ 7½″) when we were introduced and starting devouring snacks together. Frank's wife was named Henrietta, but everyone called her "Hank", thus the couple, socially, were Frank and Hank Reynolds. I was more than honored when Frank told me that night at the party he and "Hank" were big fans of my weathercasts. He also told me he thought I'd be doing the weather on GMA someday. His lips to God's ears, but that never happened. Just having that vote of confidence from him was validation enough.

Other newscasters and reporters known to national audiences and at the party that night were some who had been reporters with Steve in Vietnam. One was Dave Jane, also an ABC-TV colleague, as well as Barrie (that's the way he spelled it) Dunsmore, a Canadian (as was Peter Jennings, a fact well known to almost everyone). Roone Arledge had an affinity for hiring Canadian reporters and in my unimportant opinion, that affinity produced some first-class news people for ABC. Barrie's daughter, Lee Ann was our babysitter for over a year for Chris's daughter, Michelle. We learned from Michelle Lee Ann did cartwheels in our living room during one babysitting session and that was the end of the babysitting job. We still maintained a good friendship with the Dunsmores thereafter. I don't know if Lee Ann still has the same position, but I was told not too many years ago she was the Admissions Officer at American University (where George Clooney's father, my acquaintance, Nick, previously referenced, teaches). I've been blessed to keep in touch with Steve and Joyce. Other colleagues and friends who worked with

Steve in Vietnam included Mort Crim, with whom I got to work and know in Detroit and Sam Donaldson, who subsequently hosted and narrated three documentaries for me, more about which later. Steve recently retired as a Journalism Professor (extraordinaire) at Ball State University in Muncie, Indiana, Dave Letterman's alma mater. Once again, no degrees of separation, which continues to boggle my mind.

Frank Stallone (also one of my all-time favorite stories)—In the Ted Koppel and Steve Bell stories, above, I referred to my then wife, Chris who taught dancing to Steve Bell's daughter as well as others, in addition to her acting and voice-over work. One of the "others" was Sylvester Stallone's sister, Carla, who I got to meet, as well as Sly's mother. The most memorable meeting, to me, at least, was as follows: Chris and I were walking down an aisle in the Potomac Safeway supermarket. She said, "Oh, there's Frank Stallone." I hadn't even heard Carla's or her mother's name, so the last name Stallone was brand new to me. Chris introduced me to him. Mr. Stallone, a diminutive and soft-spoken man, said he watched me doing the weather and liked my work. Then he said, "You know, my son's in show business, too. He has a part in a movie coming out soon." I said that was wonderful, we exchanged pleasantries and that was that.

Punch line (no pun intended)—The next day, the Washington Post featured a full-page ad for *Rocky*. That dear Mr. Stallone was too humble to say Sylvester was the movie, let alone had a part in it, but it said to me, "Thank God for people like Frank Stallone." What a beautiful and humble man. I was scheduled to interview Sly one time in later years, but something arose that negated any interviews for several of us on that interview "junket". I always wanted to tell him about that day with his father in the Potomac Safeway.

Ron Canada—Ron was a reporter for Channel 7 all three years I was there. Our contracts both ended the same day. Immediately after the early evening newscast, Ron and I went to a "watering hole" downstairs beneath the station. The station had previously been a bowling alley at its location on Connecticut Avenue, NW, not far from

The National Zoo. When Ron heard my contract hadn't been renewed, he said, "Barry, you and I are among the grateful dead." I had no idea Ron had ever acted but since then he's appeared as a judge on *Law & Order, Boston Legal* and other Dick Wolf programs as well as many *Star Trek* roles (TV) and having major roles in feature films such as *The Hunted,* with the latest being *TED 2,* as a judge. Ron and I reconnected a couple years ago and am very proud to have worked with him, never forgetting his "grateful dead" comment to me.

Willard Scott—Willard was as affable in person as he was on the air. Not long after I started at Channel 7, I received a call from Willard, welcoming me to D.C., even though we were considered competitors. Thanks to his genuine welcoming, we became friends from then until now, although I haven't actually spoken to Willard since February, 2003, when he kindly did a radio show telephone conversation tribute to me for my 60th anniversary in broadcasting.

Willard's daughters and my daughters were (and are) about the same age, thus one of the times my daughters were visiting us in D.C. for two weeks one summer, Willard invited them, Chris and me to his farm in Upperville, Virginia. Willard's wife, Mary, and their amazing cook and housekeeper treated us to a wonderful day there, with Willard and me hoisting a couple of cold ones while sitting in his pool (see photos section). He told me he had lost both his parents within a month of each other. After he got *The Today Show,* he told me that call came when things were very tight financially, so his move to the network was really, he intoned, Divine Intervention. I was happy for him because he was, and is, a genuinely good and caring person.

Willard also told me a story that is known to a lot of people, but may be new to you: Willard created, and was, the original Ronald McDonald. He told me when McDonald's asked him to create the character, they offered him two choices: stock in McDonald's or $2,000. In Willard's words to me, he said he told them, "Gimme the money, baby." The $2,000 is what he got. Hindsight is definitely 20-20.

Not long after Willard and I first spoke, he and I, along with CBS meteorologist Gordon Barnes, then also local on WTOP-TV (now owned by the Twin Cities Hubbard family), decided to have as many

Monday night dinners as possible between our respective television newscasts. I can't remember who suggested it, but, regardless, it was a delight. We had those dinners at a great downtown restaurant, Duke Ziebert's. We had them as many times a month as possible, but always at least once a month.

During those halcyon days, one of my co-anchors and afterward a longtime friend, was Paul Berry. Paul was originally from Detroit and whose father would watch me a few years later during my weathercasting years in Motown. Paul owned a Rolls Royce because he enjoyed it, not for show. I was always a car aficionado, too, thus asked Paul where I could buy one, too, so we could "race" each other up and down Connecticut Avenue occasionally. I was joking, of course.

The Monday after I bought my Rolls, one of the worst cars I ever owned, mechanically, but beautiful otherwise, I called Willard and told him for our dinner that evening I'd be picking him up in a new car I'd bought. I told him to just look for a silver-colored "fancy car" and left it at that. The steering wheel was on the British side, thus when I got to WRC-TV to pick him up, he could see me as I drove up to the front door where he was waiting. Chris had bought me a blue Greek fisherman's cap, so I wore it while letting him into the back seat of the Rolls, as though I was his chauffeur. He was laughing his head off, and so was I. Willard told me years later, after he'd landed *The Today Show*, he took a cab from National Airport to WRC-TV and the cab driver said, "Oh, Mr. Scott. I once saw you and Mr. ZeVan in a Rolls Royce and you were the passenger." The cabbie was laughing and Willard told me he told the cabbie the Rolls was mine and I wasn't his chauffeur! (See photos section)

Al Roker came to D.C. from a Cleveland television station to do weather at WTTG-TV, Channel 11, the Metromedia independent station. Al looked like a fun guy and was, in those days, also drawing excellent cartoons as a sidebar to his weathercasts. I asked Willard if he thought it would be a good idea to have Al join our weather dinners, and Willard and Gordon both said it would be great. I can't remember who called Al to ask him to join us, but I think it was Willard. Thus, the following Monday, we were "The Four

Musketeeers" or "Weatherteers" or whatever you'd call us, having a mega-weather dinner at Duke's. It was the only time Al joined us for dinner. I don't know why, but it was and also the last time I ever spoke to Al. All I remember learning about him later was he is also a fellow Leo, with his birthday one day before mine, but 17 years younger.

Once in a while, Chris, my mom and I would eat at Duke's, and among the regular diners we got to know there were Mr. and Mrs. Frank Fitzsimmons. Mr. and Mrs. Fitzsimmons initially came to our table and said they liked my weathercasts. That's how we got to know them and who he was: The President of The Teamsters Union, a fellow Western Pennsylvania native and fellow Leo, too!

WTTG-TV is where another friend of ours, Maury Povich, was hosting a daytime talk show called Panorama, *later succeeded by a lady named Pat Mitchell. Pat kindly had me as a guest on* Panorama *one time, along with one of the radio personalities I idolized during my teenage years in New York, while still living in Rego Park. His name was John Henry Faulk, Another Leo, I later learned. I listened to him every afternoon on WCBS. His theme song, "Carriage and Pair" later become my radio talk show theme song more than once in later years, always paying homage to Mr. Faulk. I told him how his soothing Texas voice and philosophizing help make that then very sane world much more sane. I also told him his theme music reminded me of an afternoon carriage ride through Central Park, reflecting the first-class nature of his very cosmopolitan "New York" programs. He thanked me for being a loyal listener. In later years, I was saddened for him and angered at his accusers to learn he was accused of being a Communist sympathizer. He was later exonerated and cleared of those charges, also winning a large lawsuit. Pat Mitchell, with whom I've been privileged to keep in touch through the years, later became President and Chief Executive Officer of The Paley Center for Media (formerly the Museum of Television and Radio) in New York and the former President and CEO of PBS. Pat is also related to Ted Turner via marriage.*

Carl Stern—Within one or two days after I started on the air in D.C., I got a phone call from Carl Stern, then NBC-TV's Law Correspondent, telling me he was married to the former Joy Nathan

(Carl and Joy earlier referenced) stating he and Joy would like to get together as soon as possible. I was thrilled to know what had happened to Joy after the PCS days and honored she would have Carl call me to begin what would develop into a very close friendship to this day. Through the years, there were numerous parties at Joy and Carl's house, as well as ours in Potomac, some of them renewing and maintaining friendships with Joy's parents, Ted and Betty Nathan (who were like my "adopted" parents), also earlier referenced and who had been close to my mother during my New York high school days. Living in NW D.C., very close to the Sterns, my mother often babysat for their two sons, Larry and Teddy. (Carl's birthday is one day after mine, another Leo! Again, that never ends, apparently! My being his elder, by one day, he is very respectful to me, whimsically stated.) After retiring from NBC-TV, Carl became U.S. Attorney General Janet Reno's spokesperson. During dinner one night at Carl and Joy's house, with another guest (a former excellent female network reporter whose name I sadly can't remember) and me the only ones present, I opined it must have been great to work for Ms. Reno. Carl said she was a wonderful person and when having an occasional social dinner at their house it was fun to see her drink beer from a can. Indeed, another "real" person among those in the public eye.

Reconnecting with Joy via her marriage to Carl, also allowed a wonderful re-connection with her sister, Gay. One summer our vacation schedules jelled enough to make it possible for us to all meet in Santa Fe, where Gay lived (and still lives) (See photos section). It was during that trip I visited my first American Indian Pueblo, on New Mexico's Cochiti reservation, with Joy, Carl, Chris and Michelle. From an elderly Cochiti lady, I bought the most spectacular hand-made neck piece one could ever imagine, at a very bargain price . . . 35 dollars . . . and still have it as not only a piece to proudly wear but also as a great memory of that particular time with Joy and Carl. In later years, I would visit Gay and her partner in Santa Fe at Christmas time, also accompanied by my wife, Ellen, my younger daughter, Lisa, my son-in-law Daryl Lewis and their children (two of my grandchildren) Ryan and Chelsea. Daryl was stationed at Albuquerque's Kirtland Air Force Base during that time and we thought it would be fun (with Gay's prior permission) to have them visit a friend from my high school years. It was a very warm and memorable visit. Gay had since retired as a teacher to American Indian children in Pecos, New Mexico, not far from Santa Fe.

Bob Schieffer—Bob's wife was a schoolteacher during my D.C. days and called me to ask if I'd deliver a weather talk to her grade school class. I told her I'd be honored and did so. It wasn't until 2010 I would meet Bob, but it was quite a meeting. The meeting took place from September 30th to October 3rd that year in Bismarck, North Dakota. The North Dakota Humanities Council arranged a first-class tribute to Velva, North Dakota's Eric Sevareid, perhaps the most exemplary journalist and news analyst to ever be on the airwaves, be they television or radio. He was my news hero. I'm honored to state I got to know Eric, as did my mother. *My mother had been Eric's IRS auditor in New York and I had the privilege to interview him at length for a documentary I co-produced in 2000. He especially liked talking about his days as editor of* The Minnesota Daily, *the publication of the University of Minnesota, from which he graduated. The aforementioned Harry Reasoner also attended classes there at about the same time and both wound up working for CBS News, thanks to Murrow. As is well known by any news "junkie" Harry eventually jumped to ABC News.*

Regardless, those featured paying tribute to Eric, one of Edward R. Murrow's "boys' in London during World War Two (as well as my second cousin, Cecil Brown, who was also one of Edward R. Murrow's "boys" in London during World War Two, earlier referenced) were Dan Rather, Bob Edwards of National Public Radio, Nick Clooney (George's father and Rosemary's brother) and Bob Schieffer. When I asked Bob and Dan separately if they remembered my D.C. weathercasting days, I was honored to see their faces light up like Christmas trees after a beat of about two seconds, but both saying "Yes!" I reminded Bob about his wife having me give a school weather talk to one of her classes and he said he remembered that, very sincerely, not pretending. We then had a picture taken together (see photos section). Then I reminded Dan he'd announced my D.C. Emmy nomination at those awards for the first documentary

I produced (in the French Alps and Paris, circa 1976). He also remembered, also not in a pretending manner. We then had our picture taken together (see photos section). Last, but not least, I had a couple pictures taken with Nick Clooney after telling him about my years working with his sister, Rosemary (previously described). He wanted to talk about it in a more than passing manner and also wanted to hear more about the part of my life with cousin Cecil, since Nick had been an anchorman in Cincinnati and Buffalo during his news career. We also discussed a mutual friend of ours (to be described later), *The Hollywood Squares*' Peter Marshall.

Bob's story about news that he "lived", to say the least, was the most fascinating, in my opinion, and told to that Bismarck audience. If you haven't read or heard it, here's what Bob said, which made all of that audience gasp: It was November 23, 1963, the day after JFK had been assassinated. Bob was a reporter for *The Fort Worth Star-Telegram* in those days and the only one in that newspaper's newsroom that day because all the other reporters were in Dallas covering the previous day's terrible news.

Bob said he got a phone call in the newsroom about 9 a.m. from a lady saying she thought her son was being accused of JFK's murder but wanted to know if anyone could drive her to the jail where he was being held. Bob told her he was the only one there. She then almost begged Bob to pick her up and drive her to Dallas. She was Lee Harvey Oswald's mother. Bob knew a good scoop when he saw one, thus he agreed to pick her up and drive her to the Dallas jail. He said when they arrived at the jail, she went her separate way and he never saw her again. He also said while driving her, he could understand why Lee might have been deranged, because Bob easily picked up deranged vibes from Lee's mother during that 40 minutes in the car with her.

Bob stayed there until after Jack Ruby shot Oswald a couple hours later, still undetected as a reporter, since no reporters were officially allowed to be beyond a certain point in the jail. Bob said he might have been mistaken for an FBI man, but after Oswald was killed, a door opened in the room where Bob was seated and a real FBI agent entered the room and asked if Bob was with law enforcement. Bob said "No" and Bob said the FBI agent pointed a gun at him and said,

"If you're not out of here right now, I'm going to kill you." Bob left immediately and that was that. Obviously, Bob had not yet become a television reporter, thus his face was unfamiliar to the FBI agent. Regardless, Bob said it's as close as he'd ever want to come to meeting his Maker. Indeed.

The Concerto in 'F' For Piano and Orchestra Ballet—Although it wouldn't be until the 1980s until I'd meet and have a wonderfully long visit with Frances Gershwin (previously referenced) in her upper East Side New York City apartment, George and Ira's sister okayed (on the phone) a 1974 idea I had created for a proposed television ballet special, the music for which would be George's powerful *Concerto in 'F' For Piano and Orchestra*. Peter Nero and Ella Fitzgerald, both of whom I got to know beginning in my Las Vegas years (and previously referenced) would perform the "bookends" (opening and closing of the show). The storyboard is still in my file drawers, along with signatures of Edward (Eddie) Villella, then principal dancer for the New York City Ballet and Leslie Caron, stating they'd agree to be the stars if it got funded. The budget was then $750,000. Eddie signed it for me in person, almost dripping wet, clad only in his bathing trunks, in the front doorway of the house of a friend of his in Beverly Hills and Michael Laughlin, then Leslie's husband, returned her signature on a similar Letter of Intent. I'll never forget Leslie saying to me on the phone how excited she was about this project, then asked me, "I don't have to toe dance, do I?" I told her it would be strictly "modern", and on platforms on the streets of New York where the special would be taped. George Balanchine, iconic head of the New York City Ballet told Villella he could do it, but only if he was dancing on plywood platforms that would blend in with the color of the streets or sidewalk, and not on cement or asphalt.

I met with my proposed producer/director, Emmy-award winner, John Moffitt, director of *The Ed Sullivan Show* and other shows of note, in the Bel Air Hotel's Polo Lounge for lunch and his signing of the LOI. I paid for lunch. Tony Mordente was my chosen choreographer, with whom I would have worked in *West Side Story* on Broadway (previously referenced) but who was Chris's choreographer in the Tokyo production of that musical. He also signed. I still have the letters from ABC, CBS and NBC stating it was a beautiful project but they'd rather "program against it". I saved the letters and everything connected with the project. Culture wasn't "in" in those days in television land, although I did give the written pitch to a woman who was affiliated with WETA-TV, the D.C. PBS station and said she loved the idea. I never heard from her afterward. In subsequent years, I re-pitched to PBS and even local Twin Cities Public Television in the 1990s, but no one bought. If somehow, before I croak, I can still make that happen (with different talent of course), I will easily resurrect the choreography and hopefully have it produced. I feel if the giants I signed believed enough in the project to want to participate and make it happen, it must have had more than passing merit. (The ballet would have concluded atop the now destroyed World Trade Centers in Lower Manhattan.)

In regard to anything getting the "go-ahead" to proceed and happen in broadcasting, show business, or any business, Monty Hall once told me, during a 1999 social visit at his unpretentious but very nice home in Beverly Hills, what a nightmare it was to get *Let's Make A Deal* on the air. He said after he'd pitched and described how the first *Let's Make A Deal Show* would look, and its premise, the network executive asked, "So what would the next show look like?" Duh! (That's my comment). (I suggest reading *Tales Of Hollywood* for other nightmare stories. These stories, reprinted from *Vanity Fair*, are about 12 iconic films that almost never saw the light of day or took years to finally eke out an "okay". Grrrr.)

Gloria DeHaven—Another Leo! Chris (also a Leo, whose birthday was one day after Gloria's. but many years younger) was acting in a play in a theater near Leesburg, Virginia. One of the stars was legendary Hollywood film actress/star Gloria DeHaven. We had a house party for the cast. Gloria asked if she could use the phone on my basement office desk. I, of course, said, "Yes". She said she'd be calling California. I told her "No problem." She was on that call for at least a half-hour. Every time I see her in one of her great classic films from the 1940s and 1950s on TCM, I facetiously think "Gee, I wonder how much she owes me for that call!" Smiling here. Kathy Garver, who played Sissy on *A Family Affair*, was also a cast member who was at our party that night and was a terrific pool player as well as one of the sweetest people one could ever hope to meet. Her character in *A Family Affair* was definitely typecasting. I've lost a photo of her I took while she was holding one of our pool cues in her hand.

Bob Fosse and John Raitt—Chris and I were invited to a downtown D.C. party feting her former boss, Bob Fosse, during the time The Kennedy Center was the D.C. home to one of Bob's fantastic creations, *Pippin*. *The cast member of that production who invited Chris and me to the party was a girl Chris taught dancing, beginning at age 11, in Saint Paul. Her name was Kerry Casserly, who later performed on Broadway in later productions of* A Chorus Line *and other Broadway shows. She was also a dance partner of Mikhail Baryshnikov on a television special. She and her sisters now own a show business training school in Minneapolis.* Chris introduced me to Bob. I was surprised he was just a tad shorter than I, proving, in my opinion, creative genius has nothing to do with a genius's physical characteristics. During a visit to Chicago in the late 1970s, prior to Chris's and my divorce, Chris introduced me to Gwen Verdon, who had been Bob's wife, much taller than he. Chris had acted with, and understudied Gwen, in *Sweet Charity* on Broadway. I had known John Raitt socially and very well during my years in Las Vegas. One of his sons who lived in Minnesota became a friend during my first foray there. I had even dated, one time, during my Las Vegas years, a girl who would later become John's wife. She was a former Miss Nevada. He playfully asked me during the time we were among his party-going entourage in D.C. (at his invitation) if she and I had ever had "relations". I responded honestly and that response was a definite "No".

Colonel Sanders—I'd been asked by the city fathers of a Shenandoah Valley, Virginia, town if I'd be co-Grand Marshall of a spring festival parade and ride in an open top convertible with Colonel Sanders of KFC fame. The town was either Front Royal or Winchester, but I'm sorry to say I can't remember which. When I drove there from D.C., to actually meet at a KFC store, I parked my car, walked in and The Colonel was standing there in his trademark white suit. We shared some hello pleasantries, then he opened one side of his suit coat and I saw the interior pocket filled with standard letter-sized white envelopes. He pulled all of them out and said, "See this? These are all going to charities." He said it proudly and he should have. During my soon-to-come Detroit years, I drove to Florida in the late 1970s and stopped at his original KFC restaurant in Corbin, Kentucky. It was untouched and unchanged as he and his wife had left it after they became successful, but to my knowledge it's still there as it was when I stopped for some chicken.

Eunice Shriver—Thanks to "connected" D.C.-area fans who became friends, I received a call from one of them asking if I'd like to have Eunice Shriver on my *Washington Ski Scene* program as a guest. I said I'd be more than happy to have one of President Kennedy's sisters, who also founded The Special Olympics, honor me with her presence on that show. My friend arranged the time and day we'd be taping and all was "set". (Video of that particular interview can be seen on the Internet.) I met her in Channel 7's lobby for the taping. She was tall and elegant, but not in a "snooty" way. She was definitely a Kennedy in all her mannerisms, filled with affable, quality good humor and graciously regal. There were no pre-prepared questions, and we'd never met or spoken prior to that day, thus I think both of us were nervous prior to the interview, but as soon as we began taping, everything flowed well. One particular person Mrs. Shriver and I had in common, and discussed during the conversation, was the earlier referenced Billy Kidd, one of my closest friends, who still is, thank goodness. Mrs. Shriver talked about his help with Special Olympics in Steamboat Springs. She also told me how she created Special Olympics and the first event for them at Chicago's Soldier Field. As was the case with President Truman, it was like having a history book talk to me, but this time forever-preserved on videotape. Again, am so blessed. An offshoot of that interview occurred several years later when I was interviewing Arnold Schwarzenegger and Danny DeVito for *Twins*. It was while Maria Shriver was married to Arnold. I got off the elevator in the New York hotel where the interviews were to be taped and saw Maria standing outside the room wherein Arnold was waiting to be interviewed. She saw me and said, "Oh, my God. There's my weatherman!" She flashed me a genuinely happy smile, then went into an adjacent room, another heartwarming addition to the avalanche of my privileged and treasured memories.

Trying to help inner city kids realize it's a big world and having them "live it", first-hand, in The Rockies—Speaking of Billy Kidd, I also created an ongoing project for underprivileged inner-city kids in D.C. I was motivated to do so starting in 1975 while driving through impoverished sections of the city almost daily to do Library of Congress books-for-the-blind narrations (a paid government job in addition to my TV work at Channel 7). I felt badly about the living conditions I saw. Then I had a "brainstorm", having to do with Billy. I created "Give A Kidd A Lift", having uplifting meaning for both Billy and the kids, an annual project which would give ten inner city youngsters, aged 10 through 17, a chance to ski with Billy in Steamboat Springs, all expenses paid, for a week. Frontier Airlines, God bless them, provided the free airfare and Steamboat provided all their lodging and meals.

I selected the kids at random via the D.C. government housing authority and public school authorities recommendations who knew who to select, with the caveat to be eligible for this Rocky Mountain experience, with a qualified chaperone, they could never have traveled outside the D.C. area. I continued the program in Detroit and the Twin Cities for seven subsequent years after I left D.C. and almost every kid, after their trip, told me it gave them hope to know there was a big world out there and they would strive to break the bonds of inner city life someday, if they could. That was the purpose of my "brainstorm". I've not thought of this until just now, but perhaps my sub-conscious was reminding me I came from a poor inner city life as a youngster and was able to break the bonds to make it to the "outside and upside" world. Hmmm.

Former Vice President Hubert H. Humphrey—I first met this magnificent human being, humanitarian and world icon when I was attending a fund-raiser in Seattle in 1965, representing Channel

13 (afore-referenced) in a reportorial capacity. I gave him my card and exchanged some pleasantries after his speech. Literally a week later, I received a hand-written note from him thanking me for being there. I still have it, as he even referenced in the note what I was wearing that night. Anyone who knows anything about Mr. Humphrey knows his acumen for remembering the names and personal details about everyone he ever met was both legendary and astounding. That note was just the tip of the iceberg, as in years to follow, thanks to my moving to the Twin Cities, he became a great friend, writing me numerous letters about my career, one of which is shared in the photos section of this book. In later years, I've also had the privilege to have the friendship of his son, "Skip", and Skip's son, "Buck", the latter thanks to whom I was introduced to John Kerry during Mr. Kerry's presidential run. Mr. Kerry was kind enough to exchange several personal emails with me through the years, thanks to that meeting (see photos section). Buck also invited me to several high-profile social events through the years and has visited with me socially, not politically, at my Minneapolis home. Skip later became Minnesota's Attorney General and Buck became Al Gore's Minnesota campaign manager during Gore's Presidential bid. Skip's wife, Lee, is a direct descendant of Robert E. Lee and Buck was named after his grandmother, Muriel Buck Humphrey, i.e., Buck being her maiden name. More about Vice President Humphrey reflecting my last very memorable time with him, and Muriel, in the next story.

Senator, Then Vice President, Walter F. "Fritz" Mondale—My wife, Ellen, treated me to my 77th birthday lunch, August 5th, 2014. The treat was at my favorite Minneapolis restaurant, Murray's, truly a Minneapolis landmark for decades, and noted for some of the well-known clientele who dine there frequently. In the midst of eating, I saw Fritz Mondale approaching our table as he was walking to be seated at his. I got up, he and Ellen and I exchanged some pleasantries and I told him it was my 77th birthday. Fritz wished me a happy birthday, and then said, "Let me counsel you about age. Let me counsel you." I told him that would be fine with me. I haven't yet taken him up on his offer, but hope to soon.

I first met Fritz during social occasions between 1971 and 1974 when I was doing the weather and ski programs on KSTP-TV. A couple years after I moved to D.C. and resurrected the ski program, I called and asked if I could interview him about skiing (for the program) and he kindly agreed to the interview. He was still a Senator and had just been tapped by Jimmy Carter to be Carter's Vice Presidential running mate in the 1976 Presidential election. I went to his office in one of the Senate office buildings with my Channel 7 photographer and the first thing Fritz said to me after entering his office was, "Wouldn't it be awful if we had a war?" I replied in the affirmative and then the salutations commenced. Fritz, smiling and teasing, said a condition of Joan's acceptance to marry him was he learned how to ski. I still have the interview.

Without doubt, the greatest public honor of my life was to be chosen to emcee Fritz's pre-inaugural banquet at The Washington Hilton in January, 1977. I had been called by the Minnesota State Society in D.C. just after the November, 1976, election, and asked if I'd emcee the afore-mentioned pre-inaugural banquet. I told them it would be the greatest honor and privilege of my life, and, in my opinion, it was. As fate would have it, I had been in France with Chris and literally returned to D.C. only a few hours before emceeing that banquet. In the photos section you may notice in the two photos with Fritz (and as you'll see, signed by him, years later) I looked like I was half-asleep sitting next to the future Vice President, but I think one could describe it as more mellow than half-asleep. As has been the case often while writing this memoir, I'm smiling as I write this very fond and privileged recollection.

In the audience that night were the entire U.S. Supreme Court (including, of course, Minnesota's own Warren Burger, then Chief Justice, who graduated from Saint Paul's William Mitchell College of Law), almost every Senator and Congressman, and at the next table to ours, former Vice President, and proud to say, my friend, Hubert Humphrey and his wife, Muriel.

When it came time to introduce Mr. Humphrey, I recalled our past times together and what an inspiration he had been to me (and the nation) the morning of November 23, 1963, driving through that

afore-described snowstorm on my way back home from Arizona
to Idaho, listening to him and Rhode Island Senator John Pastore
calming the nation on national radio following the JFK assassination
the preceding day. I introduced Mr. Humphrey, he walked to the
podium and shook my hand, and in his signature ebullient manner,
said "Thank you, thank you, thank you, Barry, for that heartwarming
introduction." When Vice President-elect Mondale finished his
remarks that evening, I had a chance to visit briefly with Mr.
Humphrey and Muriel, the latter who told me she really appreciated
my remarks. I thanked her and told her they were from the heart
and she said, "Yeah, yeah." I think she'd been used to those sorts of
perpetual kudos for her husband, but she didn't say what she said
abrasively. That was almost one year to the day before Mr. Humphrey
left us. I've visited his final resting place in Minneapolis's Lakewood
Cemetery often and could never forget how blessed I was to have had
his friendship and supportiveness. Channel 7 didn't cover the event
that night.

Vice President and later Ambassador to Japan, Mr. Mondale has
been kind enough to see me several times privately through the years
and to help arrange some significant meetings or re-connections.
One of the latter was when U.S. Ambassador to Japan, former U.S.
Speaker of the House, Tom Foley, was coming to speak at an event
in Minneapolis. I told Fritz I'd known Tom during my Wenatchee
radio days (previously referenced re Tom) and would like to renew
acquaintances. Fritz arranged it and Tom and I reunited one evening
in his suite at The Marquette Hotel in Minneapolis (see photo
section). A bit more trivia, which continues to boggle my mind: I've
known as either acquaintances or friends, four U.S. Ambassadors to
Japan, i.e., Mike Mansfield, former Tennessee Senator Howard Baker
(Howard and his wife were dear social friends to me during my D.C.
days), Mr. Mondale and Mr. Foley. "Whew".

*Murray's also hosts private parties, the most recent to which I
was invited and attended three years ago, for Minnesota Senator Amy
Klobuchar's birthday. She's been a good friend and her Dad Jim, and
I, have been friends for several years, sharing at least one three-hour
lunch together in 2010, reminiscing about his stellar journalistic and*

book-writing career, the people we were both blessed to know through the years and, of course, Amy's great success as a U.S. Senator, very well liked by most people of any political stripe.

Frankie Hewitt—The former Mrs. Don Hewitt ran historic Ford's Theater during my D.C. years. She was kind enough to invite me to attend several performances there. Even though she and Don had split, Don was at one of the performances and she kindly introduced me to him. Don had created and executive produced *60 Minutes* from its inception until his passing. In subsequent years, Don accepted two suggestions I made to him regarding stories *60 Minutes* might pursue airing and kindly always took my phone calls. For a man as powerful as he was in the industry, his nose was never too high in the air to take my calls. *Regarding* 60 Minutes, *one of the reporters I got to know well during my D.C. years was Harry Reasoner. Harry was a friend of our Channel 7 anchor, former CBS correspondent David Schoumacher, thus was an interviewee on our newscasts frequently. Harry even did one of my between-the-weather-boards guest appearances one time. A native Iowan, with a dam in that state named after his father, Joe, Harry's electronic journalism career started at WCCO radio in the Twin Cities. For two years in the early 1990s on WCCO, I substitute-hosted overnight talk shows during vacation or holiday periods for the regular hosts. The connections almost never end.*

John Ehrlichman (with a huge punch line)—Shortly before he went to prison in 1976, President Nixon's counsel and Assistant to the President for Domestic Affairs, John Ehrlichman, came into our Channel 7 studio one day preparing to be interviewed by David Schoumacher on our newscast. Prior to the interview, John spotted me sitting in a dark section of the studio going over some notes and sat down next to me. He introduced himself. I told him it was good to meet him. He said he liked my weathercasts and also said, "You got one Hell of a contract." I told him I didn't know it was public knowledge but said something stating my gratitude for the job (although mixed emotions still privately reigned and may always). He then said it would be fun to keep in touch and told me how to reach him at the minimum-security prison where he'd be incarcerated near Safford, Arizona. I told him I was flattered he'd ask me to keep in touch, and he simply said, "Well, I like you. After I get out I'll look forward to seeing you again sometime." Again, regardless of his notoriety or reputation, here was another world figure welcoming me into his private circle. I continue to shake my head from side to side recalling these sorts of times and how many of them occurred.

Regardless, he and I did correspond via regular mail three times during the eighteen months he served his time. The notes were short, just stating I hoped he was faring well with him responding appreciatively, but briefly. Upon his release, he began living in Santa Fe, New Mexico, and told me if I ever visited New Mexico, he'd be glad to see me again. He also wrote his best contact phone number.

Ironically, in the early summer of 1978, I had an assignment to do a weather story in Albuquerque for WJBK-TV, the then CBS affiliate in Detroit for whom I began work in January that year, following a four-month, no-work, dry spell. I called John from Detroit and told him my itinerary, which allowed some flexible time on two of the days I'd be in Albuquerque. When the time, place and day we decided to meet arrived, I rented a car and drove the short drive to Santa Fe, meeting him at a restaurant he suggested we have breakfast, called The Pink Adobe. When John entered, he was carrying a black full-sized hardcover book under his arm, but only the back of the book was visible. I didn't think anything of it and we had breakfast, catching up on both our lives and how they had changed throughout the years.

The punch line: We finished our breakfast. John then turned the book onto its back so I could read the title. It was Richard Nixon's memoirs. John then turned to the frontispiece, where most inscriptions are written, and it was stamped, Richard M. Nixon.

Not even a "To John" or "Thanks for going to prison for me, John". Nothing. John said, "That's what I went to prison for. I caught too much Potomac Fever, and that's my thanks." He told me Nixon had sent it to John while John was still an inmate at the Safford prison. Talk about adding insult to injury. Makes one wonder.

In later years, two other very high-level people who had served in the Nixon administration, but who shall remain nameless here, told me privately, in social gatherings, not during interviews, they had nothing but disdain for him. However, each also acknowledged the positions they held in his administration set them up financially for the remainder of their lives, thus self-preservation was the motivating factor to become Nixon's "Yes men".

Senators Paul Simon, Edmund Muskie and Daniel Inouye:
Senator Simon—I got a call one night from Peter Jennings who said he was at a party not far from our house in Potomac. Why he chose to call me, I'll never know, but Peter told me Illinois Senator Paul Simon needed a ride to his house because he'd become unable to safely drive himself home. At the time, I still had my Rolls Royce. I drove to the party and two people escorted Senator Simon to my car with him remarking how fun it would be to be riding in that Rolls. It was also raining steadily and he had no umbrella. He was pleasantly, and actually sweetly, inebriated, but not enough, I thought, to need a ride home. Regardless, with his signature bow tie in place, I drove him to where he needed to be, he exited the car very easily, we said goodnight and that was that. I never saw him in person again, but any time I saw him on newscasts or in Senate proceedings on television, I remember those 20 or so minutes as his "chauffeur" and happy and honored to have been so.

Senator Muskie—During a time when an ABC radio reporter named Chris Moss, who Chris and I had met in Iran, was visiting D.C. and staying in our house, she had me accompany her to The White House for a welcoming ceremony by President Carter in The Oval Office for three new Ambassadors from three separate countries. When we got there, I was waved through after Chris had shown her credentials. The Secret Service people had kindly recognized me from my local D.C. television weathercasts. When we got to the doors leading into the Oval Office, there were two Secret Service men flanking each side of the double doors. They told Ms. Moss to go in, immediately afterward smiled and winked at me, saying, "Go ahead. You go in, too, Mr. ZeVan." This happened three times with President Carter having no idea I was standing off to the side to witness each brief ceremony. Oh, how times have changed regarding entry into The Oval Office. (I've actually been in very close proximity to Mr. Carter in later years, just two or three feet separating us, but have never introduced myself nor told him about that time in The Oval Office.)

After Chris Moss and I left The White House, she had to go to one of the Senate office buildings for a brief meeting with one of the Senators. I drove her there and parked. When we got to the floor on which her meeting was to take place, the very long majestic halls were totally empty. I had to go to the bathroom very badly and was searching for one pretty desperately. We were in front of the offices of Maine's Senator Edmund Muskie. I told Chris I would go into the office and ask if they had a restroom. They said they did and showed me where it was. After that restroom visit, I walked out the door. About three seconds later, Senator Muskie exited his office and started walking down that long empty hall. When he got fairly far down the hall, he shouted, "I enjoy you, you know!" I was so gratefully stunned I stupidly responded, "Thank you, I enjoy you, too!" He smiled then continued walking. What an honor to have that truly great man state he was a "fan". (In my opinion, had a Manchester, New Hampshire, newspaper owner's article about Senator Muskie's wife not publicly driven the Senator to tears, I think he would have won the Democratic Party's nomination for President and, again in my opinion, become one of our greatest Presidents, let alone statesmen. The aforementioned newspaper owner was sometimes a guest on our newscasts. It was difficult to be on set with him.)

Senator Inouye—Senator Herman Talmadge of Georgia was the first Member of Congress to call me about five minutes after my first weathercast on Channel 7, saying, "You have gone above and beyond the call of duty, sir!", referring to my just completed weathercast. I thanked him and then realized who some of the audience members were. I was very honored to have them honor me with their kind comments and viewing loyalty throughout the next three years at Channel 7.

About a month after I started working on Channel 7, I got a call from Hawaiian U.S. Senator (and World War Two combat hero) Dan Inouye's office saying the Senator would like to be one of those who appeared occasionally between my weatherboards as I was walking from one to the other. I said I'd be honored and the lighthearted setup would be for him to ask me why I never gave the temperature in Honolulu, to which I'd respond and then have a closing statement to the camera. I also asked them to let the Senator know I'd lived and worked in Honolulu on KGMB-TV, previously referenced in this book. They called again and said the Senator agreed to the bit I'd suggested and was happy to learn I'd lived and worked in Hawaii in 1965.

Indeed, the Senator appeared on the program (please see photos section) and my impromptu line, after I agreed to give Honolulu's temperature every night, was, "Gee, when these Senators want something, they don't mess around!" Senator Inouye smiled and that was that. In future years, we kept in touch frequently and he became one of the subjects in a documentary I'd help produce in 2000 (please see photos section). He was a first-class man in every way and it was a great privilege to have spent some non-interview times with him.

Nguyen Cao Ky—Because of David Schoumacher's former CBS news reporting history, he was able to get national-news caliber guests on our nightly Channel 7 local newscasts. The parade of the powerful was almost incessant. One of those was former South Vietnamese Prime Minister, the Vice President, Nguyen Cao Ky. Mr. Ky was a guest on our news frequently, but the first time, prior to getting on set and on the air, he saw me in the hall and said he and his family watched me every night, saying "You make us happy!" I thanked him and he continued smiling. I considered it an honor, and always awestruck, to be told by another powerful person they were a "fan". Of course, when one is seen on-air in markets where the powerful live, it's de riguer to hope they're watching, but to have them tell you they like what you're doing is very humbling, and appreciated. Even when he was on the news set prior to David interviewing him, every time we were in a commercial break, he would look at me seated to his right at my place at the anchor desk and always warmly smile.

Gloria Swanson—Ms. Swanson was on set only once, to be interviewed by David about hypoglycemic health issues and her advocacy for curing them. After her interview, she decided to watch the remainder of our news broadcast from the sidelines. She was watching while just standing in a darker section of the studio near the exit to the hallway. I was glad she was still there because I wanted to tell her my first wife, Dorothy, had suffered from hypoglycemia. I approached her, she smiled and I told her about Dorothy. She then asked, "Doesn't it make them crazy?" I told her I felt we all had mood swings from time to time, and she agreed, but then launched into a deeper analytical description about how one of her husbands was really affected by it. Her comments were very educational, based on her experiences, and now having the swings between low and high blood sugars myself, I reflect on her wisdom and genuine desire to talk more about it, one-on-one. That magnificent film star was, at most, just over five feet tall, but as anyone who's seen her performances will attest, a giant in her profession.

Sugar Ray Leonard, Jerry Brown, George McGovern, Joshua Logan and Jack Germond—All were interviewees for David during our newscasts and always stuck around for after-newscast conversations with a couple of us. Some memories of them during those times:

Sugar Ray, raised since age three in the D.C. area suburb of Palmer Park, Maryland, had recently won his Olympic Boxing Gold Medal when he was on set with us in 1976. He stated we were his favorite news team. He was one of the most personable people one could ever meet and his caring about people has resonated in recent years via The Sugar Ray Leonard Foundation to help cure Juvenile Diabetes via the JDF.

Jerry Brown was a delight while on set at least three times during his 1976 run for the Presidency. Now Governor of California (as of this writing) his demeanor "on stage" is no different from "off stage". He's the real deal and was fun with whom to verbally but pleasantly spar.

Senator George McGovern was also very real when with us during his 1976 Presidential bid. He took a few private minutes (not an interview) to speak with me about his genuine concern for this country. His compassion was real. It was saddening to learn through the years about personal family problems he was enduring. Good human being.

Jack Germond passed away two years before I started writing this. His 50-plus years as a political columnist and commentator were highly respected and legendary. He was insightful and just plain fun with whom to interact, personally and professionally. He and David were good friends, and for all his clout in political journalism there was nothing holier-than-thou about Jack. As I alluded, he was just a fun and very knowledgeable person with whom to be.

Joshua Logan, director and writer extraordinaire, was also fun with whom to be and interact. He was on our newscast only once, but held court with yours truly after the broadcast because he told me he was happy to talk about all the people we had in common, most of all Susan Strasberg, one of those he directed in *Picnic*. He was another "giant" who, in person, was as down-to-Earth as anyone could be.

Arthur Godfrey (and President Roosevelt)—In the mid-1970s, the entrance to Arthur's farm and his place of primary residence near Leesburg, Virginia, was plastered with large signs on the entry gate stating *Keep Out! This Means You!, Go Away*, etc. Arthur was a brilliant talent, not only as a television and radio show host, raconteur and singing ukulele player who put Hawaii more on the map than it would have been but also as a discoverer of major talent via **Arthur Godfrey's Talent Scouts** on television and *Arthur Godfrey Time* on CBS radio. The McGuire Sisters, Vic Damone, Julius LaRosa, Pete Barbutti and Carmel Quinn were among those for whom his shows provided their big breaks. Phyllis McGuire became a friend to me in later years (see photos section and previous reference) and told me Arthur insisted on perfection but was not mean to her or her sisters. Pete Barbutti also became a friend during and after my move to Las Vegas.

I happened to be in the lobby of the station (Channel 7) one morning when Arthur was scheduled to appear on our local version of GMA prior to GMA itself. When he entered the lobby, slowly because he walked with a cane, he was furious. Without asking him why, he asked, directly quoting here, "Why does a person have to be a bastard to get anything done in this world?" He then said he'd had some problems with his driver and the limo company that brought him to the station. As I stated earlier, and no great wisdom here, but we all do have our "moments".

In that regard, during the height of his popularity on national radio, I once heard Arthur tell this story in regard to human behavior: He said while he was a morning radio show host and disc jockey in the late 1930s, locally in D.C. (on our sister radio station, WMAL), he complained about a lot of hate mail he'd recently received. To his surprise, he said he got a phone call in the studio directly from President Roosevelt. He said the President wanted him to get to the White House at a time the President specified, later that morning, because Mr. Roosevelt had something to show him in regard to hate mail. Godfrey said he got to the White House as soon as he could after the broadcast and was welcomed by the President, who told Godfrey he was a big fan of Godfrey's but felt it necessary to show him a lot about hate mail.

He said the President led him to a large room in The White House basement that was more like a cage than a room. Godfrey said behind the fencing must have been at least ten thousand letters, stacked to the ceiling. He said the President had the aide who accompanied them to that room open the door and let the President and Godfrey into the "cage". The President then invited Godfrey to start reading the letters. He did, and said they were the most disgustingly hate-filled diatribes one could imagine, and all addressed to Mr. Roosevelt. He said the President then asked, "Now do you feel badly about your hate mail?" Godfrey said he replied, "No", and never complained about hate mail or who likes you or doesn't. It was quite a lesson from President Roosevelt to Arthur Godfrey and Godfrey said that lesson stuck with him always.

David Brinkley—David was responsible for introducing Chet to Tippi. Chet told me when he and David were getting prepared to debut NBC-TV's *Huntley-Brinkley Report*, there was a girl the network engineers used for "color balance" prior to the newscast going "live". Chet was in New York and David was in D.C. Chet saw her modeling on camera for the first time and asked David who she was. David told Chet her name was Tipton Stringer, but she preferred to be called Tippi. Tippi and Chet met shortly after Chet got to know who she was, dated and got married. More about Chet and Tippi later, but when I told Tippi I was moving to D.C., she told me to call David at NBC's D.C. Bureau and tell him "Hello" for her when I arrived in late November, 1974. (Chet had passed away March 20, 1974).

I did as Tippi suggested and called David just after Thanksgiving, 1974, in mid-afternoon. When he answered the phone, I told him my name and I was just calling to say "Hello" from Tippi. David's response was, "Thank you." I'm chortling as I write this, not out of disrespect for David, but just vividly recalling his delivery, very similar to the "Goodnight, Chet" tone and style that were two of his trademarks when signing off *The Huntley-Brinkley* report each weekday evening. I said, "You're welcome", and that was that! I called Tippi and related the preceding story and she laughed, saying, "That's David."

CHAPTER FIFTEEN

France, Iran, the U.K. and Chile

Life is being able to take the bitter with the better

—J. Allen Jensen, KID-TV General Manager

F rance, I: The "better" part of my years at Channel 7 included management's permission allowing me to produce, film, write, shoot and host my first documentary. It was aired on Channel 7's *The Washington Ski Scene* in the late autumn of 1975, filmed in the French Alps and Paris in January that year. It was produced at the request of an executive I knew at Air France in New York. I was lucky enough to have been to France three times prior to the shoot, thus "knew the territory". I filmed the entire doc with the little 16mm hand-wind Bolex H16 camera I referenced earlier in this "epic". I still have that wonderful relic, a reminder to me, of simpler and, in my opinion, a much more "quality" time. ABC-TV furnished the crew to shoot my "standup" lead-ins in Paris. During one of those shoots, Paris had an air temperature of 1 above zero, Fahrenheit, with a −20 wind chill. If you ever watch that 26-minute film, now also on the Internet, entitled *The French Ski Scene*, you'll see me almost not able to say the words because it was so cold. The scene shows the famous Eglise de Sacre Coeur at the top of Montmartre in the background, with clouds literally whizzing by, verifying that very cold wind chill. The doc was nominated for a D.C. Emmy and Dan Rather, as I previously mentioned, read the nomination at the awards the night they were presented. The "meat" of the French Alpine shots I filmed included Chamonix, Argentiere, La Plagne and Avoriaz. I also shot entering, through and outside The Mont Blanc Tunnel, featuring the Italian ski village of Courmayeur on the east side of the tunnel, then the world's longest, sitting beneath Europe's highest peak, Mont Blanc. *I had driven through the tunnel in years past, including visiting the city of Aosta, the farthest north point in Italy the Romans had built an amphitheater, which is still very well preserved and used for performances. The vineyards on the sides of the Aosta Valley mountains resonate will lush*

purple hues almost year 'round. Put that spot on your bucket list, too!
There were also city shots in Geneva as we began the step-by-step route
into the Alps. Chris was with me on that trip and shot the sequences,
in and departing Geneva from the moving rental car.

The seven-day shoot was exhausting but successful. We were to
fly from Geneva to Paris just after the shoot. At the Geneva airport,
Chris and I were so tired we went into the snack area to have a Coke
or cocoa. We sat down and watched a plane take off for Paris. It was
the plane on which we were supposed to be, but I was so tired I forgot
to look at the tickets, first and last time ever in my life to pull that
one! While watching that plane, I recall us both saying how lucky
those people were to be getting to Paris sooner than us. Right. We
luckily caught the next flight to Paris, only another hour later.

The wonderful editor for my first doc was Channel 7's Sandy
Reedy. She perfectly matched the music to the scenes and I'm sure
that was a major part of the catalyst for it being Emmy-nominated.
Sandy is now married to my friend, former ABC-TV anchor and
White House correspondent, Sam Donaldson, but much more
about Sam later. (Sandy's boss and still my friend, Jim English, later
became an executive at HBO and subsequently President of Playboy
Television. More about Jim, his HBO kindness to me, and a great
time we had in Cannes years later, later in this chronicle. Again, two
fellow Leos were Sandy and Jim. Yikes, is there any other sign?)

During the Paris part of that trip, the one who arranged for
my Paris and Alps ABC-TV sound crew was Jack Smith, then
ABC Bureau Chief in Paris. Jack was an ABC-TV news reporter/
correspondent and as class an act as his father, the iconic Howard K.
Smith. For those who may not remember, Howard moderated the
first televised U.S. presidential debates in history, i.e., Kennedy-Nixon
in 1960. I'm honored to say I was able to secure Howard's writing and
hosting services for a ten-hour documentary for which I was retained
to get all the doc's major interviewees as consulting producer in
2000, i.e., *The Remarkable Twentieth Century*, about which, as well as
Howard and his wife, Benedicte, too, will be related later.

I'm very saddened Jack died at a very early age after retiring from
ABC News and residing in a San Francisco suburb, but his sister,

Catherine (Cate), who had been a producer at Channel 7, and has been a friend since the mid-1970s, is still alive and living in Southern California. Jack was the epitome of kindness, intelligence and class.

France, II, plus QE2—My mom used to say, "Strangers are just friends we haven't met." It's been proved to me many times. One of those more significant times occurred during one of my ski writing, not filming, trips to The French Alps. There were other ski journalists there, too, representing newspapers and magazines. One of the photojournalists was a girl named Carolyn Speidel, of the iconic watchband family. Carolyn had been born in Hong Kong. I later learned she and her family were apartment building neighbors to Ted Koppel and his family, on the floor directly below. Ted many years later told me he remembered the Speidel family very well and liked them immensely. Carolyn was one of the nicest people I'd ever met, and still is. During a lull in writing action, she kindly took a photo of me atop one of the French Alps ski runs (please see photos section). We exchanged contact information. Carolyn was in the public relations arena and we kept in contact from time to time. She knew of my friendship with Tony Randall and called me one day to ask if I could arrange an interview for her for a feature story she was doing for a major publication. I gladly said, "Yes", called Tony, he accepted and Carolyn interviewed him in his 1 West 81st Street apartment.

A few months later, I told Carolyn I was asked to write a story for a St. Paul, MN, paper about cruising on the QE2. Carolyn had said she had contacts with Cunard Lines and would ask if they'd exchange a story for a one-way passage from Southampton, England, to New York. They kindly accepted, thanks to Carolyn. On October 1st, 1988, I found myself billeted in a Queen's Deck cabin, complete with my own lifeboat for the voyage previously described. Among my fellow diners each of the four nights was a man who was the executor of The Man Ray Trust, as well as another gentleman who had been private physician to former British Prime Minister Harold Macmillan. There were three or four others seated around our nightly dining table but the two I mentioned stand out most in my mind.

The North Atlantic looked smooth as glass as it was so calm for the first four days of the voyage. The captain, who I was assigned about whom to write, invited me to the bridge for the writing interview and told me he'd never seen it so smooth. We observed dolphins and porpoises jumping out and back into the water with frequency on one of those days. (The captain was the captain who a couple years later ran the QE2 aground on a sandbar on the Massachusetts coast. I felt badly for him, as he was, as the British might say, "a decent chap", and not at all imperious, viewing his position with Cunard on their then signature ship.)

I thanked Carolyn innumerable times for her kindness and we've kept in touch since. Carolyn married a man named Keith Denholm, a Scottish gentleman whose family founded, own and still maintain the shipyards in Glasgow that built the QE2 and all the other Q ships under the Cunard umbrella, including the Queen Mary. Keith is a giant in the global shipping industry. I had the major honor to visit Carolyn, Keith and their three boys in Singapore in March, 2007, while doing consulting work for a Minneapolis-based technology firm named Veritec, owned by a Vietnamese lady named Van Tran, previously mentioned. Carolyn cooked dinner for Van and me one night during the few days visit. During dinner, I looked across the massive dining room table to see Keith had the same model ancient, but in working condition, analog barometer I have sitting in my dining room in a bookcase. I asked him if he'd ever had it appraised. He told me, "Yes, recently.", and said its appreciated value was between nine and twelve thousand U.S. dollars. I thanked Keith, now, thanks to him, having the knowledge my matching piece might help me stay out of the poor house someday. I haven't had to sell it, yet.

Thanks to the work at Veritec, in the late1990s, I was able to arrange meetings for us in South Africa, previously referenced, as well as privately with Dr. Henry Kissinger, who kindly and warmly remembered me from previous social times and interviews. When Dr. Kissinger came into the boardroom in his offices at Kissinger Associates on Park Avenue, he sat next to me with our arms touching throughout the half-hour meeting and was of great assistance to Ms. Tran, along with former Ambassador Paul W. Speltz, then Dr. Kissinger's

organization's president. Thanks to, since 1977, knowing then Senator
Joe Biden, I also got us meetings with his top people to try to help Ms.
Tran's bio-ID business for U.S. security. My first meeting with Vice
President Biden in 1977, then a newly elected Senator, was at a soiree
on the Potomac, Maryland estate of then Washington Redskins owner,
Edward Bennett Williams, not far from our house. Be he Senator or
Vice President, Mr. Biden, a fellow Pennsylvania native, was and is a
very "real" person, not forgetting his roots. He was very unpretentious
with me socially and otherwise.

Iran, trip one of two—One of the perks attuned to living and working
in D.C. was (and still is, I'm certain) being watched often or regularly
on television or heard on radio by the most powerful in politics and
international dealings. There were many I was privileged to either get
to know well and or who acknowledged they were fans, which will
boggle my mind perpetually, some of whom to be later referenced.
In that regard, one day shortly before our 6 p.m. newscast, I was
standing in the hall outside the studio at Channel 7 and noticed a
cadre of gentlemen walking toward me before they entered the studio.
One of them said they all knew "who I was" and were "big fans." The
most distinguished of them introduced himself to me as Ardeshir
Zahedi, Iranian Ambassador to the U.S. I told him it was an honor to
meet him and was glad he was a viewer. He said he wanted to talk to
me after the newscast. I said that would be great, and that was that.

Following the newscast, in the hallway outside the studio, I met
with Ambassador Zahedi, who had been The Shah's son-in-law at
one time, and the four or five men accompanying him. He asked
me if I knew there was snow skiing in Iran. I told him I actually
had just learned about it the preceding month in an article in *Ski*
Magazine written by a lady named Abby Rand, a longtime personal
acquaintance and colleague of mine in what was then called the
United States Ski Writers Association. He said he was happy I
knew about skiing there because the Shah wanted to have someone
produce a film about it for U.S. and worldwide television. Ardeshir
(he requested I just call him by his first name, which I still do) said
he immediately thought of me because he watched my *Washington*

Ski Scene programs on Channel 7 and knew I'd produced the Emmy-nominated French ski doc. He said they wanted me to film in at least one of the four ski resorts The Shah had had constructed primarily for the recreational enjoyment of all the westerners who were employed at major U.S., British, French and German firms with factories and businesses in Iran. Some of the firms were Ford, GM, Chrysler (Tehran was the first place I met Lee Iacocca, then Chrysler chairman), Bell Helicopter and so forth. He asked if the station would allow me to take the time off to do the film. I told him I was sure they would. I asked and they did.

After all travel, Iranian ground transportation and lodging arrangements were meticulously made by Ardeshir's assistants at the lavish Iranian Embassy on Massachusetts Avenue, along with a couple private meetings and parties there in regard to the trip, I left for Tehran (with Chris) in late February, 1976. I still have the original Iranair ticket stubs and memorabilia from that first of what would be two trips to Iran, nine months apart, each totally paid for by the Iranian government. The Shah had purchased Boeing 747SP (Super Performance) jets and the 12-hour trip from Dulles to Tehran's Mehrabad International Airport was non-stop. We were treated like royalty, with the first-class section of the plane almost entirely empty, except for Chris and me. The route of the plane took us directly over Mount Ararat in Turkey, of course the believed site of the ruins of Noah's Ark. I looked down and saw nothing but a snowcapped peak and snow in the lower elevations at the bottom of the mountain. When we landed in Tehran, because we were guests of His Imperial Majesty, we were assigned a driver and an assistant who would be our official go-between and interpreter (when necessary) at all times at our disposal. Our assistant's name was Fereshteh (last name purposely omitted for her protection), who, I was later told, left Iran for the United States when The Shah left. Fereshteh spoke impeccable English and was a joy to have as our assistant for the entire ten days we were there.

We were billeted at The Intercontinental Hotel, very westernized with all the amenities and ample American food for all meals. Breakfast consisted of everything from pancakes and waffles to ham and eggs, as well as every Kellogg's or Big G cereal imaginable. When we awakened the first morning, at 6, I turned on the radio and Chris and I heard a very professional American disc-jockey voice saying, "Here in the nitty-gritty super city it's 65 degrees under sunny skies", then some popular American song immediately following his announcing. What was that? As my crazy life would have it, that announcer, whose radio name was Ted Anthony, was originally from Detroit and would become not only a great friend from 1978 onward, but also the catalyst for saving my life and sanity during very dark times from 1980 through 1983, more about which I'll relate later.

The modus operandi was we were to expect a call from the Niavaran Palace (the residence of the Iranian royal family) every morning at 9 to advise us about a shooting schedule for the filming. The first call came right on time and the caller said, "For sure tomorrow we'll have you meet your camera crew and go to the mountains, but today, just explore Tehran with your assistant." Okay. Indeed, we went several places with Fereshteh and our driver, noticing a flourishing and very modern city, but also noticing no one paid attention to traffic lights. We were lucky we weren't among the average 25 traffic fatalities we were told occurred every day in Tehran.

The next day, I was told the same thing, thus Fereshteh and our driver took us out and about again. This was no ordinary out and about and a spot I'd visit again in nine months with my Olympic ski champion friends, Billy Kidd and Suzy Chaffee. The "spot" was in the basement of the main branch of The Bank Markazi. It was a large room that housed the world's most extensive collection of diamonds, rubies, emeralds and other precious stones as well as at least one ancient royal throne encrusted in gold. All the jewels were encased on large, sturdy rectangular wooden tables protected with huge glass coverings. A jeweler from Switzerland who was also there said the value of the collection was incalculable, making it all worthless. The collection was to be Iran's treasury if their oil ever dried up. There's more to the story of what eventually happened to the jewels, which, out of courtesy to those who deserve that silence, I'm choosing to not tell.

There were notices to not touch the glass on any of the displays, as well as two machine-gunners at the top of the stairs that led to that basement room. There were also tear gas nozzles in the corners of the ceiling in that room. Fereshteh told us if an alarm ever sounded because of attempted thievery, a large steel gate would fall so fast, with its visible spikes all across the bottom, not even Iran's fastest runner could make it through the opening before the gate fell. She said they tested it when that security feature was installed and luckily for the runner, he couldn't beat the shutting of that large garage door-style gate.

The three other most memorable experiences that day included visiting a health club wherein men would sit for a long time in steam rooms, then lift weights. It was somewhat considered an almost religious ritual. Chris was not allowed in, thus stayed with Fereshteh for the 15 minutes I looked around. The second most memorable was seeing an open synagogue in downtown Tehran. The Shah considered himself and his subjects to be Aryan, not Arabic. The third most memorable was passing by a Wimpy's Hamburgers fast-food place and a KFC store. I was "compelled" to stop at their KFC and have a couple drumsticks. They were a close attempt at the original recipe, I didn't become ill and The Colonel, my Virginia parade partner, would have been happy about what they were serving.

Tehran's physical appearance reminded me of Salt Lake City, topographically, with desert to the west and snowcapped mountains to the east of the city, and "benches" (as they call them in Salt Lake City) where houses, apartment buildings and businesses are situated on hillsides that rise gradually, streets and roads built accordingly.

On the ninth day, the Palace spokesperson and liaison overseeing the filming plans apologized and said The Shah's and Empress Farah Diba's schedules wouldn't allow them to be filmed skiing at that time, but perhaps later in the year, thus we would be leaving Tehran for D.C. the following morning, which we did, but this story is far from over.

Iran, trip two, "thanks" to Barbara Walters, including a very special story about our one-on-one warm encounter with Queen Mother Elizabeth—On our way back to the U.S., this time with an "open jaw" one-day stopover in London, we saw headlines in the British tabloids that Ambassador Zahedi was given credit for quelling a riot at the D.C. Government Building in downtown D.C. Obviously, we were eager to see him at his soonest convenience after returning, to congratulate him and report on our trip, but first, "The Queen Mum" as follows:

Chris and I had a couple days respite between returning from Iran and getting back to D.C., thus spent those couple days in London. While standing outside Buckingham Palace, and facing The Mall, a tall and robust-looking gentleman approached us and asked if we were "Yanks". I said, "Yes." He then proceeded to tell us his name was Van Alexander and had just retired from 25 years of service "in that building" ("Buck House", as some Brits call Buckingham Palace). He then said, "Come with me over to St. James's Palace and you'll have a once in a lifetime experience." He looked trustworthy, so we said, "Fine", and walked with him a couple short blocks to the narrow road on which the back entrance to St. James's was situated. He said, "Look at all those tourists down there at the other end of the road. They have no idea what they're missing by standing there, but you two will have quite a special happening in a couple minutes." He then told us to look to the immediate right of the massive black gates that lead in and out of the St. James's Palace grounds. To the immediate right was a gatekeeper's enclosed booth. In it was a richly-dressed gatekeeper, attired in a white, very ruffled shirt, peering out the booth window from side to side, making certain all was clear for what was about to happen. Van then said, "The Queen Mother's car will be coming out of that gate. When it does, the car will turn to the left to go down this road toward The Mall, but it will be less than two feet from the curb where you're standing. When the car is parallel to you, simply wave at The Queen Mother and see what she does in return." What Van described is exactly what happened after the car, a purple Daimler limousine with the Royal crest atop the car's roof, emerged from the gates. When the limousine was directly beside us, moving very slowly, Van said, "Now wave at her!". We did. She was looking out the window, got a big smile on her face looking directly at us, and waved back. It wasn't a "Royal" wave, but rather a wave wherein you'd raise your hand parallel to your face, and flap four fingers. She saw that Chris and I were silently shrieking with delight, smiled again at us, then moved onward down that road. We thanked Van for his knowledge that would happen and then went on our separate merry ways. Every time I see an old newsreel with the Queen Mother during World War Two days, sometimes holding the hand of a young future Queen Elizabeth or walking through war-torn parts of a bombed London, I know how honored we were to have had that private moment, thanks to Mr. Alexander. God bless the people who make life so special for others. Now, back to the second trip to Iran.

I called Ardeshir (Ambassador Zahedi) upon our return and he scheduled a private supper for us a couple days later at the afore-described Iranian embassy. When we sat down to begin our supper visit, Ardeshir asked, "So how did it go?" I told him it didn't, although we were treated well, but no filming occurred. We told him what the Palace liaison had told us regarding the schedules of His and Her Imperial Majesties and he said, "Oh, this is awful. We have to get this done." Then he said Her Imperial Majesty would be in D.C. in July to have a goodwill visit with President and Mrs. Carter, thus saying he'd figure something out, but he also asked me to invite the two best U.S. skiers I knew who had been friends of mine, to be the "stars" of the film along with Empress Farah, who he knew was a great skier herself, having been raised during part of her early life in Lausanne, Switzerland. I told him I'd ask Billy Kidd and Suzy Chaffee if they'd be interested and then let him know. He said they would be great choices and we'd schedule the shoot for early January, 1977.

The next day, I contacted Billy and Suzy. They enthusiastically said, "Yes". I told Ardeshir and he was delighted. He said he'd like Suzy to meet with Empress Farah, him and me for mid-morning "tea" in July to discuss what the filming would entail six months later, with the "tea" date to be determined in June.

Then he told me he'd learned the real reason no filming occurred while Chris and I were there and which we saw on ABC-TV a couple days later: During part of one of her *Barbara Walters Special* series, Barbara publicly insulted and embarrassed The Shah during a television interview she did with him and Empress Farah. The interview had taken place during the time Chris and I were in Iran, thus The Shah wanted nothing to do with another American media person at that time. I don't blame him. Although Barbara always got directly to the bulls-eye with her questions, this time she asked a particular question very impudently, in my opinion, and the opinion of most people watching, when she asked The Shah, verbatim, "If something happened to you, would this woman be allowed to take over the throne?" This "woman" was the Empress, the Queen. The Shah was visibly taken aback and angered, saying he'd never been asked such a question and was visibly insulted by Barbara's directness. The camera cut to The Empress during this exchange, showing, very vividly, tears welling-up in her eyes and at least one flowing down her right cheek. It was a sad few minutes to watch. The bittersweet result was Barbara's actions allowed me to return to Iran, this time with Billy and Suzy, as well as my friend, ski filmmaker extraordinaire, Dick Barrymore, who I suggested to Ardeshir would produce a full-length film for ski audiences to be seen in auditoria in the U.S., similar to the venues Warren Miller showed his ski films. My film would be strictly for television. Ardeshir okayed the addition of Dick and liked my idea to amplify the visit and audiences, some of whom would hopefully book ski trips to Iran after seeing both Dick's and my presentations. Yes, relations those days were that solidly amicable between the U.S. and Iran. *In later years, I emceed two of Warren's ski film presentations at Ford Auditorium in Detroit. In two of his earlier films, he actually used some footage from ski films I had produced.*

Speaking of relations, respectfully stated, Ardeshir was dating Elizabeth Taylor at that time, but I never met her. I was invited by Rod Steiger to meet and have lunch with Rod and Ms. Taylor in later years, when Rod was dating her, while I was privileged to be visiting him at his Malibu home one morning, but more about that later. (I didn't stay to meet her later that afternoon, darn it!)

Suzy, The Empress, Ardeshir and I had that mid-morning tea at the embassy in early July, 1976, as planned. The Empress said she remembered Suzy from posters she'd seen in St. Moritz, Switzerland, featuring Suzy in ballet-skiing poses. Suzy had created ballet skiing years earlier. It was innocent fun to know we'd sort of "one-upped" Rosalyn Carter because we had tea with The Empress just before she left for The White House to have lunch with Mrs. Carter that day.

Billy, Suzy, Dick Barrymore and I left for Tehran from JFK Airport in New York again aboard one of The Shah's 747SP jets, New Year's Eve, 1976. We had the first class cabin of the plane all to ourselves. Billy and Suzy occasionally playfully danced in the aisle and we were served as much vodka and caviar as one could ingest. I've maybe had 40 alcoholic drinks in my life and didn't drink the vodka that night. We all *did* toast the arrival of 1977 somewhere over Iceland or Greenland, and afterward went to sleep in our individual wide seats. Talk about pampered.

When we landed at Mehrabad International Airport the next morning at 10, Iranian time (12½ hours ahead of U.S. Eastern Time) it was still night for us that first day of January, 1977, but we had to awaken fast to meet those who would be with us as crew and guides for the filming that would finally take place. We heard on the radio in the car that picked us up that President Carter had just concluded a meeting with The Shah and confronted him about human rights. I thought, "Oh, no, this can't be happening again!" regarding possibly no shooting. I'm glad to say it didn't cancel the shoot.

Because I always shoot to the music that's in my head, I knew every scene I wanted to shoot to match the mood and sections of each piece of the music. The music I used, and astutely suggested months earlier by Chris, was the overture from the Broadway musical, *Cyrano*, used with permission from ASCAP. That show had it's pre-Broadway opening, starring Christopher Plummer, at The Guthrie Theater in Minneapolis, not too many years earlier.

Available free on the Internet, you can see the entire four-minute vignette showing Billy and Suzy walking in front of Tehran's Shayyad Tower and mingling in The Bazaar, all the time wearing their ski outfits and carrying their skis. Billy was clad in his signature western U.S. "cowboy" outfit and classic Stetson, with Suzy in her Spandex blue ski jump suit. Billy wore the same outfit when I shot their skiing sequences on Mt. Dizin. Suzy changed into a red Spandex ski jumpsuit, wearing an American Indian chief's headdress she had owned for several years, to be used for a Cowboy and Indian chase scene she and I agreed should be used in the film for "on purpose" culture contrasts for the viewers. It would initially be seen on HBO as an intermission piece that also, I'm honored to say, received a D.C. Emmy nomination for yours truly in 1977. I shot all the Tehran and skiing sequences with my hand-wind Bolex H16 "coffee grinder".

Dizin was one of four mountains on which The Shah had had ski resorts constructed in close proximity to Tehran to provide recreation for anyone who wanted to ski. As previously stated, I shot everything with my hand-wind, Bolex H16 "coffee grinder", Dick used his Arriflex (Arri) and my backup photographer and assistant, also shooting with Arris, were provided by NIRT, National Iranian Television.

Suzy, Billy, Dick and I were driven to Dizin from Tehran (about an hour's drive) and departed the car at a spot near where The Empress's helicopter would land, depositing her, two of her children and a friend of hers. We waited only a couple minutes and then Suzy and I were reunited with Her Imperial Majesty. She gave us a warm greeting, shaking hands, then greeted Billy and Dick. Billy and Dick took a separate gondola to the summit where we'd begin shooting. The Empress, Suzy and I shared another gondola. The Empress had a slight cold that day and apologized. I thanked her for agreeing to film when she wasn't feeling that well and she said it would be fine. I was facing her in the gondola and she smiled at me several times during the two or three minute ride, as if to intone "we're finally doing this."

All the shooting went well, thanks to Billy, Suzy and The Empress having been filmed skiing hundreds (thousands?) of times. While we were positioning Suzy, Billy and The Empress for certain shots near the top of the mountain, Iranians riding the open chairlift adjacent to the gondola were giving American Indian "war whoops" while looking down at Suzy, below. Indeed, they knew what "Cowboys and Indians" were.

The primary sequence for Billy and Suzy was a "Cowboy and Indian" chase scene I had devised to be shot to a major part of the music because, from past times with her, I knew Suzy owned a beautiful American Indian Chief's headdress and asked her to bring it on the trip. I also thought it would be fun to find a place for Suzy to "hide" when Billy jumps over her head while chasing her, not seeing her hide, with her resuming the scene, chasing after him. Billy hit his mark perfectly, without seeing Suzy, jumping over her in her hiding place, then her arising to begin chasing Billy. I knew the NIRT crew was standing beside me, but for some reason, intuition told me they weren't "rolling", thus I had my little hand-wind shoot that crucial part of the scene and "got it". The NIRT photographer sheepishly told me a few minutes after we "wrapped" that day, he'd forgotten to load more film into his camera, thus my intuition was correct and, thank God, we got the scene. As I mentioned earlier, the entire film and even some outtakes can be seen on the Internet when one links to *The Iranian Ski Scene*.

A bit of trivia about Billy: A Vermont native, as is Suzy, Billy is a direct descendant of Captain Kidd, the pirate, and is also one-half Abenaki American Indian, thus, technically, the Indian wound up chasing the "Indian" (Suzy) in the last part of that skiing sequence, concluding with both of them hugging each other at the bottom of the "chase hill". NIRT's cameraman shot that zoom sequence, obviously with a new roll of film he decided to load after the preceding described debacle. Smiling here.

Around noon, Billy, Suzy, Dick, the Empress and I skied down to a mid-mountain small dark wooden cabin where we were told lunch would be provided. We learned the small cabin belonged to the Shah and Empress. When we entered, we saw two of The Shah's and Empress's children, Prince Ali Reza, then aged ten and Princess Leila, then aged four. Also present was a friend of the Empress named Lili Dashti, who, we were told, was visiting from Germany, and to whom were introduced by The Empress. I then said to Princess Leila, "Hello, your Highness". She sheepishly smiled and softly said "Hello." The same sequence occurred with Prince Ali Reza, except he didn't smile and actually looked very serious. The lunch conversation also turned into a serious discussion about Iran and The Shah.

It was near dusk when we wrapped the six-hour shoot on Mount Dizin and said farewell to The Empress, who walked to where her helicopter was waiting to take her back to Tehran. Suzy, Billy, Dick and I then got in the car with our driver and headed back toward Tehran. Prince Ali Reza, Princess Leila and Ms. Dashti had earlier departed in a Palace car after our lunch with them and The Empress.

About a half-hour after departing the mountain, our driver pulled into the parking lot adjacent to a one story building on the left side of the road. It was a nightclub named Club Varian. He said he thought we'd enjoy a brief break after shooting, thus we went in. The muted recessed ceiling purple-colored lighting and modern décor were straight out of a James Bond movie. Men were playing blackjack at tables and the dealers were all female, and, as we learned, all British, somewhat scantily clad, which I won't fully describe here. The driver told us most of the players were executives from western world countries who were doing business in Iran. After about 20 minutes, we decided to leave.

Approaching the town of Karaj, the only town of note between Mount Dizin and Tehran, our driver decided to become playful and drive on the wrong side of the road. In Iran, they drive on the "U.S." side of the road, thus he was driving on the "British" side, and now nighttime. We objected, even though there was no traffic headed toward us, and he then went back to driving correctly.

The day we got an inkling things weren't all peaceful was the day before we were to return to the U.S. The night we returned from Mount Dizin, Billy and Suzy told me they wanted to see some other part of Iran, but within easy driving distance of Tehran. I looked at a map and saw the town of Qum (Gom) was only 70 miles southwest of Tehran, so I asked our Palace driver if we could drive there so I could shoot some "flavor shots" in that town, too. The driver asked, "Why do you want to go to Qum?". I told him the simple reason and he said okay, but somewhat reluctantly.

The next morning the driver picked up all of us at the hotel and we started our little day trip to Qum. However, just a few blocks from the hotel, our driver stopped the car in an alley, got out, opened the trunk of the car, a Mercedes sedan, and lifted a couple of beaten up "regular" Iranian license plates he'd then affix, replacing the Imperial palace license plates that were on the front and back of the car. I asked him why he was doing that, and he said, "It's just better that way." I didn't pursue the subject any further.

The terrain between Tehran and Qum was like Arizona's Painted Desert, truly rich in red and purple hues and mostly flat. The first spot at which I asked to stop in Qum was in front of the mosque there. The driver said I could shoot the outside of the mosque, but quickly. Again, I didn't ask "Why?", got out of the car and started filming the exterior. Dick stayed in the car, as did Billy and Suzy. When I began shooting, there were several elderly Mullahs standing in front of the mosque who began shaking their fists at me. The driver yelled at me from the car to get back in the car as fast as possible, which I did. He told me Qum was the religious capital of Iran, thus it would be best if we did some shooting at the other end of town. The reception there, from young people especially, as is seen in my film, was enthusiastically warm and welcoming. They especially liked seeing Suzy and Billy in their respective outfits, Billy's signature Cowboy attire and Suzy in her blue Spandex ski outfit. I finished shooting and we returned to Tehran, then the U.S. the next day.

After editing, I showed Ardeshir the finished product and he was pleased. *FYI: Ardeshir is CNN news anchor Christiane Amanpour's godfather.* Jim English, our former editor-in-chief at Channel 7, became an executive in early 1978 with newly-formed HBO and used my film as an intermission piece for almost year on HBO until the Khomeini revolution occurred. The aforementioned Sandy Reedy edited the Iranian piece, magnificently. It, too, was nominated for a D.C. Emmy.

Chile—In September, 1977, after the Iranian filming earlier that year, because of my membership in the then United States Ski Writers Association, I received a call from the VP of Public Relations for Braniff International Airways. His first name was Lou and I'm truly sorry I can't remember his last name. He told me Braniff wanted to increase their ski traffic to Portillo, Chile's pre-eminently known ski resort on the Argentine border, thus asked if I'd produce, shoot, narrate and edit a film about Portillo and other parts of Chile for eventual use on television, wherever I was. Since my contract had just ended at Channel 7, I told Lou I had the free time to do the film, which debuted on my *Detroit Ski Scene* the following January and has been seen many other places since then.

There were a couple unusual highlights in regard to the trip, as follows:

- We left North America the last day of our summer, landing in Chile the last day of their winter, leaving Chile the first days of their spring and arriving back in the U.S. the first days of our autumn, all within a ten day period, i.e., all four seasons.
- Lou had timed the trip so I could film extreme ski racer Steve McKinney executing his fastest run ever for an unofficial world's record that particular day on Portillo's Roc A Jac run, clocking 137 miles per hour. (In 1978, Steve would break 200-miles-per-hour speed, also at Portillo.) Bill Rice, my great, and now sadly late, ABC-TV announcer friend and skier who was with me as I shot the film, got my film back to ABC-TV in New York via Braniff, of course, to air on *Wide World Of Sports* the following day.

I got to know Steve then and in later years. For all his expertise as the then world's fastest skier, Steve was eventually killed on a highway near Sacramento while trying to help a distressed motorist change a tire. Makes one wonder. I sent Steve's half-sister, Tamara McKinney, who was also an Olympic word champion skier, a copy of the Chilean film, featuring his then record-breaking run, after Steve's death but never received acknowledgement she'd received it. Regardless, his loss, as most all losses, was tragic.

CHAPTER SIXTEEN

Another Life, Again

You never stop paying your dues—Joel Grey to me during an L.A. interview

Even though The Washington Post gave me credit for being the only television weatherman in D.C. alerting the public to an imminent major rain storm that flooded D.C. and environs one night, and our ratings were high, station politics and egos ended my contract, as referenced in the Ron Canada remembrance, i.e., Ron saying to me, "Barry, you and I are among the grateful dead."

I was out of work from September to November when I got the nod from Detroit television station WJBK-TV, then a CBS affiliate, to be their lead weatherman, to start for $30,000 a year less than I was making in D.C. I was allowed to do what I had done in the Twin Cities at KSTP-TV, including *The Ski Scene*, Detroit version; the co-anchors were welcoming and we all got along. One of our occasional sports co-anchors was Dick Vitale who later went on to national fame on ESPN. Great guy and we had fun times.

Robert Goulet reprised his guest appearances on my weathercasts in Detroit, as did friends Louis Nye and Ed Ames, the latter, who, single at that time, asked who our pretty anchor was and they eventually dated via my "cupid" introduction. Our anchor told me they mostly visited Detroit's excellent art museums. "New" weather guests included Ray Bolger, Cyd Charisse, Tony Martin and singer Helen O'Connell. I told Helen I used to watch her perform at the Stardust in Las Vegas with co-singer Don Cornell during my TV days there. She asked if I ever got to California once in a while. I told her I rarely did and that was that.

I also began shooting more ski films for the resurrected *Detroit Ski Scene*, with the station's blessing. Following are some of those most revered memories, as well as other memories, both good and not so good, connected with my time in Detroit, not previously referenced:

224

Sophia Loren and Catherine Deneuve—On another filming trip to The French Alps, in 1978, my itinerary took me from Detroit to Paris, with a change of planes in Paris to fly to Geneva to get to The Alps. When I boarded the smaller Air France jet to Geneva, I saw Sophia Loren seated in first-class with her two children. I walked back into coach.

When we landed in Geneva, I had to wait for a small van that would take other ski journalists and me to Chamonix to begin our journalistic "chores". My cohorts were arriving on a second plane a half hour later, thus I had time to wander around the Geneva airport while waiting for their arrival. I decided to walk out into a large open patio that had no furnishings, just a cement floor. Who was standing there, actually pacing a bit back and forth, but Sophia Loren. The children weren't with her. Not being bashful, I decided to (respectfully) tell her I knew Gregory Peck and had done some work with him.

She accepted my approach, and I told her. She said, verbatim, "Oh, I *love* that man. He is one of my best friends! I'm so happy you told me!" She asked my name, after which she told me she was waiting for her driver, who had already picked up her children and were waiting for baggage. She said they were going to their "place" in the French Alps to rendezvous with her husband, Carlo Ponti. I said something mundane, like "That's great!" then told her it was an honor to meet her and said a warm goodbye and thanked her for talking to me. I started to walk away and she literally grabbed my coat, from behind, semi-gently pulled me back to her and said, "No! Stay." I want to talk *more!*" I thanked her and said I didn't know what else to say. She smiled and asked why I was there and I told her. She then said it was nice to talk and wished me good luck.

On our way to the Alps, I saw her, her children and driver in their car, paralleling our mini-bus for a while, then watched as they turned left into a road that would take them to "their" mountain place. Every time I've seen her in movies or on television, I, of course, remember that special time on the patio at the Geneva airport. *Ms. Loren was actually here in Minnesota, including the Twin Cities, acting in the film,* Grumpier Old Men, *in the mid-1990s, but I decided to not try to get in touch with her at that time. One of my longtime Minneapolis friends, former Twin Cities television personality, Shirley Hutton, who had also sold more Mary Kay products than anyone in that company's history, then owned a gigantic mansion on Minneapolis's beautiful Lake of the Isles. Jack Lemmon's wife was looking for a place for her and Jack to stay while the film was shooting. Shirley said Mrs. Lemmon came to the house and asked where all the servants were. Shirley told her there were no servants and that was the end of the possible Lemmon stay there. Shirley was related to the late "Dear Abby" via the marriage of one of her daughters to one of Abby's sons, who my wife, Ellen, also knew very well.*

One of my all-time favorite stories—On the way back to the U.S. from that trip, my seat partner and NASJA colleague was longtime *Ski Magazine* editor, Dick Needham. Dick and I had been booked into the second row in first class on the Air France flight to New York. Dick noticed that one row back from us, on the other side of the aisle, was iconic French actress, Catherine Deneuve, seated in the aisle seat, with a female companion seated near the window. We also noticed a very craggy-faced elderly-looking gentleman, seated directly behind Dick and me, frequently going back and forth between his seat and Ms. Deneuve's, showing her slides and pictures from a large briefcase. Dick said, "Look at the old geezer showing pictures of his grandkids to Deneuve." I just nodded.

After we took off, he was over there, back and forth for at least an hour. Then Dick said to me, "Deneuve's a phony. She was born in Kansas and developed this phony French accent, then moved to France and became a movie star." I told him he was wrong, and crazy. He kept insisting. Following his final insistent comment about her birthplace, I told him I'd ask her. Not being bashful about those sorts of things, but also realizing the respect factor is involved, I walked directly across the aisle, where no one was seated, put my knees on the seat, arms over the top of the backrest, and said, remembering it as if it happened today, "Pardon me, Ms. Deneuve." She looked up, anticipating what might be next out of my mouth. I then said, "My friend says you were born in Kansas." Her eyes got as big as saucers, and said "No! It is his mistake!" I told her I thought so, and apologized for the question. She got a wonderful smile on her face and told me that was fine. I then went back to my seat and Dick kept insisting he was right. Again the "geezer" was back at Ms. Deneuve's seat occasionally, still showing her some pictures and slides.

Fasten your seat belts, pun intended, for *this* punch line—About 20 minutes from landing at JFK, the flight attendant stood next to Dick's and my seat and said, "Perhaps you gentlemen would have had a much more enjoyable flight had you paid less attention to Ms. Deneuve and more attention to Mr. Cousteau in back of you." The "geezer", as Dick had described him, was Jacques Cousteau. The irony is I had worked for the ABC affiliate in D.C. until the preceding year and ABC, of course, carried Mr. Cousteau's television series, but I hadn't recognized him during the flight. When Dick and I got off the plane, there was a cadre of photographers outside the jetway, waiting for Mr. Cousteau, not Ms. Deneuve. I guess I at least have the "distinction" of probably being the only person in the world who asked Catherine Deneuve if she was born in Kansas! *Was very saddened to learn, while writing this book, Dick Needham passed away in 2012. Dick told me he had been adopted only a few days after he was born. One of the other more memorable times with him was helping him with his French when he'd lost the key to his room. He had earlier in the evening groused about my speaking French with the ski resort waitresses while ordering my supper, but when the key incident occurred told me he was happy I knew the language. We skied in many places all over the world together, from Banff, Alberta to most other Canadian and U.S. resorts to those magnificent French and Italian Alps. Spoiled was I? Indeed.*

Everett Kircher, Boyne Mountain and Big Sky, Montana—When I began writing my weekly ski columns for *The Detroit Free Press*, I got a call from a man named Chuck Moll. He was Everett Kircher's partner and General Manager of Boyne Mountain, Michigan. He and Everett invited me to be their guest at Boyne one weekend and we remained friends until both their deaths several years later. In the late 1970s, I produced a television film for them about Boyne and its history. Everett had been a Studebaker car dealership owner in Detroit. He founded and developed Boyne into several ski hills in

Northwestern Michigan, north of Traverse City and was the person who lured Norway's Olympic ski champion, and my longtime friend, Stein Eriksen, previously referenced, to the United States. Stein said he came because Everett offered him a free Studebaker! He was Everett's Director of Skiing until moving on to bigger resorts in the U.S., winding up at Deer Valley, Utah. During my Detroit years, Stein told my radio ski show audiences on WJR in Detroit, "You have done more for the ski industry in this country than anyone I've ever known." I was honored for his generous and kind statement, although I think a lot of other people who covered skiing did quite a bit, too, to cause amplified awareness for the sport. *Two years before Deer Valley opened, Stein invited me there to do some test runs on their phenomenal slopes, voted best in the U.S. by SKI magazine's editors and readers for many years after they opened in 1981. He invited me back again one year before Deer Valley opened and took a photo of me on a snowcat at the bottom of one of the runs, holding my hands in the air while saying "Yippee!" Deer Valley used that photo on their opening season postcards in 1981. In March, 1984, after moving back to the Twin Cities, I was invited to stay in Deer Valley for a couple days at one of their massive condos built just after the resort opened and before the equally massive Stein Eriksen Lodge opened. I felt like a marble in a bowling alley. Just me surrounded by at least 3,000 square feet of condo, on multi-levels. I was only the sixth guest to stay there. The guests immediately preceding my stay in that condo were Mr. and Mrs. Peter Ueberroth, the male side of that duo who had then just been named Commissioner of Baseball and was also in the throes of heading the 1984 Los Angeles Summer Olympics. Shortly thereafter, Mr. Ueberroth and I found each other attending a media event on the playing field of The Minnesota Twins at the Hubert H. Humphrey Metrodome. I tackily but playfully said to him, smiling, "I slept in the same bed as your wife!" He asked me about what I was talking and I told him he and she had signed the guest book immediately before my stay at that Deer Valley condo. He gave me a very unfriendly look over his shoulder and said, "That's not too funny, you know." I guess I shouldn't have said it, but I haven't always been the brightest bulb on the tree. Sorry, Pete.*

In 1976, Everett's Boyne Resorts bought Big Sky from Chrysler Corporation, two years after Chet Huntley died, which was three days before Big Sky opened in March, 1974. Chet had conceived the idea for Big Sky and it was tragic his cancer got to him so few days before he had a chance to witness the opening. *Some of my times with Chet and his wife, Tippy, previously referenced. One of the times with Tippy, not referenced, was being with her and actor William Conrad, whom she later married, having a good time at Big Sky's Ore House bar, several years after Chet's passing. Conrad, of course, played the original Matt Dillon on the radio version of* Gunsmoke *and starred in, among others, a television series called* Cannon. *Great actor and a great lady having a great time.*

Everett invited me to fly to Big Sky in his private jet with him, also the previously referenced Chuck Moll, his PR person whose name I can't remember and John Kircher, one of his sons, who piloted the jet at night from Kalamazoo, where we took off, through a rugged snowstorm over the mountains of south central Montana. When we landed at Bozeman's airport, I came close to kissing the tarmac, as I actually had at SFO in 1965, previously described. At dinner that evening, Everett kindly echoed what Stein had said regarding my knowledge of the ski business and global venues. I told him I was honored for his comments and came close to asking him for a job, but didn't. I didn't see him often after that trip, but have been in touch with his sons through the years. John, our Big Sky jet pilot, now runs Crystal Mountain, south of Seattle-Tacoma and Steve runs Big Sky. I was told by a mutual friend, when Everett had reached his 75th birthday, he looked very despondent. Our friend asked him why. Everett said, "Because I'm 75 and haven't done half the things I still want to do." I can identify, at age 78. More about aging later.

Major historic time with Dr. Theodore "Ted" Fujita (and flying through Hurricane David)—One of my assignments during the Detroit Channel 2 days was to interview Dr. Theodore "Ted" Fujita at his "tornado chamber" laboratory in Chicago. Dr. Fujita had created the "F"-scale for measuring the intensity of tornadoes, i.e., F-1, etc. I wish I'd had the cameraman's camera running when we walked into his dimly lighted lab at 8:30 in the morning, because he told me we were the first in the world to hear him say the following, without even saying "Hello" and almost crying: "I was wrong. Everything I've said about tornado formation is wrong. This tornado chamber is wrong. Tornadoes really form from the ground upward toward the base of the clouds, not from the clouds downward." He repeated it for the camera, but for my cameraman and me, we truly heard that historic statement and revelation uttered first.

The only other significant weather story I did for Detroit's Channel 2 was to report live for 10 hours from the inside of a Hurricane Hunter plane flying at 10,000 feet, zig-zagging back and forth in and out of the very wide eye of Hurricane David. It was during Labor Day weekend, 1979. David was a Category 5 hurricane. At 6 a.m., my cameraman and I flew out of Keesler Air Force Base in Biloxi, MS, home of the Hurricane Hunters, headed toward David, which was then just making half-landfall around the Florida Keys. I've experienced worse turbulence in commercial airliners, thus reporting and photo taking was uneventful. To me, the most fascinating sight was looking directly down over the "eye" and seeing waves spinning toward the center in an almost perfect pinwheel configuration. We got back to Biloxi at 6 p.m. after departing David when it had reached the coast of north Florida about 4 that afternoon. Our station was the only one based in Detroit given permission to be on that particular flight, thanks to the relationship Pete Storer, then Chairman of Storer Broadcasting, had with some U.S. Air Force brass. Again, it's not what you know, but who you know, that makes things happen, which is often very sad, in my opinion, leaving a lot of brilliantly talented people out in the cold. Storer Broadcasting owned our station.

Speaking of being "out in the cold", my departure from Detroit's Channel 2 was again somewhat nefarious in nature, a la "getting me another job" per WCCO-TV, previously referenced. In a nutshell, the aforementioned Sonny Elliott was fired from Channel 4. Almost immediately after hearing that news, I was told by the News Director Channel 2 would be "talking to Sonny" but my job wasn't in jeopardy. This is painful to remember, but true: I was in the weather office and got a phone call, not more than a minute after I'd been told about Sonny not being a threat to my job. The phone call was from Sonny, saying, "I wouldn't have done this to you for the world, kid. They told me it wouldn't hurt you, but I'm taking your job." I can't remember what I said to him, but hung up and told the News Director what had just happened. He had a sheepish look on his face and apologized. *During my tenure there, several of the engineers who had been part of the crew of my* Detroit Ski Scene *told me they felt my full-time talents should be devoted to documentary filmmaking, writing and narrating. Although I never filmed there, thanks to one of those wonderful people, I got to know Scotland well during some travels, and especially the village of Luss, previously referenced. Those kinds of people were the ones who truly made life stronger and more special, enriching the memory bank and mental Rolodex in perpetuity. As I think I've stated previously, they never knew how truly important they were to me then, and always.*

It wasn't a very good period of time, for a *long* time. Chris and I had divorced and I was hired, shortly after losing the Channel 2 job, as weekend weathercaster on WDIV-TV, Channel 4, which was the station from which Sonny was fired. It was a "mercy kiss" job and I knew it, but was grateful for the continued income, albeit less than I was making at Channel 2. I also started doing part-time talk show hosting on WCAR radio, one of the clients for an ad agency named D.C. Frey and Associates that had hired me to be talent as well as copywriter and VP of Creative Services for clients such as Air New Zealand, Maccabees Mutual Life Insurance, Kitchen Aid Appliances and Can-Am Travel. I and my weekend co-anchor, whose television name was Andrea Joyce, were once Grand Marshals of a parade in her hometown of Dearborn Heights, Michigan. Andrea later married broadcaster Harry Smith, who went on to national fame as a network anchor and correspondent on CBS-TV and, as of this writing, is now a features reporter for NBC-TV. I met Harry a few times in later years (nice man) and tried to get in touch with Andrea after she'd become a successful network sports reporter/anchor, but no phone calls were ever returned.

During that Channel 4 period, some pleasant things occurred. One of them was to re-acquaint with a former Twin Cities news anchor named Cathy Mann for lunch one day. Cathy had worked in the Twin Cities on Channel 9 during my KS days. Cathy called me at WDIV-TV and told me she was a native of the Detroit suburb of Livonia, where I was living at the time, and was in town visiting family. I hadn't known about Cathy's Detroit area roots until she told me. When we had lunch, she told me she was dating Fred Grandy, who played Gopher on *The Love Boat*. Fred later became a U.S. Congressman from his native Iowa.

Another privileged one-on-one lunch during those Channel 4 Detroit years was with Harry James and Betty Grable's daughter, Victoria James Bivens. During my Las Vegas years, Harry was always very generous with his time for me to visit him backstage, having first told me during a social event he was a "weather fan" of mine. What a mega-honor, to say the least. When I knew I was leaving Las Vegas for the Twin Cities, Harry told me if I was ever in the Detroit area I should look up his daughter, Victoria. She had married a Chrysler executive who was in charge of Chrysler's operations in Australia, but Harry he said he knew they'd be moving back to the U.S. in a couple years. I told him I would follow up on his kind suggestion, not knowing I'd ever be working in Detroit. Thus, as luck would have it, I decided to bite the bullet and at least try to have lunch with the daughter of two of America's most revered icons. Via networking at Chrysler, I reached Mr. Bivens, told him about his father-in-law's suggestion and he had "Vicki" call me. We arranged lunch in one of the Detroit suburbs (I think Birmingham or Bloomfield Hills) and enjoyed almost two hours discussing her famous parents, their sad breakup and her love for both of them. That was the only time I had the privilege to be with her, but she echoed the dignity of both her talented parents.

I got another employment blow just before Christmas that year: Channel 4 decided to replace me, knowing I really wasn't happy there, thus I re-connected with Ted Anthony, who had returned to Detroit from his Iranian DJ/announcing job before I landed the Channel 2 job, and was now announcing for Channel 4, asking if he had any job suggestions. He immediately called a friend of his named Chuck Costa who owned a paint store on Grand River Avenue near

Tiger Stadium, but was also heavily into great ideas to help people get jobs. Chuck told Ted I should call him "right away". I did, and Chuck saved my financial life for almost two years when I helped him create and activate *I Care, America*, which eventually was responsible for the creation of over 3,000 new jobs in the Detroit area during the early 1980s recession. Among those I got to endorse the charity were President Reagan (via my Las Vegas-borne friendship with his daughter, Maureen), Mickey Rooney, Louis Nye, Jerry Lewis and many others. Chuck also had a strong relationship with Rosa Parks and because of their friendship, she became an interviewee included in one of the documentaries I helped produce in 2000, entitled *The Remarkable 20th Century*, previously referenced and more about which later. As I write this, Chuck is hanging on to life in a Detroit hospital, as he has for at least two years. He was very philanthropic, having come to this country almost penniless at age 11 from his native Malta, becoming a successful property owner through nothing but hard work and American friends who helped him up the ladder. He would truly be a *Readers Digest* "most unforgettable people" candidate, also being a brilliant artist and thrice a Detroit mayoral candidate. His children, Gina, Pamela, Pepe, et al, were instilled with Chuck's European ethic of hard work and caring about others.

In the early 1980s, after the Channel 4 debacle, I was happy to get a call to do weekend weather on ABC-TV's answer to CNN. It was called SNC, for Satellite News Channels, and was based near Stamford, Connecticut, in wonderful studios on Shippan Point, where I'm told Ted Turner's TCM east coast studios are now on that site for Robert Osborne to do his movie introductions. They said they'd pay my travel and lodging and since I had been a member of AFTRA, our broadcast union, since 1953 (and a Detroit local union board member all six years I was there), I'd get union wages and benefits. The job was to last three to six months, but it was fine with me, being back on the air where everyone said I belonged, and I knew that was true. Thank you, God.

I did the weather cut-ins every 20 minutes and worked with genuine news giants who had previously been either on CBS, ABC or NBC radio and television, the nicest being Charles Crawford.

They were all nice, but Charles stands out the most in my little brain. Our producers were Tom Capra, son of Frank Capra, previously referenced and Stephen Bogart, Lauren Bacall and Humphrey Bogart's son. Steve looked a lot like his Dad, as did Tom resembling Frank. The most social conversation I ever had with Steve Bogart was sharing the fact that one of Chris's and my acting friends from the Twin Cities was named Grace Kaege who had acted with Steve's mother on Broadway in *Applause* and *Woman Of The Year*. He said he remembered Grace's name, and that was that.

The full-time weatherman at SNC, who had actually been on *Nightline* twice, after Ted Koppel took over from the ailing Frank Reynolds, was named Paul Douglas. He did some of the weekend shifts with me and we became fast friends with that friendship still ongoing. Paul's also a native Pennsylvanian, but from Lancaster, far from my hometown of Pittsburgh. During one of the weekends at SNC, Paul told me he received a call from an agent stating Channel 11 in the Twin Cities was interested in having him become their lead weatherman/meteorologist. He asked me if he should consider it, knowing my previous background and living experiences there. I told him I thought it would be a great career move, also stating "You'll be number one." I'm happy to state that prediction came true, in more ways than one. Paul has remained a great friend since.

CHAPTER SEVENTEEN

Twin Cities, Again

There's always a faster gun—Don Buehler, KSTP-TV reporter

Shortly after Paul Douglas got that nod, and because I was hoping to get back on the air on a full-time basis, I got a call from the aforementioned Tom Ryther, the sports anchor with whom I worked at KS. As the crazy business would have it, Tom was now working at Channel 11 in the Twin Cities, where Douglas decided he'd take the offer. That was in the spring of 1983. Douglas would start in the summer of 1983. Tom said he recommended me to News Director Tom Kirby to be full-time weatherman until Douglas and a new news and weather team debuted, then switch my duties to weekend weather and Entertainment Editor (reporter). Kirby loved it and that was how I returned to the Twin Cities television market. I was at 11 for four years. Following are some of the fondest memories:

Jerry Stiller and Anne Meara—One of my primary duties while at 11 was to review plays, as well as interview stars, directors and producers of new films on numerous junkets to and from New York and Los Angeles at least twice a month. Many of those I interviewed I'd known from years past, either as a co-actor or simply personal friend. During a feature about *Dallas*, Howard Keel said, "So *this* is what you're doing now." My heart kind of sank because I felt he knew I wasn't really happy not being able to "show my real stuff" as before in Las Vegas and at KS. Regardless, I was grateful for the work.

One of the plays I was asked to review, as well as interview some of its stars, was *Guys And Dolls* at The Guthrie Theater in Minneapolis. I interviewed iconic tough guy movie actor turned stage actor, Mike Mazurki, and a couple others, but not Jerry and I can't remember why not. Regardless, when I saw the production, Jerry's performance as Nathan Detroit was perfection. I said so on my television review. A few days afterward, I was invited to a Guthrie party to interact with the cast and it was there Jerry welcomed me as a friend. Anne's presence there was a surprise bonus. She was dynamic and first-class, no surprise there. She, Jerry and I conversed for a couple minutes about the "making the rounds" days we shared during the early 1950s around the time they made their debut on *The Ed Sullivan Show*. Their routines, written by them, of course, were classics, and still are. Their availability on the Internet and their son Ben's revival of them in a produced-for-Internet series not too many years ago has now, so deservedly, made them immortal for future generations to see how those scenes should really be executed. The from-the-heart dialogue and interaction you see between them gets straight to the sensitivities we should all feel when witnessing those sorts of performances. Jerry and Anne were, and will always be, a match unmatched, both professionally and in "real life". Jerry and I kept up most of the communication in later years.

Among the most fun times he and I had personally was during one of my junket trips to New York. We most always had the nights "free", thus Jerry suggested we see The Pointer Sisters who were performing at Radio City Music Hall. When Jerry and I met at the appointed time and place at his and Anne's apartment building on Riverside Drive, another longtime mutual friend of ours joined us: The mutual friend was singer Joe Williams. Jerry hadn't known Joe, his wife Jillean and I had been good friends during my Las Vegas years. We "Three Musketeers" caught a cab to Radio City Music Hall, Jerry bought the tickets at the door and we entered. During the opening number, the place was so overwhelmingly filled with the smoke and smell of marijuana, we all agreed we should leave. I felt badly Jerry had paid for tickets that lasted us less than three or four minutes into a performance. Regardless, he shrugged it off after correctly saying "We could get high in there just breathing it all in." and asked Joe if he had any alternate entertainment suggestions. Joe said a friend of his was singing jazz at The Village Vanguard in Greenwich Village and he thought we should go. Go we did, again in a cab, and spent a great hour there enjoying Joe's friend's performance. I can't remember the singer's name, but to play the VV, one had to be "the best", which she was. There was plenty of smoke there, too, but not from marijuana. We all took the same cab uptown, departed at our respective stops and that was that.

Another wonderful time with Jerry was when he took me to lunch at one of his and my favorite restaurants, The Russian Tea Room. Any time with Jerry was wonderful and memorable. During this particular lunch, as we were preparing to exit the restaurant, Jerry noticed playwright Garson Kanin and his wife, actress Ruth Gordon, seated in an east wall booth. We stopped and Jerry kindly gave me the honor to be introduced to them. Ruth asked what I did and I told her, briefly, it was a mixed bag and I was still trying to figure out what I was going to do when I grew up. She smiled and then said what I quoted she said just below this book's first chapter title, i.e., "I never got a good job I didn't create for myself." I thanked Jerry for the introduction, we both bade them "Adieu" and left. As we were going out the door, a man exiting directly behind us was actor/director John Houseman who had been continually ribbed by Johnny Carson regarding a television commercial Mr. Houseman had done during that era. I asked him how he felt about Carson's incessant references and he said, verbatim. "It's getting tedious." He and his female companion then continued walking out onto the sidewalk, as did Jerry and I.

Holiday cards and personal notes have been frequent through the years, but the most surprising recognition of Jerry's sincere caring about my career arrived in early January, 2001, in the form of his autobiography, *Married To Laughter*, in which he inscribed it to Ellen and me as being truly "a part of his life" and also circling my name in the acknowledgments as one of his friends, all previously referenced, but I can't mention it enough. It was truly, to say the least, an unexpected honor for this kid from Pittsburgh's projects. Jerry and Anne also honored me with annual birthday cards as well as a recorded congratulatory tribute to my 60 years in broadcasting which occurred in February, 2003, and aired here in the Twin Cities. Ellen and I also remember and remembered their birthdays and special times, a joy to do. Once when Jerry was ill, I ordered one of those fruit baskets to be delivered to him to hopefully cheer him up. When I called to ask if it had been delivered, he cheerily said, "Yes. It looks like a Hawaiian garden!" Thank God for memories and people like Jerry and Anne who make them, and life, all the more special. Sorry for perhaps over-sentimentality, but it's truly the way I feel. We can never experience enough of that genuine love and friendship, especially from people of their caliber, in my opinion.

Among the junketeers—Among those interviewers in our at least twice a month junkets to New York or L.A. were two who went very far up the success ladder. One was named Laurie Hibberd. She was a native of Canada who landed entertainment-reporting gigs in the U.S. Not long before one of the junket trips to New York, her father passed away. After a screening one night, we all gathered in The Regency Hotel's lounge. I hadn't spoken to Laurie very often, but when we did speak, it was pleasant. That night, I offered my condolences about the passing of her father, which she acknowledged graciously and sincerely. Not too many years later she became the wife of "Gelman" (Michael Gelman), Regis and Kelly's producer. Laurie went on to produce, too, numerous episodes of *Alf* and *Roseanne*, to name just two. I wish I'd known about *Roseanne*, as Tom Arnold has been a good friend to me (as well as his late Aunt Kay) since the 1980s. I met Roseanne only once while I was regularly emceeing at a comedy club in Minneapolis (Scott Hansen's *Comedy Gallery*). She was as sweet and gracious as anyone could ever be. That was during the time she and Tom were still very married to each other. I'll relate more about Tom later.

Rod Lurie was the other who really "made it" following junket-land. I always used to call him Frank because he looked so much like my close acquaintance, Frank Sinatra, Jr., previously referenced. In addition to being a television critic and interviewer, Rod was a line drawing artist for major newspapers and later directed and produced films and television series of the highest caliber starring everyone from Robert Redford to Geena Davis. Until writing this book, I had no idea of his incredible pedigree as an Israeli-born West Point graduate and too much else of note to chronicle here. Even though we had a fun and warm relationship during at least four years of junketeering, I always wondered why he looked at me somewhat wryly when I'd tease him about looking like FS, Jr. Now I know. Congratulations to Rod. I tried to reach him once during the time his TV series *The Commander* was still on the air. His agent said Rod remembered me very well, but I never got a return call from him. No problem, as he's very respectfully remembered here.

Interviewees who told me fascinating stories about their early lives were numerous, William Shatner among the most interesting and ingratiating. We shared some friends in common, thus, somewhat echoing what Henry Fonda had told me about Fonda's and Wally Cox's Salmon River fishing days during *Spencer's Mountain*'s filming in Jackson Hole, Shatner made the stories "longer" for me because I "knew the territory." Fonda had told me "because I knew him.", i.e., Wally.

The Shatner story that got to me the most was about his rough financial situation while acting in a Shakespearean production in Stratford, Ontario. He told me he was so poor he couldn't afford to rent a room, thus, for almost two weeks, slept on the floor in the cleaning room of a laundromat, between midnight and 6 a.m., undetected. Successful actors and actresses sometimes do remember their early days and hard times.

Austria—The station allowed me to occasionally shoot more segments, features and sequences for my resurrected ski program, the name of which Channel 11 changed from *The Ski Scene* to *11 Ski Country With Barry ZeVan*. One of our top sales executives named Karl Gensheimer had known I'd been to Austria previously, but strictly as a ski writer for *The Detroit Free Press*, as previously referenced, covering ski areas in Innsbruck and Mayrhofen for ten days. *The scenery in and around Mayrhofen, just six miles north of the Italian border, eclipses all the scenery shown in* The Sound Of Music. *The people there were, and are, wonderful.*

I told Karl I wanted to do a feature about Lilienfeld, the birthplace of downhill skiing, as we know it today and about which I'd, in past years, urged my fellow USSWA/NASJA journalists to more highly recognize. Karl arranged the trip with an executive friend of his at Lufthansa. A photographer from the station shot what I wanted to shoot and describe and it aired on *11 Ski Country* shortly after we returned. One of the great surprises was a close cousin of the man who invented wide skis and beartrap bindings, Mathias Zdarsky, lived in a Minneapolis suburb, thus allowed me to interview him about his famous ancestor for the feature. I had, in years past, during a USSWA annual meeting at the Chateau Lake Louise, in Alberta, written the words to a plaque that still hangs in the Zdarsky museum in Lilenfeld, acknowledging the USSWA/NASJA recognized Mr. Zdarsky as the "father of Downhill Skiing" as we know it today. If you're a skier, I'd suggest putting Lilienfeld, just 50 minutes drive west of Vienna, on your bucket list. Have visited there three times. Skier or not, this place is "magic".

I had been a continuous member of that organization since 1971, was a six-year President of the Midwest Chapter and First Vice President of the national organization of USSWA, now named NASJA. At a national meeting in the 1980s, I was lucky enough to be the first one to utter the new name after suggesting it and when it was first called the North American Ski Journalists Association. That acronym, NASJA, then morphed a few years later into the North American Snowsports Journalists Association because of the proliferation of snowboarding. As of this writing, I'm still a member, listed as semi-retired, but still writing about the sport and its history, quarterly, in The Midwest Sportster.

Manny Laureano, Henry Mancini, "Doc" Severinsen, Minnesota Governor Rudy Perpich and The Mall of Europe—Being Channel 11's Entertainment Editor happily required interviewing the cream of the crop who came to the Twin Cities and especially at Orchestra Hall, home of The Minnesota Orchestra, rightfully named the world's best orchestra by a major London, England, newspaper during tour performances in the U.K. in 2010. The Minnesota Orchestra's lead trumpeter is Manny Laureano, a native New Yorker and Juilliard prodigy. He and I have many people in common and lots to always discuss. Manny's been a great friend to me for decades. He is also . . . guess what? . . . another fellow Leo! In the mid-1990s, Ellen and I had the joy to entertain Manny and his wife, Claudette, for dinner shortly after Ellen and I were married. During the throes of a devastating Minnesota Orchestra lockout in 2013 and 2014, Manny and I discussed ideas about how we could save the orchestra. One afternoon at a private lunch at a Culver's Restaurant in a Twin Cities suburb close to both our respective houses, I came up with an idea to have the entire population of the State of Minnesota become owners of the Orchestra, similar to the citizens of Green Bay owning the Packers. Manny loved it and said he'd communicate it to the existing powers at the Orchestra.

The next morning, in the *Star Tribune*, it was noted a longtime and respected State of Minnesota congresswoman named Phyllis Kahn (also a native New Yorker, like Manny) had the same idea I'd expressed to Manny the day before. I called him and he said, "I know why you're calling. I said nothing to Phyllis. This is quite a coincidence!" I called Phyllis. She told me the *Star Tribune* hadn't told the entire story, which was Phyllis had actually suggested saving the Minnesota Twins in a similar fashion years earlier and literally and coincidentally came up with the same idea for the Orchestra I'd expressed to Manny. I told her I thought it might be fun to collaborate to get this done, thus we had a wonderful lunch and fashioned the "battle plan" and became good friends, but, happily a great solution was found without Phyllis, Manny and me going into "battle" to save our phenomenal treasure, that great Orchestra. *When The Minnesota Orchestra's newest conductor, Osmo Vanska, arrived to begin his superb work, I was invited to a welcoming luncheon for him. I knew he and I had a mutual friend in Sweden, adjacent to his native Finland. Her name is Kjerstin Hallert, a respected entertainment, television and music critic whom I'd known during times in Cannes. Maestro Vanska discussed our Kjerstin connection and he seemed happy there was someone in that room who shared a mutual friend.*

The truly great composer/conductor/musician, Henry Mancini, conducted some of his own iconic music for an Orchestra Hall performance during my tenure at Channel 11 in the mid-1980s. The station, and Orchestra Hall, had me interview him on the Orchestra Hall stage during an afternoon rehearsal break. The only people there were Henry, my Channel 11 photographer and me. Along with dissecting how he had ideas for certain music he composed (classics like *The Pink Panther* themes, *Breakfast At Tiffany's*, *Moon River*, television's *Peter Gunn* series theme, etc.), he and I discussed our native Western Pennsylvania roots. He was born in Aliquippa, just a 40 minute drive northwest of Pittsburgh, on the banks of the Ohio River, and yours truly born in Pittsburgh itself, previously noted. After the cameraman had packed his gear and left the stage, Henry and I continued talking for another couple minutes, facing each other on the chairs used for the interview and he said, "You have beautiful eyes." I respectfully smiled and thanked him for that comment, thanked him for the interview time and left. He didn't make that statement in a suggestive tone, but, to me, it was something one doesn't expect to hear every day, especially from a "giant". I took it appreciatively, not thinking anything tawdry, but thought it might be interesting to share.

Another music icon, and one of the most down-to-Earth "real" people in an industry not known for small egos, was (and is) "Doc" Severinsen. "Doc" has been The Minnesota Orchestra's guest conductor for many, many years. Channel 11 assigned me to interview him about one of the concerts he was conducting at Orchestra Hall, also in the mid-1980s. He and I discussed our mutual relationship with *The Tonight Show Starring Johnny Carson's* producer, Fred de Cordova (who had, in earlier years, also produced the hit television sitcom series, *My Three Sons*) as well as my encounter with Johnny at Las Vegas's Silver Slipper, previously noted. I asked how he got the nickname, "Doc". He told me he was born in Oregon and his father was a dentist. All the townspeople used to call his father "Doc", thus his son, who became known as Johnny Carson's, and The Minnesota Orchestra's, "Doc", became "Doc", too, but originally "Doc, Jr.". After the interview, his comment to me was so effusive and genuine, I want to share it, to wit: At the literal top of his lungs, he said (yelled), *"That was great!!!"*. I smiled and thanked him, but he repeated it to me, then adding, "I really mean that." It was a great honor from a great man.

Only a few days after I went back on the air in the Twin Cities (Channel 11) I went to Orchestra Hall to re-connect with some of the musicians I'd known years earlier following a concert featuring Mitch Miller, who, of course, gave Leslie (Uggams) her big break onto the national network stage with his *Sing Along With Mitch* television show. I wanted to say "Hello" to Mitch, too, and mention my high school times with Leslie. I went backstage to the Green Room and I heard someone softly yelling my first name two or three times while running down the long hallway behind the stage and leading to the Green Room. The person softly yelling my first name was then Minnesota Governor Rudy Perpich. He welcomed me back to Minnesota, saying he was happy I was back in the Twin Cities on the air. I had never met him, thus his kind welcome was inordinately wonderful and gratifying, to say the least. I was blessed for his friendship from that day until his passing in 1995. He even, God bless him, chose May 8, 1990, to issue an official proclamation naming that day to be Barry ZeVan Day in the State of Minnesota. The proclamation is framed and humbly but proudly hangs on one of my basement walls. I also had the privilege to know Governor Perpich's wife, Lola and their daughter, Mary Sue, the latter two who visited my house with Mary Sue's then very young daughter. I never met Rudy, Jr.

After leaving the Governorship, Rudy and I kept in touch when he, Lola and Rudy, Jr. moved to Zagreb, Croatia, to help form a post-Communist government, since Rudy had Croatian roots. We often talked on the phone while he was there. One night, during one of our phone conversations, he told me to listen to the machine gun fire outside their apartment. He was eventually asked by the Croatian government to become one of that country's top political officials (I believe it was Prime Minister), but after the gunfire episodes and also the news he'd lose his U.S. citizenship if he took the position, he and Lola moved to Paris for a year, because, I was told, Lola always wanted to live in Paris. Rudy was a consultant there. They lived on Avenue Foch, one of the most celebrated high-end addresses one can have in Paris. I spoke with him a few times while he and Lola were there, too, but was glad when they were safe and sound back in the U.S.

Rudy once invited me to a party at Mary Sue's house in one of the western Minneapolis suburbs. There couldn't have been more than 20 people there, but one of them, named Beatrice (Bea) Reitman, had a son who was slightly well known. The son's show business name was Bob Dylan. Bob's mother was a firecracker with lots of personality. She lived in Saint Paul at that time and said we should have lunch together sometime. We talked several times after that night, but I'm sorry to state we never had that lunch.

Fasten your seatbelts again—The Mall Of America, one of Rudy's many legacies as Minnesota's longest-serving Governor, opened August 11, 1992. About a month prior to that MOA opening day, I told Rudy it had always been my dream (echoing Lola's) to live in Paris. Rudy told me the Ghermezian brothers, who bankrolled and owned the MOA, were going to build The Mall of Europe adjacent to Versailles, one of Paris's suburbs. Rudy said he thought I'd be a great overseer as General Manager of the Mall of Europe, especially since I spoke (and speak) French and also worked for the Shah in their native Iran. He said he'd tell them about the meeting and would introduce me to those brothers at a private meeting about a half-hour before the MOA opened its doors. Here's what happened: I went, with Rudy, to the secluded fourth floor meeting room in the MOA, arriving exactly a half-hour prior to the official opening of the Mall. Rudy and I entered seeing the four brothers and another gentleman seated on a couch and chairs. The brothers had left Iran during another period of turmoil in that country. They immigrated to Canada and subsequently built the West Edmonton Mall in Alberta, then the world's largest (and another "warm fuzzy" connection for me with them, since I'd worked in Alberta, as previously referenced). They were all dressed in their signature black suits, wearing black ties over white shirts and wearing traditional black hats. The other gentleman, their aide-de-camp, who we learned was named Sean Samsian, was dressed in traditional western non-religious attire.

We were warmly invited by Sean Samsian to be seated. All of us were seated in a typical Middle East configuration, i.e., around the perimeter of that meeting room's primary open space. Three of the brothers were seated on a couch against a wall, the other on a straight-backed chair, next to Rudy, Samsian seated next to me, all facing one another. Rudy then reiterated what he had told them a few days earlier, i.e., that he was recommending me to become the General Manager and overseer of their Mall of Europe's construction and planning, then managing after it opened. I realized this could be an epiphany in my career and financial life. Raphael Ghermezian, the only brother who spoke to me directly, asked me to tell him and his brothers some of my personal and professional background. I obviously mentioned my times in Iran (they were pro-Shah, I was told, thus that helped my possible retention), relationship with Ambassador Zahedi, my work for Howard Hughes, the fact I spoke French well and my having also worked in Alberta. Raphael also asked my philosophy about people in general, especially when overseeing a massive project. I expressed my thoughts and he looked at his brothers, saying, verbatim, "Let's have him run it." That moment and those words will be cemented in my brain for the duration of my life. I smiled, said a million "Thank yous" and we all shook hands, with Rudy beaming for his kindness to me bearing real fruit.

Raphael told me to call Samsian at their Newport Beach, California, headquarters in three weeks and we'd sign the agreement shortly thereafter. I told him I would, we all shook hands again and went downstairs to witness the official opening of the MOA. I called Samsian three weeks later and he told me the French government had decided to not allow a Mall of Europe to be built anywhere in France, thus the locale would now be near Vienna, Austria. Samsian asked if I'd still be interested. I told him I'd been to Vienna and loved Austria, but I didn't speak German, thus respectfully . . . and sadly . . . said I wouldn't have the same interest. He told me he understood my thinking and told me the brothers would also understand but would be sorry about my decision. That was that, except for the fact Rudy told me I should have said, "Yes", anyway, because I would have been put on an immediate retainer for a very large sum for at least a year. I never was the always brightest bulb on the tree, but both Rudy and I learned about a month later the Austrian government decided to say "No" to The Mall of Europe being built in their country, thus the entire exercise concluded, but, according to Rudy, I would still have been paid very well for my availability and knowledge.

Rudy and I frequently had lunch or breakfast at a Baker's Square restaurant within walking distance of his, Lola's and Rudy, Jr.'s condo in a building called The Cliffs. Only a few weeks before he passed away, he told me he wanted me to be his "point person" to help establish, build and run, a non-Indian casino in downtown Minneapolis he knew he could persuade the legislature to approve. It would have been located in the then empty former Milwaukee Road railroad depot. I told him I'd be very interested. He said we could have a partnership agreement drafted within two to three weeks. Sadly, he had passed by then. What a privilege, honor and joy to have had him as a champion. One of his legacies is the truly outstanding Perpich Center for Arts Education, a state-funded school opened in 1985 at his urging. The school/center was originally named The Minnesota Center for Arts Education, but after his passing, justifiably re-named with his last name replacing the name Minnesota. One of those who visited the Center, in the early 2000s, was Julie Andrews. It's located fewer than ten minutes drive from my house and I've had the pleasure to visit it and those incredibly-gifted students, encompassing all art disciplines, a couple times.

Louie Anderson—I had no idea comedian Louie Anderson and his family had been among my weather fans during the KSTP-TV days, but when Louie came to town in the early 1980s to promote a one-man show he was doing at The Guthrie, I was assigned to interview him at the Channel 11 studios. He told me about him and his family watching me during those years in the 1970s. He even signed a photo, scribing, "A hunting we will go!" when he was going to cast me in a film he thought he'd be producing about hunters in Minnesota. Sadly it never materialized, but we've been together socially many times since then and he remains a friend, I'm happy to state.

CHAPTER EIGHTEEN

Unique Stories, Nuggets—Part IV

You gotta have hope!—from *Damn Yankees*

Between my last contractual days at Channel 11 in 1987 and early 1991, life was more uncertain than ever. I did some limited movie hosting on one of the Twin Cities independent television stations, with the then call letters, KTMA-TV, Channel 23. I could never enough thank the station manager, Don O'Connor, for that opportunity. My heart wasn't truthfully into anything I did at that point, having been somewhat "dismissed" by broadcasters who had no clue I still could do what I'd done previously as Twin Cities television's highest ratings-getter in 1974 at the previously stated 51 percent share of the audience. Those who did the hiring at that time also didn't realize I could do more than weather and entertainment, but any pleas were wasted and demeaning. Once, when hoping to get back to KSTP-TV, I had lunch with KS's General Manager at that time, whose name was Bob Regalbuto. Bob said something to me that was both the most wonderful and sad at the same time. It was during the Channel 11 days. He said, "You're a thoroughbred and they're making you pull a lunch wagon over there." I told him that was the most insightful and sadly true statement of which I'd ever been the recipient and thanked him for it. I knew it was true, and it made my heart sink even more. I even asked if I could be an anchor at Hubbard Broadcasting's station in Alexandria, Minnesota. He said, "That would be an insult to you." I told him I was grateful for his candor and kind compliments. Not too many months afterward, I learned Mr. Regalbuto had committed suicide. Terrible.

One of the things I did to survive during the post-Channel 11 days was to drive a cab. I'd done so, during another dark time, in Seattle-Tacoma, thus knew the routine. Driving in the Twin Cities in winter can sometimes be challenging. As if times weren't bad enough, the time that almost brought me to suicide, had I had a gun in my possession at the time, was as follows: I was scheduled to play Santa

Claus at a party following my driving shift. I'd be paid ten dollars. I had my Santa suit on, sans beard (I'd bought a cheap one several years earlier) and started my "shift". That "shift" lasted twenty hours and I made ten dollars in fares, including a tip. At dusk, I pulled over to the side of a road in the western Minneapolis suburbs, just sat there for about ten minutes and cried. Then I went to a gas station, put on the remainder of my Santa outfit and went to the party to pretend all was right with Santa and the world. Tough to write, but sadly, vividly and easily remembered.

To play even more ping-pong with my brain and life, during the last year at Channel 11, I was scheduled to work New Year's Day. A few months prior to that, I had been contacted by a friend in the oil business stating a very legitimate buyer in Beverly Hills wanted me to try to find a Bonnie Light Crude oil source and seller to unload 20-million barrels of crude into storage tanks in Rotterdam, The Netherlands, of course. Bonnie Light Crude is the world's best oil and its best source is Nigeria. Rotterdam also houses the most crude oil storage facilities in the world.

During my D.C. days, I was introduced to, and spent several pleasant social times in the five-story-with-private-elevator Kalorama section of D.C. home of Frank Ikard, then Chairman of The American Petroleum Institute. Frank had been a former Texas congressman and close friend of Lyndon and Lady Bird Johnson. One of his sons, Buck, was also married to Walter Cronkite's daughter. My cousin Cecil Brown, previously mentioned, was one of Walter's colleagues as a "Murrow boy" in London during World War Two. (The connections never end.) Ikard, his wife Jayne (a former Newsweek magazine editor) and I became good friends, thus when I was asked to get a legitimate buy for a 10-million dollar commission, I immediately contacted Frank and flew to D.C. to have a meeting about the Nigerian oil in his D.C. offices with his partner, Walter Washington, who had been a Mayor of Washington, D.C. It was determined the offer was legitimate and Frank made an appointment to fly to Lagos, Nigeria, to seal the deal with the Nigerian National Petroleum Corporation (NNPC). I still have the documents, stating the first unloading would take place January 10th, 1985, also the date we'd all be paid, including a ten-million-dollar wire transfer into my bank here in Minnesota.

The punch-in-the-face line—While perusing the New Year's Day teletype newswire services about 6 in the morning in the Channel 11 newsroom, a bulletin was printed stating the NNPC had been overtaken by a military coup in Nigeria and all deals were off regarding Bonnie Light Crude Oil purchases and deliveries. I called Frank at his other home on Martha's Vineyard, knowing he and Jayne had gone there for the Christmas holidays and where Jayne was raised. His house assistant answered the phone stating Mr. Ikard and Jayne were out for a walk. I told the assistant to tell Frank what had happened in Nigeria. He said he thought Mr. Ikard would be very upset to learn that news, but would certainly tell him. I got a call from Frank a couple hours later saying he was disappointed, as it would have been "fun", but was used to those things occasionally happening. We kept in touch until his passing in 1991. Jayne passed away in 2010.

New York television weathercasting, the casino business (again), Hollywood Update With Barry ZeVan and Comedy Central's *Daily Show*—During that 1987 to 1991 period, and somewhat beyond, continuing to rely on whatever work I could get to maintain survival, in addition to what's just been previously described, I decided to call Jim Topping. I'd worked with Jim in Honolulu, also previously referenced, who, as I also previously stated, had eventually become News Director at WABC-TV in New York. He told me they'd fly me to New York to audition for a weekend weather job at WABC-TV that would pay 90-thousand dollars a year. I arrived, did the audition, which Jim said was perfect, also saying I did exactly what he wanted me to do and, "There's no reason in this world you're not fit to do weekend weather here", verbatim. Jim approved my hire as weekend weatherman on WABC-TV, but broadcasting politics from his superiors squelched that deal before I did my first broadcast. I had, without malice, turned down a years-earlier offer from ABC-TV to do the weather at their owned-and-operated WXYZ-TV in Detroit and the superiors remembered. Ironically, years later, I was on the air in Detroit for six and a half years at two other stations, with the third station, for one month before leaving to go back to the Twin Cities, the aforementioned WXYZ-TV. Truth is stranger than fiction.

In the broadcasting and entertainment business, for those who aren't aware, thick skin is a primary element for on-air talent. There will always be insensitive or insecure detractors who will be either jealous of a certain person's successes or resent them and who will deride the successful because of the detractors' own insecurities or inabilities. It's sad for those of us who are always happy for our colleagues' successes. Eventually, one learns to put the detractors on ignore, even though that tactic is, to me, uncomfortable. As stated early in this book, I was told, by my mother, The Golden Rule is the most important of all we learn and to which we should always try to adhere. But I digress (for a change).

In the late winter of 1991, a dear friend of mine named Stan Taube, who was a lawyer and former business partner in my Minneapolis music store, previously referenced, told me he would be part of a team opening one of Minnesota's first American Indian-owned casinos. He said he thought I'd make a good public relations director for the casino and eventually others that would be owned by The Mille Lacs Band of Ojibwe Indians based near Onamia, Minnesota. Stan remembered my Las Vegas days working for Howard Hughes. I began that job July 1, 1991 and it lasted until 1999, in concert with my weekend television interviewing trips. I was busy, and exhausted, but it was a great and steady job, for which I was very grateful. *During that period of time, I met Ellen Hanson, my attorney, Tom Keller's, legal secretary. Ellen and I were married August 10, 1995, one year to the date after we met for lunch at Dayton's Oak Grill in downtown Minneapolis. As Minnesota and western Wisconsin readers will know, Dayton's later became Marshall Field's, afterward (and still) Macy's. While concluding writing this book, Ellen and I will be celebrating our 20th wedding anniversary. We renewed our fifth wedding anniversary vows on the shores of Alberta's Lake Louise, one of my favorite places.*

To get the casino's initial funding, Stan was approached by a Lac Courte Oreilles American Indian man named Dave Anderson, who had known Stan well in past years. Dave had the idea for the casino, but needed that initial funding. They went to Stan's friend, a man named Lyle Berman, whose family had owned successful Minneapolis businesses, the most successful being Berman Buckskin which eventually became Wilson's Leather. Lyle eventually said "Yes" and the two Mille Lacs Band casinos are flourishing, one near Hinckley, Minnesota and the other on the shore of Lake Mille Lacs, just north of the town of Onamia. Thanks to Stan Taube, I became one of the first 12 employees of a company that eventually employed thousands. I also emceed the ribbon-cutting opening ceremony of the Hinckley casino, but earlier that day, thanks to my friendship with Spencer Christian, *Good Morning America*'s weatherman, Spencer did his GMA weather cut-ins live from the Hinckley grounds that morning. I could never say enough good about Spencer, now into his at least tenth year as KGO-TV's weatherman in San Francisco.

Dave Anderson's knack for creating excellent barbecue sauces and the success of the casinos eventually allowed him to open world-class barbecue restaurants named *Famous Dave's*. In his offices, long before he opened his restaurants and sold his sauce products, there were at least hundred small bottles of sauces lining the shelves. I asked what they contained. He said, "You'll see someday." Lyle Berman eventually provided the funding to complete construction (and ownership) of Las Vegas's iconic Stratosphere Tower and also was the creator of television's *World Poker Tour*, the co-host for which is Vince Van Patten, one of the sons of my late friend and acting colleague, Dick. *The late Bob Stupak, who created the idea for The Stratosphere Tower, was also a native Pittsburgher and whose father was an occasional business colleague of my grandfather. Bob also dated the previously referenced Phyllis McGuire, one of the classiest "acts" I've ever had the privilege to know (please see photos section). Again, no degrees of separation!*

Comedy Central's *Daily Show*—Prior to the Minnesota casino work, in the mid to late 1980s, I was befriended by a phenomenally gifted, funny and successful Minneapolis and Saint Paul comedy club(s) owner name Scott Hansen. Scott had written for major television sitcoms, including *Roseanne* and many others. Scott had remembered

me from my weathercasting days, knew I was down on my luck
and had me become the permanent emcee for his signature club
named *Scott Hansen's Comedy Gallery*. It was the Mecca for up and
coming comedians as well as those already well-established. Scott
had given Jay Leno one of his first breaks in standup comedy and
the earlier referenced Tom Arnold was also a great friend of Scott's. I
was allowed only one joke (smiling), but I got away with telling two!
Thanks to Scott I was able to eat for over two years, as there was also
free and very good food offered to those of us performing.

One of the comics who performed at *The Comedy Gallery* was a
comedienne named Lizz Winstead. She and I learned we shared the
same birthday, August 5th, although I was much older. She became
a great friend, created Air America, a liberal talk radio network
that featured shows hosted by, among others, Al Franken, who, as
most people are aware, became one of Minnesota's U.S. Senators. I
got to know Al through the years, too. Lizz also co-created Comedy
Central's *Daily Show*, knew of my background and produced a
tongue-in-cheek, but subliminally complimentary (to those who see
it "through-the-lines"), three-minute feature about part of my career,
which appeared on *The Daily Show* and can be seen if one looks on
Google. Lizz and I have kept in touch through the years and I always
call on our mutual birthday, for which I'm certain she awaits with
baited breath every year. Seriously, am very grateful to Lizz for having
produced that *Daily Show* piece that nationally showcased some of
my eclectic show business and television life.

CHAPTER NINETEEN

Global Syndication

Life without knowing history is like saying flowers grow with no roots.
—William Bennet

I n October, 1990, I discovered a new network (new to me) called
Channel America. It was a group of 270 low and regular power
television stations in the U.S. and partially owned and founded by
former NBC-TV meteorologist, Dr. Frank Field. I called them at their
headquarters in New York, telling them I would be able to get junket
interviews with stars, directors and producers of new films for them if
they'd allow me to supply them. The Program Director, named Geoff
Andrews, immediately said, "Yes". I created a show called *Hollywood
Update With Barry ZeVan*, owned it outright, contacted the agency
here in the Twin Cities that had sent me on the junkets previously,
for the Channel 11 interviews, and they immediately "signed me up".
Thanks to the agency, Nemer Fieger and Associates, owners and a
longtime friend named Joel Thom, one of their executives, as well as
my ex-wife Chris, I was almost every weekend in New York or L.A.,
and a couple times London, to do those interviews. Joel had acted for
Chris when she starred-in and directed a local production of *Sweet
Charity* shortly after Chris and I were married. J. Marie Fieger still
runs the organization, Joel is retired and living in Florida and Chris
re-married many years ago to a good man named Paul Fournier.
Hollywood Update With Barry ZeVan debuted the first Saturday in
January, 1991 and lasted, every week, until Channel America ended
their programming in 1997. Shortly after the debut of the show on
Channel America, Geoff told me it was a success and also said, "You
made me look like a genius." I was glad.

In 1992, I met a television program syndication owner named
Bob Syers. He was introduced to me by former AWA wrestling
champion Verne Gagne, one of the nicest people I've ever known.
Bob had been the syndication guru for Verne's wrestling shows and
also a former ABC network radio Vice President. Bob's daughter Kelly

worked for Nickelodeon at that time. Bob felt he could get worldwide distribution for *Hollywood Update*, thus had me begin semi-annual trips to Cannes, France, to pitch the shows at buying conferences called MIP and MIP-TV. MIP stood for Marche International des Programmes and the events were held in The Palais des Festivales where the Cannes Film Festival is held. I attended those with Bob and his wife, Dee, for five years.

Dee also found us the apartment building where we'd stay during the conferences and where I'd eventually have a pied-a-terre to rent to own, or rent to others, but because of French bureaucracy, it never worked out as an income producer. The address was 8 rue la Verrerie, Cannes-LaBocca, France. Our apartment balcony overlooked the same railroad tracks featured in *The Red Shoes*, one of my all-time favorite movies, previously referenced. When I'd hear the sound of a train approaching and passing almost directly below our balcony, I'd always run to the balcony like the little kid I really am, and watch it speed by five-stories below. The configuration there was our building, railroad tracks, highway, beach and Mediterranean Sea. It was a topless beach, but I didn't look when occasionally walking by, at least not very often.

Among my most favorite memories during those MIP and MIP-TV times were devouring Dee's deviled eggs at small parties she and Bob would host for buyers. Eventually, thanks to Bob, my show was seen seven days a week in Thailand, for three years, as well as the entire Arabian Peninsula, except for Yemen, for at least five years. Because the sales were mostly bartered, I realized very little income from them, but the exposure was delightful. Once, on a flight from Minneapolis to L.A., I was seated next to a Middle Eastern-looking young man. Early in the flight, I asked from where he was. He told me he was from the U.A.E., then looked at me and said, smiling, "Hollywood Update. I used to watch you on television in my country. You're Barry ZeVan." I thanked him for remembering. It was a "rush" to hear him say that, then wondering how it would be to be recognized by everyone, everywhere. No wonder world-famous people treasure their privacy, but his kind recognition was, of course, very flattering and heartwarming. A Thailand network was supposed to air the programs only once a week, but my aforementioned friend, Joel Thom, was vacationing there during their run and told me about seeing it seven nights a week in Phuket. The Thais admitted it and all ended well. Thank you, Joel!!!

Also, thanks to Bob's daughter, Kelly, in 1992 I got to meet a wonderful lady named Merete Nielsen in Cannes, after Kelly had recommended me to her to have me do and submit seven character voices in English for a successful Danish children's television series Merete and her husband Elias owned, and the latter created, wrote and animated, called *The Pixies*. I recorded them here in the U.S. and Elias said I "nailed the characterizations" right away. Those voices were fun to create and record, especially the one for "Mr. Snail".

Merete pitched the show to English-speaking countries at the MIP and MIP-TV conferences every year. In later years, I had the joy to be their houseguest for two weeks in the little Danish village in which they live (on the estate of a Danish Prince, but not named Hamlet), but in close proximity to Billund, home of Lego, and for whom Elias does consulting and Merete and Elias's sons are designers there. *A bit of trivia: The Lego organization is owned by one man, whose last name is Andersen, and who invented Lego. The airport he built is one of Europe's finest. When I knew I'd be flying to Billund from Paris on Maersk Airlines to see Merete and Elias, I wondered on what sort of postage-stamp sized runway I'd be landing. No fears: it was superb and handles almost all sizes of jet aircraft.*

Merete is an accomplished landscape painter who also has made clothes for Denmark's Queen Margarethe, a lifelong friend to Merete. Part of Elias's and Merete's house includes a huge room with bolts of fabric and top quality clothes-making machines. Merete, Elias and I Skype frequently and, along with their children are among, once again, the many who have blessed me with their friendships.

CHAPTER TWENTY

The Documentaries and More

Follow every rainbow, 'til you find your dream.
—Partial lyric from *Climb Every Mountain* from *The Sound Of Music*

I n 1997, Bob, Dee and I were at a MIP-TV party for show business and television producers, show owners and so forth at The Majestic Hotel in Cannes when a young girl came up to me and said "My daddy's a millionaire. He produces documentaries about and with famous people and needs interviews for the shows. What do you do?" I told her I did precisely what he needed regarding interviews, as well as about my lifelong friendships with a lot of people who had become world famous, but knowing them and "living it" with them before most people knew who they were.

She was ecstatic, told me her name and introduced me to her father, the owner of the company based in North Hollywood a couple blocks from the Toluca Lake border. I'm purposely not stating their names since in later years they had some problems and I don't want to embarrass them. Suffice it to say, as a consulting producer and their Vice President of Program Development, I got them the most recognizable and world-famous interviewees for a ten-hour series that ran on PBS affiliate stations for at least two years. Another of the documentaries . . . one of three I wrote and produced for them . . . involved Lucy and Desi's writers, previously referenced.

I also voiced other documentaries and series they'd already produced and was with them from early 1998 until early 2001. During that time, I lived three weeks each month in the owner's mother's guesthouse across the street from the production company and then came back to Minnesota for a week each month. Suffice it to say regarding world-renowned celebrated actors, actresses, producers, directors and political leaders, the days with many of them were as much social as professional, also resurrecting my personal life with many of them before they became iconic. Following are some of the more outstanding memories of those years:

General Colin Powell—Thanks to a great friend named Rick Kiernan, former PIO for The Pentagon (U.S. Army) and an official for the 1996 Atlanta Summer Olympics, I was able to secure an interview with General Powell in his Alexandria, Virginia, offices in 2000. General Powell was as gracious and kind as one would expect and allowed me to ask an additional question prior to the conclusion of the interview, after I asked if it would be okay. Before the interview, I had a few minutes to roam around the offices and noticed a closet that was wide open. In the closet was one of General Powell's famous little red Radio Flyer wagons that he uses to identify with his charity, America's Promise, focusing on helping youth. It was inscribed to Texas Governor George W, Bush. I couldn't resist taking a photo of it (please see photos section). Also please see the photo of General Powell and me in the photos section and his kind inscription to me above his signature. A very blessed boy am I. *When General Powell became Secretary of State, I sent him a congratulatory note, to which he kindly replied. Please see photos section.*

General John W. Vessey—For the same documentary, I was blessed to make fairly rapid contact with General Vessey, former Joint Chiefs of Staff Chairman, coincident with timing that was necessary for all the D.C.-based interviews. General Vessey, who lived and lives in Minnesota, said he remembered me from my KS weathercasting days, for which I told him I was very appreciative. The only time General Vessey could carve for the interview was 11 p.m. in private officer quarters he used when visiting Fort Meade, Maryland, of course within the confines of the D.C. metropolitan area. He said he had a meeting the next morning and had not even unpacked his suitcase when we did the interview. Anyone under his command must have been eager to serve. He was, and is, a "'real" person and stated he knew he'd been blessed to be acknowledged enough to become Joint Chiefs Chairman.

Tony Randall: Addenda very worth reading, especially about the ups and downs of talents in show business—Even though Tony was like a mentor to me from the *Peepers* days until his passing, he was never so candid to me regarding show business and how it affects the sensibilities of performers as he was during a videotaped conversation in his sixth floor, 1 West 81st Street apartment during an interview for my documentary, *Television: The First 50 Years*. My cameraman and I arrived about 15 minutes early. The apartment elevator door opened into a small waiting area as Tony's and Heather's 6,000 square foot apartment comprised the entire floor. I rang the bell and Tony answered in his slim underpants saying, "You're early!" I apologized and said we'd be willing to wait, but he told us to come in and set up while he got fully dressed (please see photos section). Tony's second wife, Heather (we've kept in touch occasionally and cordially since Tony's passing), had recently given birth to Tony's and Heather's second child, Jefferson. Heather wasn't present for the taping, thus with just Tony, my cameraman and me in the room, as well as Tony and Heather's youngest child, Julia, at about age one-plus, silently crawling on the floor nearby, Tony opened up completely about everything from his U.S. Army service in World War Two to how *Mister Peepers* changed his life forever to owning *The Odd Couple* with co-star Jack Klugman and the afore-referenced agent, Abby Greshler. Tony also psychoanalyzed what a lot of actors and actresses go through when they're rejected for parts as well as relating how his passion for opera developed. Following, almost verbatim, is what he told me in regard to the above:

Tony was born in Tulsa, Oklahoma, nee Leonard Rosenberg. He told me he went back to Tulsa for a personal appearance there (after he'd become world-famous) and no one was there to even just meet him at the plane. He said, "So much for fame. It really means not much in the grand scheme of things." Prior to joining the U.S. Army in World War Two, Tony told me he had dabbled in acting and knew he was good at it, determined to re-start his acting career when he got out of the service. Tony told me his best pal in the Army was Eli Wallach. *Mr. Wallach was also one of the interviewees for the documentary for which I was interviewing Tony at that time, i.e.,* Television: The First 50 Years, *previously referenced.*

Tony said when he and Eli were discharged at the end of the war, they both kept in touch but went their separate career ways. Tony told me for a while he became a radio announcer and local radio drama cast member at WTIC in Hartford, Connecticut, while Eli went straight back to stage acting in New York. Tony's radio career then evolved to national prominence beginning in 1949 on one of radio's most famous dramas, entitled *I Love A Mystery*, where he had a permanent ongoing role as a character named "Reggie". *While listening to him at age 12 on that radio program via KQV in Pittsburgh, I had no inkling he would become a mentor and friend to me for over 50 years, commencing in 1952.* Tony also became a stage play director and actor, Off-Broadway.

Tony then told me, "Things were going very well for me. I was happy to be a regularly working actor and director. In early 1952, I got a phone call from a man named Fred Coe." *Fred Coe was already a highly-respected producer in the relatively new medium of television, which debuted nationally in 1948, two years after yours truly started performing on television, as referenced much earlier in this book.* Tony continued, "Fred said he'd just created a television sitcom idea with a part specifically written for me and I should definitely grab the chance to be on the new show. He told me the show was called *Mister Peepers*, about teachers, students and their friends connected to a school named Jefferson Junior High. He also told me a new actor who would become a sensation would play the title role and that actor's name was Wally Cox. I told Fred I was not interested, four times on four phone calls within a week. I told him my directing obligations at Circle In The Square were far more important to me."

Tony then told me Fred called him to talk to him a fifth time, *begging* Tony to take the part of Wally's character's sidekick who would be named Harvey Weskit. Tony said he gave in to Fred, thinking if he was pushing Tony so aggressively, it must be truly worth exploring. "Accepting the part on *Mister Peepers* was the most important and life-changing career decision I ever made in my life", Tony told me. He continued, "None of us then knew the power of television. I began to know it two weeks after *Peepers* debuted when, one Monday, I was walking down a street in Philadelphia. I was there to visit friends. All of a sudden, people kept pointing at me with a few of them saying, 'You're Tony Randall! We just saw you on

Mister Peepers last night!' or other recognition statements similar to that. I was shocked but then realized this could be big." Thanks to Tony's deserved launch onto the national scene he became not only a television star, but also shone brightly in feature films, one or two of them with my dear friend and other mentor, the afore-referenced Louis Nye. It's an almost incestuous business sometimes and somewhat an elite "closed club", which, in my opinion, is a sad reality.

When Abby (Greshler) got Tony and Jack *The Odd Couple* series, the three of them owned the show and rights, as previously mentioned. That ownership gleaned Tony enough money to create his National Actors Theater and house it in the former Lyceum Theater near Times Square, which he also owned thanks to *The Odd Couple* income. The NAT later moved to Pace University where Jerry and Anne also appeared in plays for Tony's NAT.

Several times, aside from *Peepers*, and in later years, Tony and I would find ourselves in close proximity. One fun time was when Tony was starring in *The Music Man* at McCormick Place in Chicago. I went backstage to say, "Hello", and Tony paraded me out of his dressing room, arm in arm, stating to a good-sized crowd waiting to see him, "Ladies and gentlemen, I've known this distinguished looking almost bald-headed man since he was a young boy with thick bushy hair!" Everyone laughed. Tony continued telling them we had acted together on *Peepers* and remained friends ever since. Tony also acknowledged our *Peepers* years on a radio tribute he did for my 60th anniversary in broadcasting *previously referenced with Jerry and Anne, Peter Jennings, Peter Nero, Art Linkletter, Willard Scott, Elliott Gould, Dick Van Patten and Frank Sinatra, Jr., also kindly helping me with that career milestone.*

During the apartment interview, Tony also spontaneously launched into stating how cruel the business can sometimes be. For those reading this who are in "the business", hopefully his wisdom, forthcoming, will bring comfort to knowing "you're not alone" when it comes to being rejected for parts. He said, but for the grace of God, he could have been one of those who became bitter and angry about being either ignored or dismissed because they weren't chosen for parts. He said he personally resented the insensitivity of many casting directors and producers regarding their somewhat elitist attitudes and treatment toward actors, actresses, singers and dancers. As "above it all" as Tony's characters most often were, he, as a human being, was the exact opposite. One of the illustrations of Tony's humanitarian side was Tony suggesting Abby sign me as an acting client in later years, which Abby did. Abby's corporation, Diamond Artists, Ltd., was located in The Luckman Building on Sunset Boulevard, catty-corner from the massive apartment building where the aforementioned Oscar and June Levant lived, immediately adjacent to the Beverly Hills city limits. Abby, his son Steve and their right-hand assistant, a Chicago native named Lillian Miceli (who also shared my August 5th birthday) all were very kind to me but I was never submitted for a part. Not Tony's fault, that's for certain. Steve Greshler once told me I'd make a great villain. That's as close as I got to being submitted, but I was grateful for Tony championing me enough to get me signed with Diamond Artists. Tony's last representation was under the wing of The William Morris Agency's chairman, Norman Brokaw. Brokaw and I spoke only once prior to the emergence of the new agency, William Morris Endeavor, now lead by Chicago Mayor Rahm Emanuel's brother, Ari.

Tom Arnold—Prior to the interview at his Calabassas, California, mansion, Tom didn't know his Aunt Kay and I had been very close friends (nothing else) during our MIP and MIP-TV times in Cannes and exchanged Christmas greetings every year. Kay was an excellent actress who had a recurring part on *Roseanne* while Roseanne and Tom were married. Kay was also widowed, having been married to the Vice President and General Manager of WPIX-TV in New York during that station's most profitable years. She lived the last years of her life in Passaic, New Jersey, but not in as much comfort as one might expect, since she was one of Bernie Madoff's Ponzi Scheme victims, very sad to learn. Kay, Tom and their respective relatives had been born and raised in Ottumwa, Iowa.

Tom had known me from my Twin Cities television days and as previously referenced, he, Roseanne and I met at Scott Hansen's *Comedy Gallery* when I was emceeing for Scott, and Tom and

Roseanne were still very much in love, openly smooching (just kissing and hugging) one night in the back row of the club during performances and my emcee chores.

Tom has always been very gracious and kind to me. After the interview, he said, "Take a dip!" The "dip" would have been into a pool that rivaled that of San Simeon, with marble statues throughout. I respectfully declined because I was fully dressed, had no swimming suit with me and had to get back to the North Hollywood offices.

Betty Friedan—Ms. Friedan allowed us to interview her in her D.C. apartment, saying she used to watch my D.C. weathercasts in the mid-1970s. She actually seemed puzzled that I'd be interviewing and producing and asked me why I wasn't still doing the weather. In essence, I told her that life went on to a different dimension, she nodded and that was that. Similar to President Truman, listening to her respond to my questions was like listening to a history book talking. She was diminutive in size but a giant in every other way. Her very large apartment was replete with hundreds of books and papers scattered about, everywhere, but, in my opinion, reflected the depth of her successes and missions in regard to female equality. As the powerful and very non-nonsense lady she was, I was very grateful she'd agreed to have the time together.

Rod Steiger—My cameraman and I arrived around 10 a.m. at Rod's unpretentious Malibu house on Zumirez Drive to do one of the interviews I'd arranged for *The Remarkable 20th Century* (please see photos section). What he offered following the interview is worth continuing to read! Among the most personal stories he told me was about his affection for my aforementioned friend and former acting and drama school colleague, Shirley Jones, during the filming of *Oklahoma!* Rod said he unabashedly tried to hit on Shirley but she wouldn't give him the time of day. He told me he eventually got over it, but was really smitten with her. In Shirley's memoir, published in 2013, she referred to the *Oklahoma!* filming days, also referencing her relationship with Rod being cordial and remaining so until his passing. Rod also referenced the power of television, similar to what

I previously wrote about Tony Randall's experiences in that regard. Rod said he had acted in the live television dramatization of *Marty*, actor Ernest Borgnine's successful feature film vehicle. Rod told me the morning after it aired, he couldn't walk more than two steps down any street without a cab driver, bus driver or pedestrians telling him what a great acting job he'd performed the night before. Some people even called him "Marty" instead of Rod.

Punch line for which worth waiting—When the interview concluded, Rod told my cameraman and me, "Elizabeth's coming over with sandwiches in a few minutes. If you want to stay, you're welcome to." Elizabeth's last name was Taylor and Rod was dating her at the time. Stupidly, my cameraman and I respectfully declined the offer, with me saying, "Thank you, but that's your private time." Rod repeated his offer but we told him we had to get back to North Hollywood on a deadline (which was true), but in retrospect, having a private lunch at Rod Steiger's house with Elizabeth Taylor being the food provider would have been one of the all-time special times. Rod later told me we should have stayed, as Elizabeth would also have agreed to be interviewed. One of the "Duh" times in my life, of which there are many.

Eddie Albert, Peter Graves, Tippi Hedren and Arlene Dahl (please see photos section)—Peter and Arlene were born and raised in Minneapolis. Eddie was born in Rock Island, Illinois, but the family moved to Minneapolis when he was one-year old. Tippi Hedren was born and raised in New Ulm, Minnesota.

Eddie Albert's house was on a street in Pacific Palisades. His house was also very identifiable because of the corn and other vegetables planted in his front yard, a la *Green Acres*. He told me the neighbors didn't like it but he didn't care. It was also not anathema to any city ordinances, thus he decided to create a mini-*Green Acres* "farm" in front of his house. He was very down to Earth, no pun intended, and we enjoyed a good hour talking about his long career.

Peter Graves' house in Santa Monica had an almost baronial interior. The living room was heavily laden with rich very dark wood paneling, definitely not purchased at a do-it-yourself store. There was also a large crest above the huge fireplace. Peter was as distinguished in his manner as the characters he portrayed on television, especially akin to *Mission: Impossible.* He told me he and his brother always had an affection for their hometown, Minneapolis, and didn't consider themselves competitors because each had their own acting styles and personas. I was aware he'd come to the Twin Cities frequently, especially to speak to classes at The University of Minnesota, but had never met him prior to the Santa Monica interview.

Tippi Hedren has made caring for injured wild animals a decades-long passion. I had the joy to be with her twice for interviews at her Shambala Preserve near Acton, California, just north of L.A. Tippi told me she was "discovered" when stepping off a bus near Donaldson's department store in Minneapolis. Tippi was a model at Donaldson's and truly stunning in appearance. We never discussed Alfred Hitchcock's unwanted advances toward Tippi as that episode in her life had already been widely chronicled. She did tell me her passion for helping injured wild animals was almost a lifelong dream. Her daughter, actress Melanie Griffith and son-in-law, actor Antonio Banderas, help fund The Shambala Preserve. I interviewed Melanie several times for *Hollywood Update,* She's also a fellow Leo (of course!) very pleasant with whom to speak and down-to-Earth, as well.

For those reading this who may be unfamiliar with the following fact, the Twin Cities and The State of Minnesota have given birth to an inordinate number of some of the world's most talented and respected stars and world leaders, some of them Minnesota *transplants.* I've had the joy and privilege to have very private times, having nothing to do with interviews, with almost every one of them, and some of their offspring (some previously referenced), including Grand Rapids, Minnesota-born Judy Garland; Doland, South Dakota-born Minneapolis Mayor, U.S. Senator and U.S. Vice President Hubert H. Humphrey and his wife Muriel (as well as his son Skip and grandson Buck); former Senator, Vice President and Ambassador to Japan, Walter F. Mondale; Velva, North Dakota-born Eric Sevareid; Iowa-born Harry Reasoner; Gretchen Carlson; James

Arness; Peter Graves; Arlene Dahl; Lea Thompson; Kelly Lynch; Joel and Ethan Coen; Illinois-born Eddie Albert; Tippi Hedren; Jesse Ventura; Jerry Bowen; Bob McNamara (CBS News); Robert Vaughn; Brooklyn-born Senator Al Franken and many more.

Arlene Dahl and I had a longtime mutual friend named Shirley Eder. Shirley was a syndicated entertainment columnist, based in Detroit, and with whom I worked at WJBK-TV in Motown. Shirley's father was a New York State Supreme Court Justice. Shirley was also heiress to the Nathan's hot dog fortune, but for all her privileged life, she was very "real", too. Shirley and her husband took at least one cruise a year with Arlene and her husband, cosmetics industry executive, Marc Rosen. The first time I was with Arlene and Marc was at their Nyack, New York home (please see additional photos section). It had been the brainstorm of Channel 11's newsroom secretary, Karen (whose last name I'm saddened to not remember) to produce news features about famous Minnesotans who were still alive. When she suggested Arlene Dahl I was especially delighted because of my friendship with Arlene's and my mutual friend, Shirley Eder. As I stated, that interview took place at Arlene's Nyack home, with Marc nearby. The interview went well, with Arlene, mostly reminiscing about her Washburn High School days in Minneapolis and how she became a major MGM star. At the conclusion of the interview, Marc said he wanted to show me his 1970s-era Rolls Royce he had just purchased and had been shipped from a dealer in St. Louis. You'll see him, Arlene and me posed beside it in the photos section of this book. Having owned a Rolls in D.C. (previously mentioned) I didn't have the heart to tell Marc he'd been "had" by the Rolls dealer, because what they shipped him was a Bentley, to which they attached a Rolls grill and hood ornament.

The next time I interviewed Arlene was in her and Marc's New York City apartment (please see another photo in the photos section, with Arlene, her Shih-Tzu and yours truly). She and I talked mostly about her astrology columns in the National Enquirer as well as how she proud she was of her actor son, Lorenzo Lamas. Arlene, another Leo, has been married six times. Her marriage to Marc Rosen is, as I write this, now in its 31st year. Marc is a genuinely nice and brilliantly artistically gifted person, now primarily designing perfume and cologne bottles for the world's most celebrated fragrances. During the Nyack days, Marc was an executive with Helena Rubenstein cosmetics.

The Sunshine Boys (follow-up from previous reference)—In 2001, following my North Hollywood documentary retention, I returned to the Twin Cities full time to explore more survival possibilities. I learned from a friend in "the business" that a production of Neil Simon's *The Sunshine Boys* was being cast to go on a national tour for almost a year. It was under the umbrella and ownership of a production company in Minneapolis named Troupe America. The producer, Curt Wollan, had been a KSTP-TV weather fan of mine in his youth.

I learned from Linda Twiss, Troupe America's publicity, media and public relations director, and a supportive longtime friend, that the stars of the show would be my childhood friends, Frank Gorshin and Dick Van Patten. Frank and I walked to Friendship School together for our fifth grade year, living just one block from each other in that Pittsburgh enclave of Bloomfield, earlier referenced. *That fifth-grade year was the only year I didn't go to grade school at H.C. Frick in Oakland.* Dick's mother, Jo Van Patten, was one of my agents during the New York television acting days and I got to meet Dick frequently during *I Remember Mama* rehearsals, since he also acted with my high school friend, Judson Rees, on that show.

Knowing it would be like "old home week" if I would be able to work with Frank and Dick, I called Curt, read for him and got a part as "The Patient" as well as double-understudying both Frank and Dick, previously referenced. We started rehearsals in Detroit in August, 2001. We were to be the second performers to open a brand new theater across from Ford Motor Company's World Headquarters in Dearborn, September 12, 2001. Melissa Manchester, previously married to a former agent friend of mine named Larry Brezner, was the opening act, September 11th. *I had known Phil Caldwell, former President of Ford Motor Company, socially, during and after my Detroit television days, thus was happy to see where he'd hung his professional hat.*

The morning of September 11, 2001, we all know what happened. Curt called all of us to a meeting that afternoon, telling us he'd met with the Mayor of Dearborn, as well as the new theater's owners, and they all decided the show must go on. Melissa's show played to five people, ours, the next night, to three. Lou Rawls was to perform the next night after our show, and did. To say 9/11 put a damper on the show's audiences and our spirit would be the proverbial understatement. We toured until April, 2002, concluding the tour, ironically, in my former "stomping grounds", Idaho Falls, Idaho. After the show, I had a reunion dinner with my former news anchor, Dave Wayne (Siebenmark) and his wife, Pat. Dave was originally from Minneapolis, thus we had even more to discuss than the "good old days" in Idaho Falls. Pat, his wife, was originally from Storm Lake, Iowa, and had been, before she met Dave, the high school girlfriend of Al "Dix" Lohman, who would become one-half of the future Los Angeles successful radio team, Lohman and Barkley. Dave and Pat were two of the nicest people I'd ever known. Both have now passed away.

There were several memorable performance stops on the tour. One of them, in Palm Desert, California, had Boris Karloff's daughter, Sarah Karloff, visiting us in The Green Room after a performance. She's as class an act as her father and we chatted for more than a few minutes about her Dad and especially how un-Frankenstein-like he was in real life. The aforementioned Larry Brezner was also there and whom I'd known well when his agency was handling my friend Tom Poston and acquaintance Woody Allen.

Frank had his own bus for half the play tour because he smoked. He was convinced to just take smoke breaks for the second half of the tour. We got a holiday break for Thanksgiving and Christmas after performing in Athens, Georgia. The cast was going to fly back to Minneapolis. Because of 9/11 airplane fears, I elected to drive, taking a cab from Athens to the Atlanta airport, renting a car and driving from 6 a.m. Eastern Time to 11 p.m. Central Time, non-stop (except for fast food and bathroom breaks) arriving at our Minneapolis house in 17 hours.

One of the documentaries I produced, wrote, production designed and directed in the 2000s included the 2006 Telly Award-winning *American Indian Homelands: Matters Of Truth, Honor and Dignity, Immemorial*, hosted by my longtime and very revered friend, Sam Donaldson. The first time I met Sam, in 1977, for about a half-second, was when I was walking in the basement of The White House toward the press briefing room and Sam was walking in the opposite direction ready to pass me. He said, "Hello, Barry." I said "Hello, Sam", and that was that. One should never assume anything is always "that was that" and our future relationship validates that "wisdom", to wit:

Sam's 2004 offer and retention to host and narrate the documentary had its genesis because I had (and still have) a great American Indian friend named Joe Valandra. At the request of my longtime Minneapolis friend and primary attorney, Tom Keller (previously acknowledged), I had helped Joe get a good executive position with the Grand Casinos corporate hierarchy in the early 1990s. Through the years, Joe's and my friendship was strong. During one of my very down times, he immediately hired me to do public relations work for a billion-dollar company of which he had become CEO. He had me accompany him to London for some meetings, as well as others in Seattle and Las Vegas. Unfortunately, Joe's position ended and we were both out of work. Regardless, the Lord never gives us more than we can handle, as the saying goes and in which I firmly believe, thus we survived the ups and downs.

As fate dictated, Joe phoned me one day in the late winter of 2004, suggesting I call a man named Cris Stainbrook who was CEO of the Little Canada, Minnesota-based Indian Land Tenure Foundation. He said he thought Cris would welcome the idea to have me produce a documentary about that Foundation's work. I called Cris, we met with him and his executive staff and after submitting a sample script, my production company, Vanbar Productions, was retained to produce the work.

I chose an American Indian named Brad Johnson to be my Director of Photography and editor. Brad, who lived fairly close to me, was introduced to me by a fellow named Bob House, a brilliantly talented writer with whom I'd worked during our Mille Lacs Band of Ojibwe Indians' Grand Casino years. Brad's shooting and editing in the 14 states we shot, as well as D.C., were first class.

I had always been a champion for American Indians and the justice they deserved but hadn't had the chance to visit as many reservations as Brad and I did during the two-plus months it took to shoot. The purpose of the 78-minute documentary was to bring heretofore un-publicized awareness about Indian lands taken by the federal government and what's since been done to recover not only the lands but also monetary reimbursement to thousands of Indian families for the loss of their properties, putting so many of them into almost perpetual poverty. The primary culprit was known as The Dawes Act, signed into law in February, 1887. Our documentary dug deeply into its history, its raison d'etre, i.e., to virtually eliminate the American Indian population and the ramifications thereof, still stinging in the 21st century. Two of my Senatorial interviewees were Senators John McCain and Tom Daschle, both empathetic to the plight of American Indians. Senator McCain even reminded us during his interview about how the Pilgrims brought blankets laced with smallpox to these shores, thus also introducing disease to a previously healthy American Indian population.

Sam did his on-camera stand-ups and voice over narration a few feet from his house on one of three ranches he owns in southeast New Mexico, bordering the Mescalero-Apache reservation. He kindly invited Brad and me to stay overnight in one of his three first-class guesthouses prior to the following day's taping session. Each bedroom had it's own full bath and shower and each guesthouse was actually larger than Sam and his wife Jan's main house. The guesthouses are on a hill overlooking the main house.

One of Sam's ranch hands had committed a murder on Sam's property only three weeks prior to our taping, with the incident covered by all the national media. Sam was still justifiably a bit shaken because of the incident, but went ahead with the taping as the professional he is.

If anyone would ever doubt Sam's strength, energy and great sense of humor, they'd be very incorrect. For supper, Sam cooked us some great ribs his wife Jan had picked up in nearby Hondo, New Mexico, that afternoon. Both Sam and Jan said they were the best ribs anyone could ever wish to devour and they were correct. We also had corn on the cob. During supper, after relating some personal stories and reminiscences, Sam jovially asked me, "Is there anyone you don't know?" I replied I knew I'd been very blessed and my memory retention was almost a curse, but I just enjoyed sharing the very fortunate blessings and stories married to my friendships and acquaintances, hopefully considered entertaining rather than boastful. Sam said he understood, but my litany was still a bit overwhelming. I told him he, as an actual icon, could definitely eclipse any relationship memories I had, and that's true, not false praise.

We ate outdoors, but after supper came into the main house and sat around the kitchen table discussing various subjects including world events of the day. It was still daylight and Sam noticed one of the front tires on Jan's car was flat. He said, "I'll fix that!" Sam then proceeded to drag a nearby cinderblock to sit next to the flat tire and literally lifted the left side of the car with his bare hands, pushing the large cinderblock underneath where it needed to rest while he removed the tire, replaced it with the spare and let the car settle down on it's own after replacing that tire. No one would ever want to encounter Sam in a fight. As might be said by natives of that part of the country, "He's one tough hombre!"

I had met one of Sam's very successful contemporaries, a ranch owner and oil man named Rolla Hinkle, two years earlier, during *The Sunshine Boys* play tour (previously referenced) when we performed in Alto, New Mexico, ironically not far from Sam's ranches, but before I asked Sam to host and narrate the documentary. Sam and I discussed Rolla, too, during our taping visit. Rolla was very proud of Sam's achievements.

Sam was born in El Paso, but raised on his mother and father's farm/ranch in southeast New Mexico, very close to where his own ranches are today. Sam's father passed away when Sam was young, thus he had to become "the man of the house" unexpectedly.

Sam has since hosted and narrated three additional docs, two for me and one for some friends of mine in Texas to whom I recommended Sam. Their names are Arturo and Deborah Ruiz-Esparza. "My" docs, taped in 2014 and 2015, were about the Mandan-Hidatsa-Arikara tribe in North Dakota, entitled *MHA*

Nation Tomorrow and the other a pending-distribution doc entitled *Introduction To 25 Words*, a documentary about a documentary produced in China, about how and why it was made. The original doc won a Houston international Film Festival Award in 2012. My friends Raul Carrera, Chuy Carrera and Tim Corder, all based in Austin, had me executive produce that doc and we taped Sam's on-camera work in San Antonio, Texas. Sam's on-camera and voice over work for the *MHA Nation* doc was taped in comfort indoors in D.C. after Brad Johnson and I taped the other parts of the doc and interviews in New Town, North Dakota during the almost coldest ten winter days in their history, circa January, 2014.

CHAPTER TWENTY-ONE

Unordinary Nuggets, Thoughts and Lessons

That's all there is. There isn't any more.—Actress Eleonora Duse

Other disparate and unordinary life-shaping occurrences also come to mind as I conclude recollections of my life's adventure to this date:

1946—During the second trip to New York with my mother (previously referenced) I think it might be fun to know my mother, Barbara Walters's father, Lou Walters and I had some interaction on his Latin Quarter nightclub dance floor, as follows: My mother was unconventional and somewhat a free spirit, thus took me to a show at The Latin Quarter, one of the world's most celebrated nightclubs, at that time, when I was nine years old. After the show, the orchestra started playing for dancing. My mother took me up on the stage and had me as her dance partner, slow dancing. About a minute later, a man came up to us on stage and told my mother young children weren't allowed to dance on that stage. The man was Lou Walters. My mother didn't argue, but I always wondered if Barbara might have been sitting in the light booth above, watching the encounter as a teenager. I was told in later years that could have been the case, since Barbara has openly described her childhood as somewhat lonely, often including "hanging around" The Latin Quarter.

1952—One of my occasional after school and Saturday jobs when not acting or rehearsing was to assist a small grocery store owner in Rego Park. His name I can't remember, but he was an elderly Jewish gentleman who taught me how to do things I never thought would matter in later life. One was how to open a sealed, flapped box correctly and easily, every time. The other was how to "candle" eggs, making certain they were fit to eat. I consider those sorts of memories among the most important and life affirming. Blessings to all the teachers in my life who didn't know they were teaching me how to be "street smart" and otherwise somewhat wiser.

1953—Even though I was making some income acting on *Peepers* and other occasional shows, I still needed to make as much income as possible, thus was told The Roxy Theater was hiring extra ushers to escort higher-ups to their seats for the world premiere of the film *The Robe*, the first film ever shot and released in Cinemascope. I was doing some part-time ushering at The Astor Theater at the time, thus put in my bid to usher for *The Robe*. I got the job and two of those I was assigned to escort to their seats were Mr. and Mrs. Spiros Skouras. Mr. Skouras was then President of 20th Century Fox, who launched Cinemascope. In my heart of hearts I wanted to tell him I was an actor and ask him to guide me to a big screen audition, but of course, didn't. He and his wife were very pleasant on that trip down the Roxy aisle. *For Minnesota readers, or any others who aren't aware, The Roxy Theater, one of New York's most prestigious movie theaters, was named after a Minneapolis native named "Roxy" Rothafel, who also created Radio City Music Hall's Rockettes. In addition, since Minneapolis-Saint Paul trivia is fun to "trumpet", the famous gilded statue of Prometheus, adjoining the ice skating rink in Rockefeller Center (where I learned to ice skate badly), was designed by a Saint Paul, Minnesota-born sculptor named Paul Manship.*

1957—The first date I ever had in Missoula was with a girl named Jan Owen. Someone at the television station (Channel 13) said they thought she and I would make a good twosome. I took her to see *Around The World In 80 Days* at a small movie theater there. Jan's family owned and operated a private flying service, based at the Missoula Airport, replete with its own hangars. I was earning 60 dollars a week, as earlier noted. She was a pretty girl, nose not high in the air and the date was pleasant, but I think Jan knew it wouldn't go any farther than that first very platonic date. Sadly, so did I. I've always wondered with whom she finally wed, if at all. Throughout much of my life, those sorts of thoughts have permeated many hours, but, as I think I stated earlier, one of my credos is the often stated, "God has us where we're supposed to be."

1968—During my earliest Las Vegas television days, I received a phone call from a lady named Marguerite Knickerbocker. She told me she and her husband, Al, a former movie studio stuntman, lived in a little spot in the road near the Colorado River named Nelson, Nevada. She also told me her brother was the once very famous film actor, Jon Hall, who had also been married to singer Frances Langford for over 20 years and who, after divorcing Hall, married the scion of the Evinrude outboard motors fortune, Ralph Evinrude. She told me she and Jon had been born and raised in Lausanne, Switzerland (where I've been blessed to visit several times in later life) and both she and her brother were the niece and nephew of Paul Gauguin. I visited them several times in their eclectic Nelson house, surrounded by nothing but desert and scrub on a very steep hill leading to the river. The house had three giant refrigerators and the same number of freezers, with dirt floors covered by very expensive Persian rugs. The legacy and memory they kindly gave me that still exists was a then almost 100-year old perfectly preserved copy of The Old Farmers Almanac, which I still have. Marguerite and Al both had terrible diabetic health issues and passed about ten years after we had lost touch. They would definitely qualify as two of Readers' Digest's most unforgettable people subjects. My blessings have been many.

Because I've always had an interest in almost everything enlightening life has to offer, some of the most interesting exploratory times occurred during my Las Vegas days from 1967 through 1970, as well as some untold "star" memories in subsequent years, and are chronicled in the following "snapshots":

Hoover/Boulder Dam, Monument Valley, Ted Danson—At least once every month for four years, following the conclusion of our 11 p.m. newscasts on both Channels 8 and 13, I'd drive to Hoover (Boulder) Dam, park my car above the middle of the Dam, get out of the car and look down to the bottom of the construction and into Black Canyon's waters. The Dam's iconic spillway was lighted in an orange-ish hue. At about midnight, I was usually the only person there, straddling the Nevada-Arizona line on the sidewalk, marked by a plaque affixed to the retaining wall. All one could hear was the whirring of the turbines across the road and firmly ensconced into the waters of Lake Mead. I usually stood there, looked and thought for about 15 or twenty minutes, with the midnight temperature at about 95 degrees in the summer, got back into my car and drove back to Las Vegas. It was a good "thinking spot" for me. Although I was always considered myself to be a "people person", the isolated times always brought me to a meditative sense of calm and almost religious sense of contemplation. The same occurred for me when I'd pick rocks on weekends alone, beginning about sunrise, in the quiet isolation of Death Valley or in Monument Valley, on the Utah-Arizona border. If you haven't been to those places or at those times of day or night, please put them on your "bucket list". Those experiences will add much deeper dimension to your life and reason for being, as well as a lot of humility, in my opinion. *Actor Ted Danson's father was curator for an American Indian museum in Flagstaff, Arizona, where Ted was raised. Once, while interviewing Ted,, I told him I knew that territory very well, having even driven through snowstorms there in late August. He kind of shrugged it off, politely, but after the interview, I also told him I used to go to The Mittens, those majestic red-colored monoliths in Monument Valley, as one of my favorite thinking places. He then said, "Wow, you really DO know that territory. That's one of my favorite thinking spots, too." In my opinion, never "dismiss" anyone until you hear "the rest of the story", as Paul Harvey used to say.*

Death Valley, Tom Williams and Marta Becket, London Bridge—I referenced picking rocks many weekends in Death Valley. I began going there frequently after interviewing on my Channel 13 talk show two of the most interesting people I'd ever met. Their names were Tom Williams and Marta Becket and had just been featured in a National Geographic Magazine story about their Opera House at Amargosa Junction, at the south end of Death Valley, California. Marta had just retired as top New York City Ballet dancer for George Balanchine and Tom an executive with BBD&O advertising in New York. (Marta was also another fellow Leo. Yikes! How many of us *are* there?) While driving on their way to L.A. from New York, their car broke down in Amargosa Junction, California, near the Nevada state line, while exploring the Death Valley area. They saw an abandoned theater for sale while waiting for the car repairs to be completed, bought the building and converted it into a theater wherein Marta decided to perform whether or not there was an audience. She painted a mural of audience figures around the walls, set up a tin can for donations in the entrance to the theater and an iconic institution was born. They had visitors from all over the world and were featured in international news stories on all the most powerful media outlets (please see photo section). Marta and Tom eventually divorced, even though he was the emcee, replete with tuxedo, for her ballet performances. They lived right next door to the Opera House in part of an abandoned motel they also cleaned up for tourists and visitors to stay. Marta had 13 cats the last time I visited her in the 1980s. That dear and wonderful legend, and friend, died in 2005.

A broadcaster named Lee Shoblom, a Duluth, Minnesota, native, had been a broadcast talent in Las Vegas when I first arrived there in early 1967. He and his wife, Linda, moved in late 1967 to the then very fledgling Lake Havasu City, Arizona, to build and own LHC's first radio station, . Lee invited me to visit one weekend and gave me some of the large pieces of the interior of the original London Bridge that was being dismantled with the exterior preserved to create the resurrection of that fabled bridge as an attraction for the soon-to-be popular town of Lake Havasu City. I still have those large pieces and great memories of Lee and Linda, who I visited a couple more times while I was still living and working in Vegas. Lee sold his LHC radio station and is still going strong as a "voice" and respected presence in the broadcasting arena.

Speaking of "presence", the first time I interviewed Pierce Brosnan was for the film, *Mrs. Doubtfire*. When I entered the room, even before I said, "Hello", Pierce's first words to me were, "You're an actor, *aren't* you?" I was respectfully taken aback at his question, but then said, "Yes, I *was*, at one time." He then said, "I know. You have a presence about you." I was again humbly honored for someone of that caliber recognizing there was a bit more to me than "surface". His kind comment made the interview even warmer than it might have been. In later years, I knew a girl he was dating. She said she and Pierce loved skiing. At that time, when I still had some clout with international ski areas, I arranged for them to have free skiing and lodging at Whistler-Blackcomb Mountain, British Columbia. As was the case with Peter Jennings in Avoriaz, France, previously referenced, Pierce could have *bought* Whistler-Blackcomb, but the resort was happy to have *his* "presence", gratis.

Regarding those interview days, in my opinion, it would be incorrect to not express gratitude for the kindness Johnny Depp afforded me when I interviewed him for the film, *Ed Wood*. It was the one time I interviewed him, and it would not have happened had he not cared that I got to do the interview. I was the last one scheduled to interview him late that day, long past the timeframe the studio had set for him to do interviews. I'd been sitting on a chair alone just outside the interview room. He came out of the interview room and asked, "Are you waiting to do an interview?" bypassing and interrupting a gatekeeper who had begun to tell me there was no time left in Johnny's schedule. I told Johnny, "Yes", and he told me to come into the room. He gave me double the usual four or five minutes and in his soft-spoken manner actually apologized for my having to wait so long, emphasizing no one should be pushed aside because of time constraints. Every time I see him doing all his great work I vividly remember how genuinely sweet, gentle and kind he was on that late and dark afternoon. He wasn't acting, and, as Jerry Stiller would say, "not a faker".

Also, during my Channel 11 Entertainment Editor days, I was assigned to screen a movie starring former wrestler turned actor (and eventually turned Mayor and Minnesota Governor), Jesse Ventura, which premiered at a small theater in Brooklyn Park, Minnesota, a Twin Cities suburb, where he had been Mayor. It was raining lightly as a got out of my car to walk a few blocks to the theater, when a limo pulled up alongside me and I heard, "Hey, Barry. Get in." It was Jesse offering me a ride to the entrance, which I happily accepted. When we got out of the limo, Jesse and his wife, Terry, invited me to a private party with them and only family members following the screening. I gladly accepted and it was a wonderful party. After he became Governor, he was one of the interviewees for my *20th Century* documentary, telling me afterward to "keep up the good work." He, as so many others in comfortable positions, had no idea every month presented me a struggle to survive.

Las Vegas and other "nuggets" not previously addressed nor all Vegas related: "Uncle" Lou Handman, one of the founders of ASCAP and previously mentioned, treated me to see Judy Garland perform in a one-woman show at The Palace Theater during my teenage acting years in New York. The theater, surprisingly, was almost empty and I had a front row seat. Without hyperbole here, Judy was fewer than 20 feet away from me, seated on the lip of the stage, and sang *Over The Rainbow* directly toward me for almost the entire song. Little did I know the following: That her daughter Liza would watch over/babysit my daughters in her dressing room at The Sahara for almost an hour in Las Vegas in 1970 during an emergency I had in the midst of interviewing Liza for radio. Coincidentally, Liza and her then husband, Peter Allen, lived in an apartment building named La Fonda, as did I at that time. Regarding The Palace, my mother would eventually live directly across the street from The Palace's stage entrance beginning in the late 1950s. In earlier years, during my mom's and my first trip to New York, I also had the privilege of Dinah Shore singling me out to sing to me from the stage of The Paramount Theater because she'd asked for audience requests and couldn't fulfill mine. I don't remember what I requested, but I remember her saying, "I'm sorry, honey. I don't have the charts for *that* one, but I'll sing to you anyway." My mom, sitting next to me, was beaming.

Others with whom I had *private* interaction in New York included Eddie Cantor's daughter, Marilyn, to give her something my family owned and she wished to purchase, having to do with my grandfather's former "agent" life. She had contacted me through Actors Equity. We met in front of one of the more popular Fifth Avenue stores. In later years, I met Eddie briefly in Hollywood, by accident, and told him about my meeting with Marilyn and what she wanted for sentimental reasons. He was very warm and unaffected.

During some time with Jack Benny at the Channel 13 studios, while he was sitting on a couch waiting to be interviewed by the afore-mentioned Joe Delaney, Jack was laughing about the introductions he got at The Sahara's Congo Room. He said, in his signature delivery style, "They call it the world-famous Congo Room. Right. In downtown Rangoon, that's all they're talking about." Fun.

Jack E. Leonard, to me one of the funniest comedians ever, also said, at a different time, while sitting on that Joe Delaney Green Room couch while waiting to be interviewed, his agent told him because of taxes, Jack wasn't allowed to collect his paycheck for two more weeks. "Fat Jack", as some in the business used to affectionately call him, said some other things that can't be repeated here. His "insult humor" was phenomenal.

I was blessed to also get to know comedian Myron Cohen fairly well during those Las Vegas years. One of the classic stories he told was about a Texan and an Israeli talking about the sizes of their countries. The Texan asked the Israeli, "Do you know, boy, you can get on a train in Texarkana, bound for El Paso, and ride all day, ride all night, ride all the next day and ride all the next night and still be in Texas?" The Israeli replied, " Aw, what's so great about that? We have trains in Israel that go that slow, too."

I once interviewed Gore Vidal about a film he'd produced. The interview took place shortly after his relative, Al Gore, became Vice President. I asked him his opinion of Gore, thinking he'd praise him. He said, verbatim here, "He's a charmless clod."

William F. Buckley, one of Gore Vidal's most vitriolic detractors, was a next-to-me seat partner of mine on a flight and day I had been upgraded to first class. He was totally focused on the laptop on which he was typing and we never uttered one word to each other, but it was fascinating to see his fingers flying rapidly on that keyboard.

Speaking of prolific writers, a nephew of New York Times Washington, D.C.-based columnist, William F. Safire, married a former WJLA-TV reporter/colleague/friend of mine named Maralee Beck. Bill Safire's nephew was (and is) named Andy Safir (spelling it without the "e" at the end) and he, Maralee and I have kept in contact to this day. Andy was a valued member of the Nixon White House staff. When I temporarily lost track of Ambassador Zahedi following the Iranian revolution, I asked Andy for his Uncle Bill's contact information to allow me to try to re-contact Ambassador Zahedi (Ardeshir) again. Andy kindly gave me that contact information, his Uncle Bill gave me Ardeshir's address in Switzerland and the reconnection has lasted very well to this day. In July, 2012, a great friend and sometimes employer named Eugene (Gene) Chase, took me to visit Ardeshir again in Switzerland. It was both a business and pleasure trip. Ardeshir is still energetic and currently writing his fourth autobiographic volume regarding his Ambassadorial days in D.C. Gene's story could fill another book, but suffice it to say he's one of the most remarkable people one could ever know, providing sustainable agriculture action for countries such as Ghana (where he's a Chief) to The Maldive Islands to Haiti and beyond, almost single-handedly.

I had mentioned being VP of Creative Services for an ad agency in Detroit. As I also previously mentioned, my Seattle-Tacoma boss, J. Elroy McCaw, told me I was the best idea man he'd ever known. While I think I'm not even close to being the best at anything, here are some of the things I've created, past and relatively present:

Polish slogans—Trademarked and copyrighted in 2013, and what I created because of a relationship with Polish friends here in America named Mario and Oliver McKay (their Anglicized names), following are two slogans that are antidotes to Polish jokes, and featured in a large Chicago *Sun Times* article in November, 2013: *Poland: It's Not A Joke. Never Was* and *Being Polish. It's Not A Joke. Never Was.* The slogans are on merchandise with the names of famous Polish people marked above the slogans. Proceeds from the online sales of the merchandise are given to Polish orphanages via a Polish-government authorized Foundation Mario, Oliver and I established called The Optivus Foundation, based in both Warsaw and here in Minneapolis. Thanks to my Chicago agent, Dr. Judith-Rae Ross, the *Chicago Sun Times* feature article appeared. Dr. Ross has been instrumental in getting many good career moves to be successful since 2010, and her husband, Allan, went to the same U.S. Air Force weather school as I did in Illinois, but at different times.

Peter Molson—During a 1980 travel documentary producing and filming trip for the Mont Tremblant Resort Hotels Association in Quebec, (during which I almost fell out of the open small airplane door from which I was hanging and filming directly above the summit of Mont Tremblant) I was introduced to Peter Molson, then primary heir to the Molson brewing fortune. It was suggested to Peter by one of the resort owners, named Serge Dubois, that I might be a good problem-solver for a challenging personal issue he was having. Peter invited me to his house on Lac Tremblant to privately discuss the matter, for which I was honored and hoped to be of assistance. When I entered the house, Peter asked if I wanted a "Golden" (Molson's Golden, of course). I playfully asked if he had any Budweiser. He gently laughed and knew I was purposely teasing. I immediately said, "Yes, of course, and thanks." to the Golden offer and we sat in his living room . . . just Peter and me . . . for almost two hours, discussing and apparently solving his problem. In later years, we spoke a couple times about businesses in which he may have had interests in adding to his empire, and the conversations were always cordial. I later learned my private time with him was very rare since he was a very private person, and as noble as they come. One of Peter's other residences was in St. Jovite, not far from Tremblant. My thanks to Serge Dubois for that magic and privileged private time with Mr. Molson.

Budweiser and Neutrogena—Neither of these companies allow "outside" marketing or advertising suggestions. Both their agencies have told me the slogans I created and suggested for them are blockbusters, shown to them with confidentiality agreements, but could not go any farther because of company policies. In a nutshell, and condensed, for Budweiser, my basic slogan was, "Beer wiser, Bud? Budweiser beer." For Neutrogena, it was, sung to the tune of *Carolina In The Morning*, "Nothin' gets you cleaner than a little Neutrogena in the morning." Oh, well.

A few things I've learned from this jam-packed life so far, not necessarily in order of import:
- Never *stop* learning. It's the essence of keeping us alive and vital.
- Always try to give everyone one hundred percent credit for character and trustworthiness, from the beginning. If they eventually work their ways down to zero, they will have been

the ones who caused that destination to arrive, probably hurting you in the journey, but sometimes unintentionally.

- Life is, unfortunately, not always, or maybe ever, an MGM musical. If it *is*, it's sometimes not worth a review.
- Insensitive people need human being lessons.
- Trite, but true: It's nice to be important but much more important to be nice.
- *Really* listen to what people have to say. It will serve you well throughout the journey.
- *Hope* people will really listen to *you. Everyone* has a relevant story. Everyone.
- There is definitely a higher power, in my opinion, and, obviously the opinion of billions of us. Look at the stars and planets some dark night and realize none of this could have happened by accident, also realizing our daily problems, except for facing terrible trauma or painful death, are minutiae.
- Be thankful for every breath you take and every blessing you have, especially if you don't live in or amongst constant poverty. We're among the most blessed passengers on this ride, even if only having *one* break in life.
- Apologize and be contrite for mistakes you've made, especially if unintentionally hurtful to other people, always trying to live by The Golden Rule, but knowing the maturity process is constant and sometimes never fully realized nor achieved. Heaven knows *I've* never reached that long-sought goal, but it's definitely on my bucket list.

What am I doing now, as I conclude this chronicle? I'm happy (and honored) to state I've been retained to put my eclectic career and life experiences to hopefully good use as a public and media relations, strategic alliances, awareness and development consultant for The Masgutova Foundation/Svetlana Masgutova Educational Institute, based in Orlando, Florida and Warsaw, Poland. Founded decades ago by a brilliantly-talented Russian Ph.D. after whom the Foundation and Educational Institute are named, and aligned with her American-born counterpart, Pamela Curlee, I've had the privilege to witness their work that has revitalized those with cerebral palsy, autism and multiple other neuro-physical issues, as well as the health of trauma victims, performed globally from Newtown, Connecticut (The Sandy Hook School massacre) to Chernobyl, Ukraine. To be able to be of service to them and those they serve is a wonderful way to possibly conclude the professional part of my life.

Thanks, again, to dear and wonderful Jerry Stiller for urging me to write my story. A lot has been omitted because I didn't want to make it the length of *War And Peace*, but I think you may have gotten the picture: Life for me has included a lot more than weather reports, but thanks to those, perhaps other parts of my life may not have occurred. I hope those parts have been interesting enough for you to have further explored.

Appreciation for reading this is gratefully and very humbly conveyed to you.

The Photographs...

Professional life...

The current
serenity-se
Seinfeld.
him as one-half of
Meara. But, as his
reveals, Jerry Stiller
with entertainment.

Growing up
Brooklyn and on M
Jerry Stiller discove
when, as a child, he
an audience. Jerry's
vaudeville performa
that he, too, wanted
studied drama at Sy
charismatic professor
he could achieve his
cessful actor. After S
New York to begin a

Jerry soon met Ar
fell in love with her, h
able person. At first th
in their separate per
they began doing a
houses of New York's
created a brilliantly
characters who were
themselves. Before lon
The Ed Sullivan Show,
program of the day.
smash hit.

To Barry Zevan —
To Ellen Zevan
You are very much
PART OF MY Life
Love
Jerry
Stiller
1/2/2001

(continued)

Above: *Jerry with me
following documentary
taping meeting at New
York's Edison Hotel, 1998.*

Left: *Jerry Stiller's
note to Ellen and me,
handwritten in his
autobiography,* Married
To Laughter—
A Love Story Featuring
Anne Meara. *I didn't
know he had written
his book until it arrived
in the mail as a gift to
us, January, 2001.*

Jimmy Durante and me following his two-promos Las Vegas filming session for me for KSTP-TV, which he did for no charge, as he said to me, because he was a "fan".

Woody Allen and me following his two-promos Las Vegas filming session for me for KSTP-TV, which he did for no charge, saying he, too, was a "fan" of my weathercasts.

Sammy Davis, Jr. and me following his two-promos Las Vegas filming session for me for KSTP-TV, which he did for no charge. Sammy was like a brother to me for over 30 years.

Chet Huntley, Chrissy and me at a St. Paul. MN, social event three months prior to his death. He was touching me on the shoulder while teasingly chastising my urgings to audiences on The Ski Scene to send him good wishes about his health. He said he received an avalanche of cards and letters. Below: Note to me from Tippy, Chet's widow, in his autobiography frontispiece, which she voluntarily sent to me shortly after Chet's passing. I didn't know he had written a book until it arrived.

For Barry,
Chet's friend,
Tippy Huntley

THE
GENEROUS YEARS

Remembrances of a frontier boyhood

CHET HUNTLEY

A FAWCETT CREST BOOK
Fawcett Publications, Inc., Greenwich, Conn.

288

Longtime friend. Emmy-award winning network journalist and producer, Linda Ellerbee, following documentary interview with me at her Lucky Duck studios in New York.

NBC
Entertainment

A Division of
National Broadcasting Company, Inc.

Thirty Rockefeller Plaza
New York, N.Y. 10020   212-664-4444

2/10/86

Dear Barry,

Nice talking with you last week. Thanks for your time and all your help. Let me know if you need anything. Thanks again.

David Letterman

Handwritten note David snail-mailed to me following a reminiscent satellite interview he and I did for KARE-TV in Minneapolis-St. Paul, during which he, at that time, acknowledged what I've later chronicled in this book.

NBC
Entertainment

1410 W./Letterman
National Broadcasting Company, Inc.
Thirty Rockefeller Plaza
New York, N.Y. 10020

WUSA
441 Boone Avenue North
Minneapolis, MN 55427

Attn: Barry Zevan

January 20, 1995

Dear Barry,
I have been trying to figure out who it was in
this office who was so rude to you.
Outrageous.
I wish you had persisted and told me
at the time. I think I know who it was.
They have gone on to greener pastures, which
with any luck will turn brown to their touch.
Thanks for your note. Come and see me next
time you are here. Judy, my assistant and
Gretchen, my overseer are wonderful people
and will welcome you with open arms, provided
you do not park your Rolls in front of the
building.
As for your friend in Minneapolis.
Same invitation. If she's here and would like to
have a coffee, I am sure I would enjoy it.
Though she shouldn't park
her Rolls in front either.
Seriously, you are both welcome here,
but you especially.
All the best.

*Letter from Peter and
memorial service
invitation referenced on
page 109. Peter was a
true, dear friend to me,
both here in the U.S.
and overseas. I can't
believe he's gone.*

PLEASE JOIN THE FAMILY OF
PETER JENNINGS
REMEMBER AND CELEBRATE HIS LIFE

TUESDAY, SEPTEMBER 20, 2005

11:00 A.M.

CARNEGIE HALL

57TH STREET AND SEVENTH AVENUE

NEW YORK

DOORS OPEN AT 10:00 A.M.
THE ENCLOSED TICKET IS FOR YOUR PERSONAL USE AND WILL BE REQUIRED FOR SEATING.
BECAUSE OF SECURITY, PLEASE DO NOT BRING CAMERAS, BRIEFCASES OR BACKPACKS.

Nearby Maryland neighbor Ted Koppel and me just sitting in his driveway one weekend afternoon. He was and still is a good friend, I'm honored to state. He and his wife, Grace Anne, are very down-to-Earth and have great senses of humor.

Ted and Grace Anne Koppel (center) at one of my Potomac, MD, birthday parties, circa mid-1970s. Others in the photo include husband and wife reporter/anchors Chris Curle and Don Farmer (before they co-anchored at CNN), ABC News correspondent Barrie Dunsmore and his wife and yours truly.

Today Show weatherman Willard Scott and me in Willard's pool at his farm in Upperville, VA, just before Willard got the nod from Today. Willard was and is one of the nicer people in broadcasting and I'm proud to have his longtime friendship.

With my Rolls Royce just prior to selling it back, 1975

With friend Carl Stern, NBC-TV Law Correspondent, sitting on sister-in-law Gay Nathan's Santa Fe, NM patio, mid-1970s

Below: *Re-uniting with CBS-TV's Bob Schieffer in Bismarck, ND, at a week-long October, 2010, tribute to North Dakota's Eric Sevareid, and about which described on pages 66, 188 and 264. Bob's wife, and elementary teacher had me give weather talks to her students during my D.C. television days.*

Re-uniting with CBS-TV's Dan Rather in Bismarck, ND, at a week-long October, 2010, tribute to North Dakota's Eric Sevareid, and about which described on pages 66, 188 and 264. Dan announced one of my Emmy nominations in D.C. in 1977.

Below: *With Nick Clooney, George Clooney's father and my friend Rosemary's younger brother, in Bismarck, ND, at a week-long October, 2010, tribute to North Dakota's Eric Sevareid, and about which described on pages 66, 188 and 264. Nick enjoyed my reminiscences of Rosemary during her and my* Perry Como Show *years and subsequent times together.*

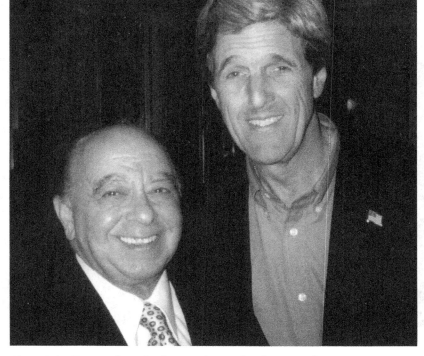

Above: *John Kerry and me, thanks to Buck Humphrey's camera, during 2004 Presidential campaign in Minneapolis. Secretary Kerry was very gracious (and very tall!). We kept in touch for several months.*

Below: *With friend Peter Marshall in front of his home in California, 2010. Peter and his wife, Laurie, are two of the nicest people, in or out of show business.*

Senator Daniel Inouye (D), Hawaii, after having fun teasing me about the weather, standing between my weatherboards on Channel 7 in D.C., mid-1970s

Senator Daniel Inouye (D), Hawaii, in his office following my interview with him for a 20th century themed documentary for which I was consulting executive producer, 2000.

Left: *Thanks to Carolyn Speidel's camera, per her kind suggestion, me at the summit of one of France's alpine ski resorts, mid-1970s.*

Below: *Lifelong friends to me, Frank Gorshin, Dick Van Patten and me during our 2002* The Sunshine Boys *play tour, taken in Amarillo, TX.*

296

Before he sent it to then Texas Governor George W. Bush, in an office ante-room, I snapped this photo of the Radio Flyer wagon General Colin Powell would be sending to "W" and inscribed to "W", just prior to my interview with the General.

General Colin Powell and me following my interview with him as consulting executive producer for The Remarkable 20th Century *documentary.*

With lifelong friend, colleague and mentor Tony Randall in his and Heather's 6th floor, 1 West 81st Street, New York apartment, circa 1998, following my interview with him for the documentary, Television:the First 50 Years, *which I wrote and executive produced.*

Rod Steiger and me at his Malibu home, circa 1999, following a reunion with him from our early TV acting days together. He invited me to stay to have lunch with him and Elizabeth Taylor, who he was dating at that time and he said was "coming over with sandwiches", but I respectfully declined. He later told me I should have stayed. He was correct.

Right: *Actress Arlene Dahl and me in her New York apartment following a social visit and interview for a documentary. The Minneapolis native and I earlier shared other social times at her and husband Marc Jacobs's Nyack, NY, second home. A truly wonderful lady and fellow Leo!*

Below: *Acting in* The Happy Time *at The Corning Summer Playhouse in Corning, NY, circa mi-1950s, with Joe Ruskin, one of my former Pittsburgh Playhouse drama teachers. He later had regular parts on* The Untouchables *and other series. The lady who played our maid in this production was Barbara Barrie, who later played the wife of* Barney Miller *on the TV sitcom series of the same name. The connections never end.*

Left: *With lifelong NYC high school years friend, Elliott Gould, re-uniting at a film retrospective in his honor in Minneapolis, early 2000s. His inscription, if you can't read it, includes stating I'm the one wearing the tie. Elliott's a good person and more multi-talented than most people are aware.*

Below: *Jerry Lewis and me during one of our many professional and private times together. This photo was taken in Las Vegas after an interview with Jerry for wrestling champion Verne Gagne's syndicated television show. He kindly signed it, "To Barry, A dear old friend". Jerry and I kept in touch for a very long time and he's still a friend, I'm proud to say.(see pages 7, 52, 53, 74, 76, 77, 233)*

The City of Thunder Bay
Ontario, Canada

Know all Men by these presents, that by the Authority vested in me as Mayor of the City of Thunder Bay, I do hereby name

Barry Ze Van
Honorary Citizen

I was made one of only 12 Honorary Citizens of Thunder Bay, Ontario, in 1975, thanks to my friend, Paul Drombolis, head of their tourist office. He presented it to me live on Channel 7 in D.C

My 60th birthday proclamation from The City of Thunder Bay, Ontario, noting my status as an honorary citizen in the copy. (Thunder Bay is also home to television orchestra leader, Paul Shaffer, formerly with SNL and Late Night With David Letterman. The Drombolis's lived two houses away from the Shaffers when Paul was a youngster.)

On behalf of
The Council and Citizens
of the
City of Thunder Bay
Sincere congratulations
are extended to

Barry Ze Van
our honorary citizen since the year 1975

on the occasion of your
60th Birthday

His valuable contribution to the enrichment of harmonious relations between our two great countries will be long remembered. We wish him continuing happiness, prosperity, and good health.

August 5, 1997

Mayor David Hamilton

To B— — my friend
Walt Mondale

One of the photos Vice President Mondale kindly signed for me after I emceed his pre-inaugural banquet at the Washington Hilton for the Minnesota State Society in January, 1977. That was quite an honor and quite an evening. I thank him for the additional honor of his endorsement of this book.

With longtime Minnesota friend, Loni Anderson, the day before she was going to move in with Burt Reynolds, pre-marriage. I'm sorry it didn't work out for them. I met him only once. Loni and I share the same birthday, August 5th, although I'm seven years her elder.

From age 2 through 4, including photo with my Mom and Grandpa, the latter outside the apartment building on South Millvale Avenue in Pittsburgh, where I would live my late pre-teen years with them

Joan's sweet note to me when flooding prevented her from being a guest on my D.C. TV weathercast one night.

My older granddaugther, Maritsa, her husband, Gunnar and me flanking dear Joan just a year before her untimely death. Maritsa and Gunnar were huge fans of Joan's, thus I was glad to make the introduction. This photo was taken backstage at Mystic Lake Casino in Prior Lake, Minnesota, a Twin Cities suburb. Joan and I reminisced very profoundly that night about our early Las Vegas days together. It was a very sentimental evening recalling old friends, especially those no longer alive. (She also told me she loved the tie I was wearing in this photo. Great words from the head of The Fashion Police. I miss her.)

HUBERT H. HUMPHREY
MINNESOTA

United States Senate
WASHINGTON, D.C. 20510

September 20, 1971

Mr. Barry ZeVan
The Weatherman
KSTP-TV
3415 University Avenue
St. Paul, Minnesota

Dear Barry:

How very good of you to retain such fond memories of
the program we did a few years ago. As I told you out at
the fairgrounds, I personally feel you are a very exciting
television personality. Don't be discouraged if it takes
a little time for the "numbers" to come your way in the
rating race.

Minnesotans are many times hard set in their traditional
patterns. I know because I was the first Democrat they
sent to the United States Senate in decades. But once they
get to know you and get accustomed to your entertaining
style, you'll have them in your corner.

I've often felt that Minnesotans have a sort of masochistic
trait about their weather. For some reason they never
brag on the inter-seasonal beauty of our state. Instead,
most of them boast of the extreme conditions of weather,
especially the snow and cold of our winters. This, of
course, does little to attract new industry and new people
to our state.

I deeply appreciate your long and enduring friendship, and
I am honored by your support and encouragement.

Sincerely,

Hubert H. Humphrey

The first of seven personal letters Hubert Humphrey would write to me over the course of several years. He was a giant in every way and, in my opinion and the opinion of so many, would have made one of the best Presidents of the United States in all our history. I often visit his final place of rest at Minneapolis's Lakewood Cemetery, remembering.

★ ★ ★ ★ ★ ★ · ★ · ★ ★ ★ ★ ★ ★ ★ ★ ★

FISHBAIT MAY 16, 1977

TO THE FAMOUS THE ONLY
BARRY ZEVAN AND CHRIS.

Best Wishes,

FishBait Miller

William "Fishbait" Miller was as popular on Capitol Hill and in the halls of Congress as any figure who had ever served as House doorkeeper, or in any other capacity. He gave me his autobiography, entitled Fishbait, *when I was visiting a Congressional friend on The Hill one day and inscribed it as you see it. I was proud he was a viewer and fan, and thanked him profusely (I didn't know he'd written his book).*

Joe Yule, Mickey Rooney's Dad, messaged this photo to me in 1949 after I had the honor to perform with him in Finian's Rainbow during part of a national tour, thanks to him getting me the part. (See page 36) He was another giant, an original, with a heart bigger than he was. Thank you, Mr. Yule.

Right: *As noted on page 153, Gregory Peck and me following my first time to be with him. It was at The Krupp Ranch, a few miles west of Las Vegas, during a pause in the filming of The Stalking Moon, May, 1968 and after interviewing him for KLAV radio. Several weeks after this photo was shot, it was a thrill to see how he signed it, calling me his "podner".* Below: *Gregory Peck and me in the studios of KSTP-TV, Twin Cities, June, 1974, just concluding a session wherein he did two promos for me and my weathercasts. He was laughing at something I was saying, and I think the expression on his face notes he was enjoying the moment, which was an honor for yours truly. One of the promos I'd written for him to say was,* "Barry ZeVan, The Weatherman, is alive and well. Let's just say he's alive, and leave it at that." *He, God bless him, whimsically changed the last utterance to say,* "Let's just say he's well, and leave it at that." *Loved it, we kept it and aired it. Great sense of humor from the classiest man one could ever meet, and know. What an honor and blessing. He kindly remembered me several years later at a function at The Kennedy Center in D.C., smilingly stating,* "You and I worked together a couple times."

Thanks to agent Judith-Rae Ross and portrait artist John "Nico" Nicolosi, DDS, I was able to reunite in May, 2013, with my 1948 through 1951 Pittsburgh Playhouse Drama School pal, and fellow performer, Shirley Jones, during a postage stamp unveiling in the office of Omaha, Nebraska's, Mayor, where these photos with her were taken. Shirley and her co-star, Gordon MacRae, were being honored for the 50th anniversary of Carousel *with their portraits affixed to the new stamp. As you can see, Shirley kindly signed both photos shown, very warmly, with the inscriptions, "To Barry, The last of the big-timers! Love, Shirley" and "Hey, Barry! You were a real blast! Love, Shirley". Those kind comments were, in my opinion, among the most gratifying anyone could ever receive. Thank you, Shirley.*

Family section,
1890s through 2012...

The 1890s—Great Grandpa and Great Grandma Nossokoff. They started all of it.

Below left: *Mom in 1908,* Below right: *"Nana" Rachel Broida in 1900*

Brig. Gen. M. Nossokoff
U R K O F P
201 S. Evaline Street,
Pittsburgh, Pa.
PHONE: MONTROSE 6228

*Brigadier
General
Morris
Nossokoff,
1900s and
Mom,
autographed
to Grandpa
John, 1920)*

Clockwise from above:
*Grandpa John, 1920s;
Grandpa John in Atlantic
City surf, 1920s ; Mom in
the late 1910s ; Mom, early
1920s; Mom, mid-1930s*

Clockwise from above: *Mom, late 1920s; Mom, 1935; Mom, me and Grandpa John, 1939; Great-Grandpa Nossokoff and me, 1940s*

Left: *1920s Violinist Dave Rubinoff, Agent Grandpa John's prodigy.* Below: *"Aunt" Florrie in her and Lou's basement bar and rec room, 1950s*

My favorite photo of Grandpa John, 1940s

Below left to right: *Mom's half-brother Donny, late 1930s, who died at age 14; Aunt Arlene and Uncle Phil, 1940s; Me with Aunt Arlene, early 1950s*

The 1940s: (Left to right) Me at Coney Island, NY, 1945 (first trip to New York City), shots of NY from the roof of the Edison Hotel,

Above: *Mom and me in the center of the Armocida family's Thanksgiving dinner table, late 1940s. They feted us with their lavish Pittsburgh Italian hospitality every year for at least ten Thanksgivings. They were raucous, generous and wonderful people.* Below: *In first local play* (Strange Bedfellows) *at Pittsburgh Playhouse, 1948*

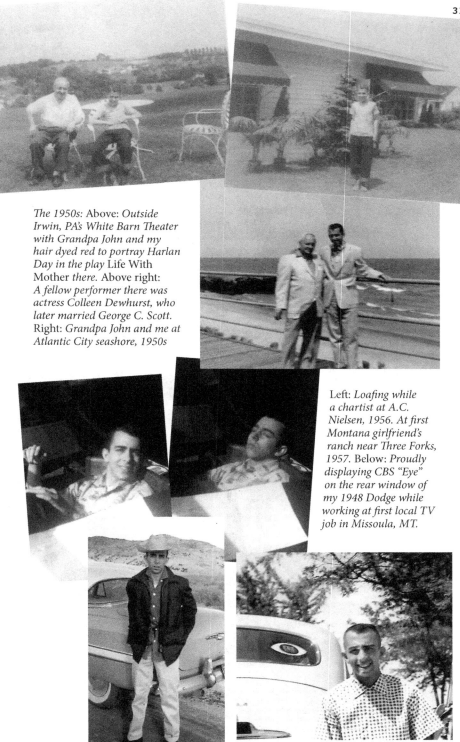

The 1950s: Above: *Outside Irwin, PA's White Barn Theater with Grandpa John and my hair dyed red to portray Harlan Day in the play* Life With Mother *there.* Above right: *A fellow performer there was actress Colleen Dewhurst, who later married George C. Scott.* Right: *Grandpa John and me at Atlantic City seashore, 1950s*

Left: *Loafing while a chartist at A.C. Nielsen, 1956. At first Montana girlfriend's ranch near Three Forks, 1957.* Below: *Proudly displaying CBS "Eye" on the rear window of my 1948 Dodge while working at first local TV job in Missoula, MT.*

Above: *Older daughter
Shaunda, at age one, in
Mom's arms outside her
apartment building in
New York, Summer, 1962.*
Above right: *Shaunda
at home, Idaho Falls,
Christmas, 1962.* Right:
*Shaunda and me outside
Idaho Falls house, 1962*

*Shaunda (front) and
Lisa (back) after
Dorothy's and my
divorce, 1965*

315

With Shaunda and Lisa during
a trip to Edmonton, Alberta, to
visit Eric and Barabra Neville,
late 1960s. I wore the toupee only
briefly, but still wish I had that
much natural hair.

Christmas, 1973, St. Paul, MN,
with Mom, Shaunda and Chris's
daughter, Michelle.

My pal Paul Drombolis, like a brother to me, enjoying piloting a boat and also, center of bottom picture with wife Helen, being honored at a 2005 national SKAL event in Thunder Bay, Ontario, which I was honored to attend and at which asked to speak glowingly about Paul and Helen, which I did, gladly.

My 75th birthday party, August 5, 2012, at the Minneapolis, house, thanks to Ellen. Left: Lisa and Shaunda with me. Right: Shaunda, Maritsa (my older granddaughter), Gunnar and Hunter Hamilton, with me, the very happy birthday boy.

From left to right: *Shelbea, Tracy and Chelsea (my younger granddaughter) and Abby Rose Ransom, Lisa, me, older Grandson Ryan Lewis, his son Wesley, significant other Abigail, younger grandson Brady, Ryan and Abigail's daughter Reagan, and Abigail's daughter, Emma. Since these photos were taken, three additional great-grandchildren have been added to the family!*

Facebook	Page 1 of 1

Subj:	**Vera Goulet mentioned you on Facebook**
Date:	10/9/2013 6:49:26 P.M. Central Daylight Time
From:	notification+pkm-vv1_@facebookmail.com
Reply-to:	e+09ym3pz000000gbryib0070b⬛⬛⬛⬛⬛⬛zg3lxmqz0⬛⬛⬛⬛⬛0002gl53@reply.facebook.com
To:	bnz1@aol.com

facebook

Vera Goulet **mentioned you in a comment.**

Vera wrote: "Barry, it is so good to hear from you. I hope you and your family are well. Yes, it an incredible recording. He was only seventeen years old and already he was just amazing. You know that he cherished tour friendship and had tremendous respect for you."

My thanks to Vera Goulet acknowledging on Facebook Robert's kind thoughts about me long after his passing. Very gratifying, to say the least

The Index...